Memory and Amnesia

Memory and Amnesia

An Introduction

ALAN J. PARKIN

Basil Blackwell

Copyright © Alan J. Parkin 1987

First published 1987

Basil Blackwell Ltd
108 Cowley Road, Oxford, OX4 1JF, UK

Basil Blackwell Inc.
432 Park Avenue South, Suite 1503
New York, NY 10016, USA

British Library Cataloguing in Publication Data

Parkin, Alan J.
Memory and amnesia: an
introduction.
1. Memory   2. Neuropsychology
I. Title
153.1   BF371
ISBN 0-631-14868-X
ISBN 0-631-14869-8 Pbk

Library of Congress Cataloging in Publication Data
Parkin, Alan J.
Memory and amnesia.

Bibliography: p.
Includes index.
1. Memory.   2. Memory, Disorders of.   I. Title.
[DNLM: 1. Memory Disorders.   WM 173.7 P247m]
BF371.P275   1987   153.1'2   86—17637
ISBN 0-631-14868-X
ISBN 0-631-14869-8 (pbk.)

Typeset in 11 on 13pt Garamond
by Columns of Reading
Printed in Great Britain by Billing & Sons Ltd, Worcester

Contents

Preface

Interest in amnesia has increased greatly in the last twenty years. The various phenomena exhibited by amnesic patients have become of great interest not just to clinicians, but also to experimental psychologists concerned with explaining normal memory function. One aim of this book, therefore, is to provide an introductory text which can be read by psychology under-graduates pursuing a course in the psychology of memory or neuropsychology. The nature and consequences of memory loss are, however, of interest to other professional groups, most notably neurologists, neurosurgeons, psychiatrists, speech therapists, occu-pational therapists, nurses and lawyers. Accordingly, the book also offers an account of memory and amnesia which can be followed by professionals with no previous experience of psychological approaches to explanation.

These aims have necessitated a book divided into two parts. The first part provides a basic account of psychological theories about the nature of human memory. The study is somewhat selective in that it concentrates on those aspects of research and theory which are central to the subsequent discussion of memory disorders. Furthermore, some of my colleagues will note that the account is rather traditional, with no discussion of more recent theoretical developments such as distributed processing models. The reason for this lies in the current relationship between most research on memory disorders and theories of normal function. Attempts to explain amnesia have drawn, almost exclusively, on theories of normal function as their starting-point. As a result, theorizing in amnesia research tends to lag behind that in the normal field and accounts of amnesia have yet to embrace more recent develop-ments.

The second part opens with an overview of assessment procedures followed by an account of the various kinds of memory disorders. Most space is given over to the amnesic syndrome, despite its comparative rarity in the clinical population. This reflects the considerable theoretical importance that the syndrome has acquired within experimental memory research. The rest of the book covers ageing and dementia, transient disorders, psychogenic memory loss, and remediation. In providing a bibliography I have tried to strike a balance between thorough coverage while avoiding mass citation. I hope that most of the references cited will lead the interested reader to more detailed information on a particular topic, and I have also made suggestions for further reading.

Finally, many people have helped in the preparation of this book by commenting on various sections. In particular I would like to thank Nick Leng, Andrew Mayes, and Barbara Wilson. In addition, Pete Clifton, Sue Leekam, Bronwyn Moorehouse and Nicola Stanhope provided useful comments. Much of the material for the book had to be obtained from sources outside my own university and I am indebted to Shirley Kirby-Turner and Jenny Marshman of Sussex University Library and Judy Lehman of the Brighton Postgraduate Medical Library for their help in obtaining references. Last, I must thank Sylvia Turner for all her work preparing the manuscript, Philip Carpenter for his encouragement, and Jean Van Altena for her very thorough copy-editing.

Alan Parkin
Sussex University, July 1986

Acknowledgements

I am grateful to the following for permission to redraw and reproduce figures: Academic Press (1.2, 1.3, 1.4, 1.5, 2.1, 4.3, 6.4, 6.5); Blackwell Scientific (6.3a); Cambridge University Press (1.1, 6.6b); Harper and Row (3.2); Masson Italia (6.7, 7.2); Pergamon Press (4.2, 6.3b, 6.6a, 6.9).

The significance of the cover illustration is attributable to R. Sorabji's work *Aristotle On Memory* (London: Duckworth, 1972). Aristotle's contribution to the philosophical understanding of memory is widely acknowledged. It is to Cicero that we owe the legend of Simonides and the invention of the method of *loci* – a mnemonic technique that has recently been applied to the treatment of memory disorders.

Abbreviations

AD	Alzheimer's disease
BRMT	Boston Remote Memory Test
CAT	Computerized axial tomography
CVA	Cerebro-vascular accident (stroke)
ECT	Electro-convulsive therapy
EEG	Electro-encephalogram
HC	Huntingdon's Chorea
LTS	Long-term store
MQ	Memory quotient
NART	New Adult Reading Test
PE	Post-encephalitic
PI	Proactive interference
PTA	Post-traumatic amnesia
RA	Retrograde amnesia
RBMT	Rivermead Behavioural Memory Test
RI	Retroactive interference
STS	Short-term store
TGA	Transient global amnesia
WAIS	Wechsler Adult Intelligence Scale
WCST	Wisconsin Card Sorting Test
WISC	Wechsler Intelligence Scale for Children
WMS	Wechsler Memory Scale

Part I

The Nature of Memory

1

A Model of Memory

One response to the question 'How does memory work?' might be to look at the anatomy and physiology of the brain. After all, memory is located there, so our knowledge of brain function might be expected to provide the answer. The brain is composed of millions of *neurones*, whose basic structure is illustrated in figure 1.1. Communication between neurones occurs by the transmission of nerve impulses along the *axon* of one neurone to the *dendrites* of another. The point of communication between an axon and a dendrite is called a *synapse*. Essentially it consists of two membranes separated by a minute gap. The impulse is transmitted by means of a chemical substance known as a *neurotransmitter*, which is released from the *pre-synaptic membrane* and travels to the *post-synaptic membrane*, where it sets up a new impulse. The level of interconnection between neurones is enormous, with a fully developed neurone averaging over a thousand dendritic and a thousand axonal synapses. The neuronal network therefore provides an ideal basis for the complex processes of memory.

In recent years neuroscientists have made major advances towards an understanding of the nervous system, but they have not reached the point where they can provide answers to the kinds of questions psychologists ask about memory. Thus we may be able to identify certain brain structures and neurotransmitters as being implicated in memory, but this does not tell us how memory is organized, how memories are retrieved, or why one learning strategy is better than another. We know that the neural networks of the brain underlie these activities, but unless we have a *theory* about how they are organized, we are no better off than someone who knows nothing about electronics trying to understand the circuit diagram of a television.

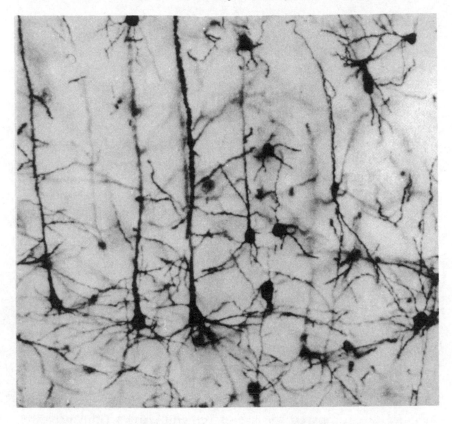

Figure 1.1   Cross-section of brain tissue showing neuronal network

Because the workings of memory are not apparent from the physical structure of the brain, explanations of memory must be based on analogies with things we do understand. The earliest and perhaps most famous example of a description of memory by analogy comes from Plato, who asks us to:

Imagine . . . for the sake of argument that our minds contain a block of wax, which in this or that individual may be larger or smaller, and composed of wax that is comparatively pure or muddy, and harder in some, softer in others, and sometimes of just the right consistency . . . and say that whenever we wish to remember something we hear or conceive in our own minds, we hold this wax under the perceptions or ideas and imprint them on it as we might stamp the impression of a seal ring. Whatever is so imprinted we remember and know so long as the image remains; whatever is rubbed out or has not succeeded in leaving an impression we have forgotten and do not know. (*Theaetus*, translated by Hamilton, 1961, p. 897)

By means of a simple analogy, Plato provides a basis for discussing the formation of memories, memory capacity, and individual differences in learning ability, and distinguishes between different explanations of forgetting. Another analogy appears later, when Plato describes memory as an 'aviary', in which pieces of knowledge are represented by 'birds' which have to be 'hunted down' if that knowledge is to be used. This argument extends the wax tablet analogy in two important ways. First, it conceives of memory as a space in which individual memories are stored at specific locations, and second, it makes a distinction between storing information and the active search processes required to retrieve it.

The origins of recent memory models can be traced back to William James (1842–1910). Although he relied entirely on introspection, James had many important ideas about memory and other psychological processes, and we will refer to him at a number of points. Like Plato, James used a spatial analogy to describe memory; he compared the act of remembering to the way we 'rummage our house for a lost object'. However, James introduced another important distinction, noting that new experiences do not disappear immediately from consciousness but linger in awareness for a short period of time. He termed this phenomenon 'primary memory', and suggested that its contents did not need to be retrieved; hence, 'an object of primary memory is not . . . brought back; it was never lost; its date was never cut off in consciousness from that of the immediately present moment . . . it comes to us as belonging to the rearward portion of the present space of time, and not to the genuine past' (James, 1890, pp. 646–7). In James's system the contents of primary memory pass into 'secondary memory', a large repository within which all our acquired knowledge is permanently stored. Information in secondary memory, unlike that in primary memory, has to be retrieved before it can be used. Unfortunately, James's important insights into memory were ignored for more than half the twentieth century. This was largely attributable to the pervasive influence of *behaviourism* on the course of experimental psychology at this time. The behaviourists viewed any explanation which embodied consciousness as a concept unworthy of scientific interest; thus James's dichotomy, with its emphasis on the relationship between consciousness and remembering, failed to attract any experimental investigation.

THE 'MULTISTORE' MODEL OF MEMORY

Analogies used to explain memory are now referred to as *models*. These models still conceive of memory in spatial terms, but they tend to compare the organization of memory with that of a computer. Figure 1.2 shows a typical example of this approach. Memory is seen as a series of 'stores', each representing a different stage in the processing of information. New information first enters a 'sensory store', a form of memory whose existence has been confirmed only by means of modern experimental techniques. New information enters the nervous system via one or more of our senses. Experiments have shown that the pattern of stimulation set up remains for a short period after the stimulus itself has been terminated. For visual information this form of sensory storage is known as 'iconic memory', and its existence was elegantly demonstrated by Sperling in 1960. In his experiment, subjects were shown three rows of letters, such as TDR, SRN, and FZR, for only 50 milliseconds. When the subjects were asked to name all the letters, they could report no more than four or five. Alternatively, subjects were shown the array, and immediately afterwards were given a signal indicating which of the three rows should be reported, they then named all three letters correctly on most trials. Since the subjects had no advance warning as to which row they would be asked to report, they must have had the whole array available when the signal was given, even though the stimulus itself was no longer present. Sperling examined the time course of this 'partial report' advantage, and found that it could be obtained only with intervals of less than a second between terminating the stimulus and giving the report signal, thus confirming that iconic memory is extremely transient. Sensory storage in other modalities has also been

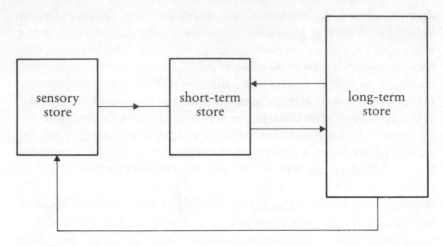

Figure 1.2   The 'multistore' model of memory (after Atkinson and Shiffrin, 1968)

investigated, but discussion of this topic goes beyond our present concern.

During the period of sensory storage, information undergoes basic processes of identification before it passes into short-term store (STS). This store is conceptually equivalent to James's primary memory, and provides the basis for our conscious mental activity. STS is the locus of control within the memory system; it determines what information is attended to and how information is processed, and governs retrieval of existing memory. STS can hold only a certain amount of information, and we refer to this capacity as our 'span of awareness' or, more typically, our *memory span*. Measurement of memory span is most commonly undertaken using the *digit span* technique. This measures the number of randomly arranged digits that an individual can repeat back in the correct order immediately after hearing or seeing them. In normal adults, digit span is around seven (plus or minus two).

The need for an STS is evident from consideration of a number of different tasks. When reading, for example, the earlier parts of a sentence must be kept in mind for the sentence as a whole to be understood. In performing a mental calculation, the outcome of one stage may need to be held while the solution to another stage is derived. Anecdotal evidence suggests that information in STS is vulnerable, and can easily be lost if some distraction or aversive event occurs. The everyday experience of being distracted and then being unable to remember what you were just saying is one example, as is the inability of concussion victims to remember events immediately preceding their accident.

Once in STS, information can have one of two fates: it can be transferred to long-term store (LTS), a structure of large capacity analogous to James's secondary memory, or it can be forgotten. How transfer occurs will be considered a little later. For now it is sufficient to note that effective transfer of information to LTS involves the formation of a permanent *memory trace*, which subsequently provides the basis for restoring that information to consciousness. In figure 1.2 you will notice that there is an arrow going directly from LTS to sensory store. This acknowledges that LTS is needed for the identification processes carried out. These early processes are extremely complex in themselves, and include word identification and object recognition. Thus, by the time information reaches STS, a considerable degree of processing has been achieved. We are not aware of these initial processes, however, what passes into consciousness and hence into STS is just their end result. This relationship implies that only information that has been consciously perceived passes from STS to LTS. In general we will assume this to be the case, but allow for the possibility of remembering some things we are not aware of (e.g., see Eich, 1984).

EVIDENCE FOR THE STS/LTS DISTINCTION

The distinction between STS and LTS is one that has strong intuitive appeal, but it is important to show that these hypothetical stores are separable components within the memory system. We will see later that evidence from amnesic patients bears on this issue, but for now, only experiments on normal memory will be considered. A number of techniques have been used, but we will concentrate on the *free recall* paradigm. This involves the sequential presentation of a series of items, usually words, followed by the instruction to recall as many of the items as possible in any order.

The results are displayed by plotting the probability of an item being recalled as a function of its position in the list; figure 1.3 shows the resulting *serial position curve.* The first few items are remembered quite well relative to the items in the middle of the list; this is called the *primacy effect.* The best recall is obtained for the last few items in the list; this is termed the *recency effect.* The middle portion of the curve, where recall is poorest, is known as the *asymptote.*

Psychologists were quick to explain this result in terms of the STS/LTS distinction; the recency effect was interpreted as the output of STS, while recall from earlier in the list was thought to come from LTS. However, before this interpretation could be accepted, additional experimental evidence was required. If the serial position curve represented the joint operation of STS and LTS, it was necessary to show that the two parts of the curve responded differently when certain factors were manipulated. If one could isolate a factor which influenced recall from earlier parts of the list but had no influence on the recency effect and, by contrast, a factor which only affected the size of the recency effect, this would be consistent with the operation of two memory stores with different characteristics.

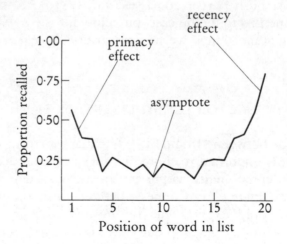

Figure 1.3   Typical finding from a free recall experiment, showing the three components of the serial position curve (after Glanzer and Cunitz, 1966)

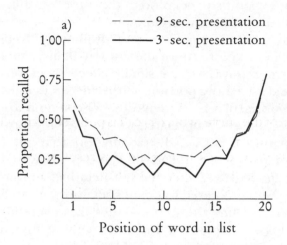

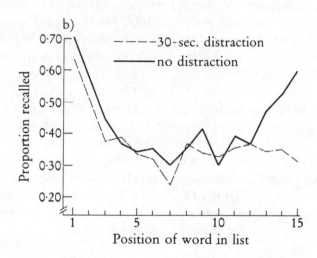

Figure 1.4   a) The effect of presentation time on the serial position curve. Presentation for 9 seconds improves recall relative to presentation for 3 seconds for early list positions, but does not influence the size of the recency effect. b) The effect of distraction prior to recall on the serial position curve. With distraction for 30 seconds, the recency effect disappears, but there is no effect on recall from other parts of the list. (After Glanzer and Cunitz, 1966)

Subsequent experiments explored the serial position curve under a number of different conditions. Figure 1.4a shows that longer presentation time improves recall from early list positions but has no influence on recall of the last few items. A number of other factors were shown to have similar effects. Thus, recall from the primacy and asymptote portions of the curve was greater with word lists comprised of related items or more common words than with lists of uncommon or unrelated words. The only factor found to have the opposite effect was distraction prior to recall. This was shown by comparing the recall of subjects allowed to start remembering immediately after the last item had appeared with that when they were required to count backwards in threes for 30 seconds before recalling the items. Under these conditions, the recency effect was completely eliminated, without any change in recall from other parts of the list (see figure 1.4b).

These results are most readily interpreted by assuming that recall from different parts of the list reflects the output of different memory stores. The ease with which the last few items are recalled and the susceptibility of this effect to distraction support the existence of an STS from which new information is immediately available, but which is vulnerable to disruption. Conversely, the fact that distraction does not affect recall from earlier in the list indicates that this information has achieved permanent storage in LTS. The identification of factors which influence recall from this part of the list but fail to influence the recency effect also supports the multistore interpretation of the serial position curve. Furthermore, the variables influencing recall indicate factors that are pertinent to the operation of LTS itself. For example, the finding of enhanced recall when items are meaningfully related confirms what we might expect, that memory is more effective for organized material.

If we conceive of memory formation as the transfer of information from STS to LTS, we must consider what factors might influence this process. The most obvious of these is that the brain itself should be working normally and the consequences of brain malfunction on memory constitutes a major part of this book. However, normal individuals often fail to remember things, and, under certain circumstances, this could be attributed to an ineffective transfer from STS to LTS. Proponents of the multistore model have suggested that successful transfer may depend on the amount of *rehearsal* the information receives. This concept stems from our natural tendency to repeat new information, either aloud or silently, in an effort to remember it. The relationship between rehearsal and memory was demonstrated by Rundus in 1971, using a modified version of the free recall technique. Subjects were presented with a list of words and were encouraged to repeat them out loud during presentation. Figure 1.5 shows both the recall data and the number of times words at each list position were rehearsed. For the early serial positions, recall was highly correlated with rehearsal rate, but this was not observed for the last few items. The transfer of information from STS to LTS therefore seems related to the amount of rehearsal each item receives; it thus offers an explanation of the primacy effect in terms of higher rehearsal rates for the first few items. Furthermore the increased recall with slower presentation rates stems most probably from the extra rehearsal time made available in that condition.

Although rehearsal affects how well we perform in the free recall task, it is of little broader significance. In everyday life we are seldom aware of rehearsing new information, yet we remember large numbers of new facts every day. Coupled with this, certain

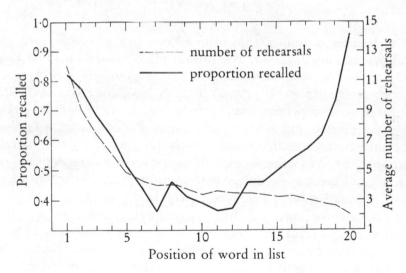

Figure 1.5   The relationship between the serial position curve and the number of times each word was rehearsed (after Rundus, 1971)

types of information, such as faces and smells, do not seem amenable to rehearsal. Finally, the rehearsal concept places too great an emphasis on the role of intentionality in learning. It is a perverse fact about human memory that we often remember things we would rather forget and forget things we want to remember. The writer Annie Dillard (1982) gives her own observation on this problem:

I . . . looked at the painting on the hotel room wall. It was . . . a detailed and lifelike painting of a smiling clown's head, made out of vegetables. It was a painting . . . which you do not intend to look at but alas you never forget. Some tasteless fate presses it upon you. . . . Two years have passed [and] I have forgotten a great many things I wanted to remember – but I have not forgotten that clown painting or its lunatic setting in the old hotel. (p. 85)

Forming new memories depends on more than the conscious intention to do so. In later chapters we will consider what these other factors might be.

CONSOLIDATION AND THE TRANSFER OF INFORMATION FROM STS TO LTS

The transfer of information from STS to LTS involves a process known as *consolidation*. The notion of consolidation has a long history, but modern ideas about the process derive mainly from the work of Donald Hebb (1949). Hebb's basic idea was that new information is represented initially by means of a temporary trace. He conceived of this as a specific pattern of activity within a group of interconnected neurones, which he referred to as a *cell assembly*. At this stage, storage of information is considered to be *active*, because any disruption in the pattern of activity will result in the information being lost completely. However, if this activity is maintained for sufficient time, structural changes in the cell assembly will occur, resulting in a permanent memory trace. Once this has been formed, there is no longer any need to maintain the initial pattern of activity, and the information is considered to be in *passive* storage.

It seems entirely reasonable to suppose that permanent

memories are formed by structural alterations in neurones; but what exactly is the change that occurs? When the nucleic acids *deoxyribose nucleic acid* (DNA) and *ribose nucleic acid* (RNA) were discovered, there was considerable speculation that they might be involved in memory. DNA and RNA are present in every living cell; DNA resides in the nucleus and forms the basis of the cell's genes, and RNA is the means by which information coded in the DNA is transmitted to the various organelles within the cell. It was suggested that RNA, as well as carrying information about cell function, could be the basis of memory storage.

Support for this theory came from a study by Hyden and Egyhazi (1962) in which rats were trained to walk a tightrope to obtain food. It was found that those who had acquired this skill had more RNA in their brain-stems than rats who had learnt nothing. Furthermore, the composition of the RNA in the trained group was different from that in the controls. Because these changes were found only in trained rats, it was concluded that RNA must be the basis of memory. Unfortunately, there is an alternative explanation. The processes underlying consolidation, like all others in an organism, are regulated by enzymes whose synthesis is controlled by RNA. One can assume that learning involves a pattern of enzymatic activity which differs from that in an animal that is not learning anything. It is not surprising, therefore, to find that the RNA of trained rats is different from that of rats that have not learnt, because different processes have taken place in the brain. What this evidence shows, therefore, is that certain patterns of RNA activity are *correlated* with learning; it does not allow us to conclude that RNA is the basis of memory.

Although many biochemical processes are known to be correlated with consolidation, the notion of a 'memory molecule' is no longer taken seriously. Instead, modern ideas regarding the basis of memory have focused on the structure of neurones. Hebb believed that the structural change underlying consolidation involved an alteration in the pattern of synaptic connectivity, and this view is still favoured, for at least two reasons. First, modification of synapses appears to be the only mechanism capable of storing the huge amounts of information that memory contains. It has been estimated that the brain contains 10^{13} synapses, a number that is adequate to handle the levels of information storage in memory.

Second, synapses make very low demands on energy, requiring only that the basal metabolic rate of the brain be maintained – thus accounting for the preservation of memory during periods of coma, when the brain's electrical activity is substantially reduced. The exact means by which synapses are modified is not yet known. One possibility is that changes occur in the amounts of neurotransmitter released at particular synapses; another is that memory formation involves the growth of completely new synapses.

An important feature of Hebb's explanation of consolidation is that the active and passive modes of storage make use of different underlying mechanisms. This being so, performance based on the active storage of information should continue even when the mechanisms of consolidation have been made inoperative (note that the reverse is not possible, because passive storage relies on the input provided by the active storage mechanism). Thus we might expect to observe situations in which information can be recalled immediately because it is in active storage but has been forgotten after a few minutes. In this book you will find many examples of this dissociation in various pathological disorders of memory, but for now we will restrict ourselves to experimental evidence from normal individuals.

One of the earliest neurotransmitters to be discovered was *acetylcholine*, and neuronal pathways in which it occurs are known to be implicated in memory function. There are a number of drugs that inhibit the action of acetylcholine, and administration of these would therefore be expected to affect memory adversely. Drachman and Leavitt (1974) gave one of these drugs, *scopala-mine* (hyoscine), to volunteers, and then examined their performance on a number of memory tasks. One of these was *digit span* which presumably relies mainly on active storage. Drachman and Leavitt found that scopalamine had no effect on digit span, but that performance on tasks requiring retention over longer time periods was impaired. These findings agree with a number of other studies (e.g. Cooper, 1984), and confirm that immediate recall of information, as in the digit span task, is mediated by a different system from that underlying longer-term recall, because only the latter is affected by inhibiting acetyl-choline.

So far the distinction between active and passive storage maps nicely on to the STS/LTS distinction. Information in STS seems to be supported by active storage, and transfer to LTS represents the formation of a permanent memory trace by the process of consolidation. If we interpret the free recall task in these terms, we are led to conclude that memory for recent items, which is disrupted by distraction, has not been consolidated, whereas memory for earlier list positions has gone into permanent storage. In a typical free recall experiment, the time that elapses between presentation of the first and last items is around 30 seconds. Thus, if recall from the early list positions is based on permanent memory, we must conclude that the process of consolidation is extremely rapid. Some physiologists have proposed that consolidation is indeed that fast, but others have suggested that it is much slower. Hebb himself suggested that the process took between 15 minutes and 1 hour, and others have suggested even longer periods. Electroconvulsive therapy, for example, causes a massive disruption in brain function, including the processes of consolidation. Patients are always amnesic with regard to events prior to the shock, suggesting that memory has failed to consolidate. However, the amnesic period is normally greater than a few seconds, indicating a longer time course for consolidation than that inferred from the free recall task.

Discrepancies of this kind can be resolved by supposing that consolidation involves a number of stages. One proposal is that there is an initial, rapid consolidation process which sets up a basic permanent representation, and that it is this mechanism that underlies the transfer of information from STS to LTS. Once in LTS, the newly formed trace is subject to additional consolidation processes which serve to integrate the new information with the existing contents of LTS. Traces formed by the rapid process may be sufficient to sustain recall in the free recall task, but more durable memory depends on the efficient implementation of the latter process (Squire et al., 1984).

Explanation of memory in purely biological terms is not yet possible. We know that complex patterns of neuronal activity underlie memory function, but the manner in which memory works is not evident from this alone. Psychologists have constructed models of memory by drawing analogies between memory and entities we do understand. Current theorizing conceives of memory as a series of stores with different characteristics. We have been concerned primarily with the distinction between STS and LTS, the former representing a limited-capacity system underlying conscious mental activity, the latter a permanent repository of all our knowledge. A number of lines of evidence support this distinction, particularly that derived from the free recall task. Transfer from STS to LTS involves a process known as consolidation, in which structural changes in the neuronal network give rise to a permanent memory trace.

2

Beyond the Multistore Model

The multistore model provides a basic account of how the memory system is organized. The dichotomies proposed in the model seem intuitively sound, and there is both psychological and physiological evidence to back the model up. However, there are many more issues that must be addressed if we are to have an adequate understanding of memory. The first of these concerns the organization of LTS.

THE ORGANIZATION OF LTS

In any individual, LTS contains a vast amount of information, and to be effective, it must be organized. The question of organization can be approached in many ways. Psycholinguists, for example, may be concerned with how we represent our knowledge of words and their meaning. Our approach will be more general, and will be based on the proposal that information in LTS takes one of three basic forms. This view is favoured because it provides the most appropriate framework for understanding certain phenomena which we will encounter in our subsequent discussion of memory disorders.

As a starting-point for discussion, let us return to the serial position curve in figure 1.3. This shows that subjects remembered only about 20 per cent of the words from the middle part of the list. Clearly memory has failed here; but what exactly has gone wrong? Free recall experiments involve common words, so the failure to remember cannot be because the subjects no longer know the words. Memory fails because the subjects are unable to remember that a given word was presented at a particular time.

In 1972 Tulving put forward a conceptual view of memory which provides a framework for discussing forgetting in the free recall task. He proposed that memories in LTS could be classified as either *episodic* or *semantic*. Episodic memory is described as an 'auto-biographical' memory responsible for storing a record of the events in our lives. It enables us to answer questions such as 'What were you doing yesterday?' or 'When did you last go to the cinema?' Semantic memory is our store of general knowledge about the world, concepts, rules, and language. The essential feature of semantic memory is that it can be used without reference to the events that account for its formation in the first place. Thus, when using language or doing arithmetic, we are not aware of the original circumstances under which we learnt to do these things; they are simply something we 'know'. Returning to the free recall task, the forgetting of words can be considered as a failure of episodic memory, since the locus of difficulty is in remembering a specific past event – namely, that a particular word was presented in a list we saw or heard at a specific time.

Semantic memory can also store information about ourselves. When we are asked what we do, what our opinions are, and so on, we do not have to remember specific past experiences in order to answer. Instead, we have access to a general account of ourselves, which is often sufficient to answer a wide range of personal questions. In normal individuals, this information is used in conjunction with the recollection of specific past experiences to provide a more detailed answer to a question. Thus, when asked your opinion about a particular piece of music, your positive reaction might be reinforced by recounting some occasion when you found it particularly enjoyable.

More recently Tulving (1985), among others (e.g. Anderson, 1985), has argued for an additional form of memory, a form that has been termed *procedural memory*. This can be defined as information in LTS that cannot be inspected consciously. Riding a bicycle, for example, is a complex skill that most of us acquire, but if we try to explain how we do it, we can give only the most superficial explanation. Similarly, native speakers of a language can usually give no account of the complicated grammatical rules that enable them to produce correct utterances. This type of memory is contrasted with episodic and semantic memory, both of which can be inspected consciously and both of whose content can be described fully to another individual.

Although it is necessary to distinguish them conceptually, episodic, semantic, and procedural memory represent a highly interactive system, and, at any one time, the behaviour of a normal individual may be directed by information from one or more of these sources. In addition, the contribution of these different memories in determining behaviour may change across time. The formation of new semantic memories may depend initially, for example, on information from episodic memory. Consider the problem of learning computer terminology. To newcomers, the jargon is wholly unfamiliar and difficult to assimilate. Thus the instruction to 'boot' the system is rather mysterious unless you remember that on a previous occasion it meant to start up the computer. However, with repeated use, the term becomes part of your general knowledge, and can be defined without recourse to episodic memory. These kinds of interactions also occur while learning skills. Take learning to type, for example. At first, this involves having to remember the layout of the keyboard in order to place your fingers correctly. However, as practice continues, the skill becomes increasingly automatic and independent of our ability to remember the keyboard's layout. At this stage, typing has ceased to rely on episodic and semantic memory, and has become incorporated in procedural memory. Indeed, when skilled typists are asked to recall the layout of the keyboard, they often find it difficult, remembering the location of some letters only by trying to type them and noticing where their finger is placed (Posner, 1973).

Tulving's account of memory is essentially introspective, with each form of memory being associated with a different kind of conscious experience. We are not consciously aware of procedural memories; their existence is inferred from the fact that an organism responds in a consistent manner to a particular stimulus. Because of this, it is a form of memory that we can assume to be present in any organism capable of learning, and for this reason it is thought to be the most primitive kind of memory. Semantic memory is open to conscious examination, because we can inwardly contemplate the features of the external world. Its contents are confirmed and altered in the light of new experience. For example, someone might believe initially that all cars run on petrol, but then he or she encounters a car that runs on diesel. This new observation then modifies that person's knowledge about cars. Episodic memory is associated with an additional and qualitatively distinct conscious awareness. It has a self-referential quality, enabling us to be aware of ourselves in the past and to imagine ourselves in the future. The truth of episodic memories is determined entirely by their sub-jective familiarity, rather than by observation. When we recall personal experiences, we do not have external proof that our memories are correct; the manner in which they enter our consciousness seems to assure their authenticity.

Semantic and episodic memory are assumed to be higher and more recently evolved forms of memory, and are inextricably linked with consciousness. As yet, we cannot establish whether other animals experience consciousness, which makes it difficult to consider these memory systems in relation to species other than man. Many psychologists have proposed conceptual distinctions similar to Tulving's, and there is agreement that a classification of this kind makes intuitive sense; but experimental evidence to support the distinctions is only beginning to emerge. At present, major support for this view comes from studies of the human amnesic syndrome, which will be considered in chapter 6.

Figure 2.1 represents our revised view of human memory; the multistore model is retained, but with the addition of a tripartite division of LTS into episodic, semantic, and procedural memory.

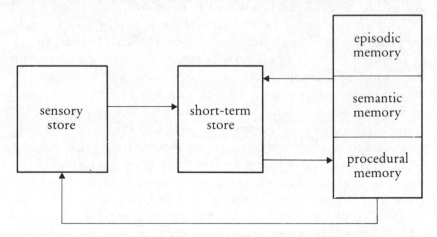

Figure 2.1   Revised multistore model, showing tripartite division of LTS

This division seems generally acceptable (but see chapter 6 for an alternative view); but for further understanding of memory, we must go beyond the fundamental question of organization and consider how the various parts of the system work. Unfortunately, the multistore model has not proved useful for pursuing these additional questions.

PROBLEMS WITH THE MULTISTORE MODEL

So far it has been assumed that the recency effect represents the output of STS, but recent research has challenged this view. It has been shown that the recency effect can survive long periods of distraction and that recency effects occur when people recall personal events extending over several months (see Baddeley, 1986). One could argue that these recency effects are different from those found in free recall but this explanation lacks *parsimony*. Some workers now believe that all recency effects are due to an *ordinal retrieval strategy* whereby memory can be accessed by a kind of 'looking back' process which becomes more inefficient as the items to be located become more distant. For very similar items, such as words in a list, this process is not particularly good and only the last few items can be retrieved effectively. However, for more distinctive events the process can extend back over much longer time periods.

Unfortunately not all the evidence favours this parsimonious view. Later we will see that most kinds of amnesic patient show normal recency in free recall but a grossly defective recall of information over any longer period of time. If the recency effect reflects an intact ordinal retrieval strategy one would not expect such a clear-cut impairment. The debate over recency has yet to be resolved, but for now we will assume that the recency effect in the free recall task is at least consistent with the existence of a separable STS. However, interpretive difficulties of this kind have placed limitations on the serial position curve as a fruitful means of exploring the STS/LTS dichotomy.

Another attempt to develop the STS/LTS dichotomy involves the idea that the two stores employed different forms of *encoding*. For a new memory trace to be formed, information must be translated into a *code*, which, to be effective, must allow that information to be reconstituted at a later stage. The concept of encoding can be applied to all kinds of information, but is most readily understood by considering how we remember words. Three basic dimensions of words can be specified: orthographic (visual features), phonological (acoustic features), and semantic (features having to do with meaning). The multifaceted nature of words allows some flexibility in how they can be represented in memory. Thus, on trying to memorize the word TABLE, a code based on its orthographic, phonological, or semantic properties, or any combination of these could be derived.

In 1964 Conrad reported an experiment in which subjects were shown a sequence of individual letters and were asked to repeat them back immediately in the correct order. The sequences were only six letters long, so the test mainly assessed memory span and could be assumed to rely principally on STS. Half the letter sequences were liable to phonological confusion (e.g. T E G V C B), while the remainder were not (e.g. S Y K H L O). Subjects made more errors on the former than the latter. It was concluded that this difference arose because subjects were making active use of a phonological code to perform the task, so letters that sounded similar were more likely to be confused.

Conrad's finding led to the idea that STS might rely primarily on a phonological code. Baddeley (1966a) subsequently presented lists of five words and asked subjects to recall them immediately in the correct order. There were two kinds of word lists, one composed of phonologically confusable words (e.g. MAD, MAP, MAN), and one of semantically confusable words (e.g. HUGE, GREAT, BIG). Recall with each of these lists was compared with that of a control list which was neither phonologically nor semantically confusable. The results showed that recall of phonologically confusable lists was substantially impaired, whereas that of semantically confusable lists was hardly affected. In a subsequent experiment, Baddeley (1966b) examined the effects of phonological and semantic confusability when recall was delayed for 20 minutes. Under these conditions it was only the recall of semantically confusable items which was worse than that of the controls.

Using the logic applied to Conrad's experiment, one might conclude that STS relied on phonological coding, whereas LTS represented information by means of a semantic code. However, a moment's thought indicates that such a simplistic distinction between the two stores will not do. Earlier we defined STS as a memory system capable of supporting our conscious mental activity. If STS represented information only phonologically, how could we understand immediately what was said to us, perform mental calculations, or recognize faces and smells? Moreover, a number of subsequent experiments have shown evidence of semantic coding in STS and phonological coding in LTS. Thus, attempts to distinguish STS and LTS in terms of encoding have failed. However, some of these experiments, especially those showing phonological confusion in immediate recall, have proved interesting for other reasons, which will be discussed later in this chapter.

LEVELS OF PROCESSING

The difficulties encountered with the multistore model led Craik and Lockhart (1972) to propose *levels of processing* as an alternative approach to understanding memory. Contrary to some accounts, they did not reject the basic multistore model outright. They simply argued that the model was unable to provide any further insights into the operation of memory, and that attempts to develop it further would be counterproductive.

The levels of processing concept is based on the assertion that the memory trace represents a record of the analyses carried out during the conscious processing of new information. It follows, therefore, that memory function can be explored by investigating how variations in the way new information is processed affect our subsequent ability to remember it. This idea was formalized by suggesting that analysis of a new stimulus proceeds through a series of levels, each representing a different dimension of the stimulus. The analogy was then extended by suggesting that more complex processing occurs at 'deeper' levels than simpler processes. For words, three levels were conceived: orthographic, phonological, and semantic, the latter representing the deepest level. Processing of new information was said to be under the control of a 'central processor' (see figure 2.2). This entity, like STS, represents the locus of conscious mental activity. However, the concern of Craik

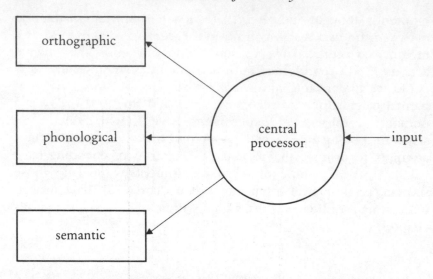

Figure 2.2　The 'levels of processing' approach to memory. Processing of new information is controlled by the central processor and can occur at one or more levels. Diagram shows how the theory relates to verbal memory

and Lockhart was not with the processor's structural aspects, but with how variations in its deployment might affect the retention of new information.

To explore this issue, Craik and Lockhart made use of the *incidental learning* technique. This involves presenting subjects with a series of items and requiring them to make a decision about each one. By manipulating the type of decision required, it is possible to create various *orienting tasks*, each of which addresses a different level of processing. The following are examples of orienting tasks involving orthographic, phonological, and semantic levels of processing: Is the word in capital letters? (orthographic) Does it rhyme with 'grog'? (phonological) Does it hop about? (semantic). All these would evoke a 'yes' response for the word FROG. For convenience, orthographic and phonological tasks are classified together as 'non-semantic'. An important feature of incidental learning is that the subjects do not usually expect their

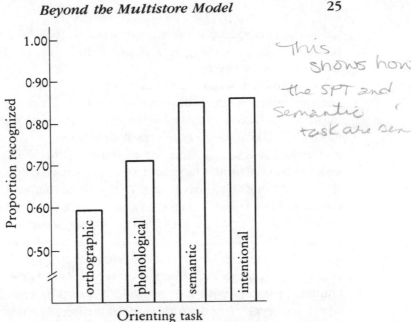

*Figure 2.3   Typical effect of different levels of processing on memory
performance (data from Craik, 1977a)*

memory to be tested; hence, the pattern of retention observed can
be attributed to the processing evoked by the orienting task, as
opposed to subjects' own attempts at deliberate memorization.

Figure 2.3 shows the results of an incidental learning experiment
involving memory for words. It employed not only semantic and
non-semantic orienting tasks, but also a control task whereby
subjects were instructed to learn the words. The most important
result is that the semantic orienting task produced much better
memory performance than the non-semantic tasks. However, note
also that the semantic task was as effective as the control condition;
this emphasizes the point made earlier that the intention to
remember is not an important determinant of whether or not we
remember something. On the basis of these findings, it was asserted
that 'deeper' semantic processing gave rise to a better, more
durable memory trace. The superiority of semantic over non-
semantic processing was demonstrated in numerous studies and

led to the generation of a principle: namely, that the probability of remembering something is a positive function of the depth to which it was processed.

Craik and Lockhart's approach grew in popularity with the demonstration of levels of processing effects for different types of information. This contrasted with experiments on the multistore model, which had been concerned almost exclusively with verbal memory. Winograd (1976), for example, showed subjects a long sequence of unfamiliar faces and required them to make a decision about each one. This involved either a judgement about physical characteristics (does he have straight hair?), personality (does he look friendly?), or role (does he look like an actor?). Subsequently the subjects' ability to recognize the faces was tested, and it was found that judgements about physical characteristics produced poorer recognition than the other types. This finding resembles findings in studies with words, since it shows that memory is best when subjects attend to meaning during learning. However, subsequent research has shown that the relationship between different orienting tasks and facial memory is more complex than originally thought (e.g. Winograd, 1981; Parkin and Hayward, 1983).

More subtle distinctions than that between semantic and non-semantic processing levels can be made. Craik and Tulving (1975) maintained that within the level of semantic processing, one could distinguish between different degrees of *elaboration*. This concept arose from experiments showing that the more extensively subjects processed the meaning of information, the more success-fully they remembered it. The importance of elaboration in memory was recognized by James (1890), and his account captures the essential point:

The more other facts a fact is associated with in the mind, the better possession of it our memory retains. Each of its associates becomes a hook to which it hangs, a means to fish it up by when sunk below the surface. . . . The 'secret of a good memory' is thus the secret of forming diverse and multiple associations with every fact we care to retain. (p. 662)

In modern terminology, elaboration can be described as the formation of a more richly encoded memory trace, which is more easily accessible because there are many different ways of contacting it in the process of retrieval.

Depth and elaboration were just two of a number of concepts that arose from the levels of processing approach. But interest in the approach subsided when certain methodological problems surfaced. The most important of these concerned the explanatory power of the levels concept. In the experiment illustrated in figure 2.3, subjects in the semantic orienting condition remembered more words than those in the non-semantic groups. This effect was explained by arguing that the semantic task produced a 'deeper' level of encoding. But how could we assume that? The answer was: 'Because it produced better retention.' Unfortunately, this argument is circular, since differences in depth are assumed on the basis of differences in retention, while this, in turn, is explained as a consequence of different depths of processing. The problem of circularity has proved a major stumbling block in developing the levels of processing concept. I have demonstrated some ways of overcoming it, but progress has not been great (Parkin, 1979; 1984).

Despite these difficulties, the levels of processing idea has made a significant contribution to our understanding of memory. Prior to its development, memory theories tended to oversimplify the psychological factors involved in the formation of new memories. Work with the multistore approach had identified only rehearsal as a significant factor in remembering. However, as we noted in chapter 1, this is a rather limited concept, which can account for only a tiny fraction of what we learn. The recognition that acquisition is not a rigidly defined process and that variations in the way information is handled can affect how well it is remembered has had an important impact on the way psychologists investigate memory. In attempting to explain a wide range of memory phenomena, it is now accepted that changes in the *processing strategy* adopted by the subject may provide the basis for an explanation.

WORKING MEMORY

The working memory model of Baddeley and Hitch (1974) represents a third framework for studying the operation of memory.

Its aim is to establish how memory is organized so as to support the kinds of mental activity that characterize our everyday life. Essentially it is a development of the STS concept described in chapter 1. The major difference is that STS is no longer a unitary system. Instead it is conceived of as 'an alliance of temporary storage systems co-ordinated by an attentional component [termed] the *central executive*' (Baddeley, 1984a). The model is outlined in figure 2.4; two temporary storage systems can be identified, the *articulatory loop*, and the *visiospatial scratch pad*. The bulk of conscious mental activity is handled by the central executive. When the need arises, however, certain types of information can be transferred to one of the specialized storage systems. The visio-spatial scratch pad is assumed to be a specific device for manipulating visual images, but research on this aspect of the system has only recently commenced. In contrast, the articulatory loop has received substantial investigation.

Earlier we considered experiments showing phonological confusions in the immediate recall of verbal information. It was findings such as these that led, in part, to the concept of the articulatory loop. This loop is seen as a structure of limited capacity that is

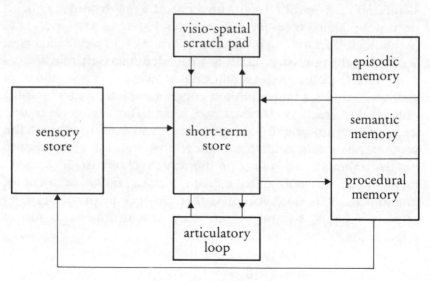

Figure 2.4   Multistore model revised to incorporate the concept of working memory

capable of holding a small amount of phonological information. Thus, in Baddeley's immediate recall experiment, the poorer recall of phonologically confusable words stems from subjects' reliance on the articulatory loop as an aid to performing the task.

The role of the articulatory loop has been explored mainly by using the *articulatory suppression* technique. It is assumed that the loop utilizes some of the internal mechanisms responsible for generating speech. Thus, if a subject is speaking, it is not possible to use the articulatory loop. In articulatory suppression experiments, subjects are required to perform a mental task while reciting nonsense (e.g. coca-cola, coca-cola, etc.). Their performance is compared with that of a control group who perform the same task without suppression. The contribution of the articulatory loop to performance of the task is then assessed by comparing the suppression group with the control group.

There seems to be good evidence that the human memory system has a specific capacity to store temporarily a limited amount of phonological information, but what do we use it for? One proposal is that the short-term storage of phonological information plays a role in silent reading. In general, experiments have shown that the suppression of articulation during reading affects only the more difficult aspects of reading, such as drawing inferences. Baddeley (1984b) has suggested that one role of the loop is to help preserve word order. This may be useful when dealing with difficult texts such as legal documents, but unimportant with easier material.

The concept of an articulatory loop has gained considerable popularity as an explanatory construct. It provides us with a basis for discussing and understanding the involvement of phonological information in STS function. In terms of the entire working memory system, however, it is a very small component. Experiments with articulatory suppression have shown impairments on a number of psychological tasks, but subjects have never been incapable of performing them. At best, the articulatory loop is a useful adjunct to the complex processes underlying conscious mental activity, but it seems that we can get by without its contribution. What is more difficult is to explain how the central executive operates, but this has so far received little attention.

In this chapter we have extended the multistore model by dividing LTS into three separate forms of memory: episodic, semantic, and procedural. We have noted that the multistore model is limited as a means of explaining how various parts of the system work. Two alternative approaches have been considered: levels of processing and working memory. Both of these approaches still embody a distinction between some form of STS and LTS but the emphasis is different. Levels of processing concentrates on how different processing strategies affect memory, whereas working memory considers how STS might be adapted to support our various mental activities.

3

Remembering and Forgetting

The act of remembering involves the location of memories in LTS and their restoration to consciousness. Theoretical explanations of this *retrieval process* must explain how we are able rapidly to access specific memories from among the vast amount of information stored in LTS. For this to occur, retrieval must be guided in some way; thus William James (1899) writes: 'Suppose I am silent for a moment, and then say ... "Remember!, Recollect!" Does your ... memory obey the order, and reproduce any definite image from your past? Certainly not. It stands staring into vacancy, and asking, "What kind of a thing do you wish me to remember?" ' (pp. 117–18) James's point is that retrieval is a *reconstructive* process, in which currently available information serves to initiate and direct the search for memories in LTS. Modern retrieval theories have attempted to offer a more detailed explanation of how this interaction occurs.

MODERN THEORIES OF RETRIEVAL

Before we can discuss retrieval, it is necessary to distinguish three different kinds of remembering. Figure 3.1 describes a hypothetical experiment in which subjects have attempted to learn a list of words. Condition A represents *recall* when the subjects try to remember the words without any external information to help them. Condition B represents *cued recall*, in which the subjects are given some explicit information to help them remember (e.g. one of the words you are trying to remember begins with WA ...). Condition C involves *recognition*, the subject being presented with a word and then asked whether it is one that he or she is trying to

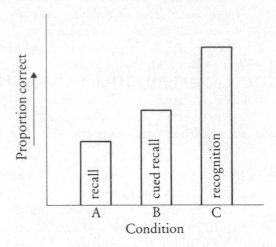

Figure 3.1   Typical relationship between different types of retrieval test

remember (e.g. was WATCH on the list?). The results are typical of the many experiments that have tested memory in these three different ways: performance is best with recognition testing, followed by cued recall, and then recall. These findings concur with our everyday experience of memory. We may fail to recall the answer to a question, for example, but recognize it immediately when it is shown to us. Similarly, we may be unable to name someone, but remember the name easily when we are prompted with their initials.

Any theory of retrieval must account for the superiority of recognition over recall. One explanation is to conceive of memories as varying in 'strength' and to say that greater trace strength is required for recall than for recognition (Kintsch, 1970). However, this explanation is not consistent with certain experimental findings. One of these is that lists of common words (e.g. TABLE) are recalled more easily than lists of rare words (e.g. SPOOL), whereas in recognition testing, rare words are identified more readily than common words. A 'strength' theory of memory cannot account for this, since it would predict that words recalled best should also be those most easily recognized.

The identification of factors which have different effects on recall and recognition has led to the idea that the latter are separate processes. This proposal forms the basis of the *generation-recognition* theory of retrieval (e.g. Anderson and Bower, 1972). According to this theory, retrieval involves an initial search stage in which possible 'targets' are generated. Each of these is then subjected to a recognition process, to determine whether it is the information required. For recall, both stages must be implemented, whereas for recognition, only the second stage is required. Recall is therefore less reliable, because there are two stages at which it can fail, compared with only one for recognition.

The generation-recognition model can be explained using the example of an experiment in which a subject is required to learn a list of ten words. Memory traces corresponding to these words are laid down in episodic memory, and when the instruction to recall the words is given, STS retrieves information from semantic memory in order to generate possible targets. Under free recall conditions, the subject must initiate this process by first accessing the relevant portion of episodic memory. When a word is retrieved, this can then serve as a further possibility for generating associations. For example, subjects may have remembered words in relation to other words on the list, so that retrieving one word provides a cue to another word. As each word is generated, it is subjected to a 'recognition check' to establish whether it is on the target list. If the check is positive, the word is recalled, if negative, it is not. The advantage of cued over free recall arises because a cue provides specific information about the nature of the target information. Thus the generation process is more likely to come up with the appropriate target word. Recognition is even more efficient, because the generation stage is bypassed entirely.

Generation-recognition theory provides us with a testable prediction. For a memory to be recalled, both the generation and recognition phases must have been successful. From this it follows that any information that can be recalled *must* be capable of being recognized. Thus, if we are able to recall WATCH from a word list, we should also be able to recognize it, since, in recalling WATCH, the act of recognition was carried out.

In 1973 Tulving and Thomson carried out an experiment which examined this prediction. The experiment consisted of four phases. In phase 1 subjects were presented with target words to learn. Each of these was accompanied by a 'cue' word which the subjects were asked to attend to but not deliberately try to remember. A typical example might be the target ENGINE paired with 'black'. In phase 2 subjects were presented with another list of words, for each of which they were required to generate associations. The stimulus words were carefully chosen so that there would be a high probability of their generating one of the targets learnt in phase 1. Thus for the 'black'–ENGINE pairing, the word 'steam' might be a stimulus in phase 2. As a result a large number of phase-1 targets were produced. In phase 3 subjects had to look at the words they had generated and pick out any that were targets in phase 1. In phase 4 subjects were presented with the cue words from phase 1 and asked to recall the target word that accompanied each one. The most important result was that in phase 4 subjects often recalled words that they failed to recognize in phase 3.

The experiment failed to confirm the prediction that we must be able to recognize any word that we can recall. This led to a rejection of the generation-recognition model by Tulving and Thomson, who replaced it with the *encoding specificity principle*. The essence of this view is that recall and recognition are not separate stages of the retrieval process. Instead, retrieval is viewed as a single process in which information currently available interacts directly with the contents of memory. The success of retrieval depends on overlap between the stored information and that currently available. The greater the overlap, the greater the likelihood of a memory being successfully retrieved. To explain the usual superiority of recognition over recall, it was argued that recognition tests typically present subjects with more information about what they are trying to remember. But then, why did Tulving and Thomson find cued recall better than recognition? Their explanation centred on the manner in which the target had been encoded. It was argued that the phase-1 cue words led subjects to encode the target words in a specific way. When these cue words were subsequently generated in phase 2, it was in response to different cues; thus, the target words were presented in a different *context* to that in which they were originally learnt. Thus, in the recognition test there was less overlap with the target memory trace than with the original cue, and it was this difference that led to cued recall being better than recognition.

The encoding of contextual information is an essential prerequisite for an efficiently organized LTS. Contextual information can be defined broadly as the information associated with a memory that enables that memory to be distinguished from all others. Hewitt (1973) has proposed a distinction between *intrinsic* and *extrinsic* context. A change in intrinsic context arises when some aspect of the target itself is changed (e.g. the colour of someone's hair), whereas in a change of extrinsic context, the target itself remains the same, but the information accompanying the target is different. A good example of the latter is meeting someone you know very well in an unexpected place. There may be nothing different about their appearance, but the fact that you do not normally meet them under such circumstances can make it more difficult to recognize them.

An important feature of episodic memory is its capacity for answering questions requiring location of a particular point in the past. Episodic memory must therefore have some form of organization which distinguishes events in time, but how is this achieved? Logical constraints obviously play a role – e.g. schooldays must have preceded college days. Similarly, 'key events' such as getting married can be used as 'landmarks' for identifying events as having occurred before or after such an event. But there are numerous occasions on which our ability to remember an event requires more sophisticated discrimination. Consider the question 'What did you watch on television last night?' This is presumably something you have done many times before, so how do you distinguish the events of last night from those of previous similar occasions? To explain this ability, it has been proposed that contextual information has a specific temporal aspect which defines a given event in time. Psychologists label this *temporal context*, but there are no strong theories of how LTS represents this information.

Recently the encoding specificity idea has come in for serious criticism. Consider a hypothetical experiment in which a subject learns some new information. Two cues, X and Y, are then presented successively, but only Y enables the subject to remember the target information. The encoding specificity principle asserts that a retrieval cue will be effective only if it has information in common with the memory trace. It would thus be concluded that Y has an overlap with the memory trace whereas X does not.

However, if X were the only effective cue, the opposite conclusion would be reached. This circular line of reasoning has led many psychologists to reject encoding specificity as a valid scientific theory. There are also 'ecological' objections to it. By arguing that cues are effective only if they have some informational overlap with a memory trace, considerable inflexibility is attributed to the retrieval system, since novel information cannot be used to access memories. By contrast, the generation-recognition model allows for completely new information to facilitate recall, provided it guides the generation process in an appropriate manner.

Although the encoding specificity principle is limited as a scientific theory, it was important in drawing attention to the role of context in the retrieval process. Earlier theories of retrieval had taken little account of contextual influences. Tulving and Thomson's demonstration that altering the conditions under which target information is presented can lead to failure of recognition ensured that all subsequent theories of retrieval would specifically address the effects of context.

The generation-recognition model can be adapted to accommodate the effects of context (Reder et al., 1974), but this still does not make it an adequate explanation of the retrieval system. One difficulty is that our memory does not normally seem to generate possibilities prior to recall. Most of what we remember appears to come to us effortlessly, and it is only on rare occasions that we apply a conscious generative strategy to help us remember. Related to this is the problem of specifying how the generation process starts. This may be straightforward when a specific cue is presented, but this situation is not characteristic of normal memory. The generation-recognition model provides an account of how retrieval operates when explicit information is available about the memories to be recalled. This does not deny the basic contention that retrieval is a reconstructive act, but the normal process of retrieval is more complex than that specified by the generation-recognition model.

RECOGNITION VERSUS FAMILIARITY

So far we have considered recognition as a unitary process, but more detailed analysis shows that this is not the case. The literal meaning of the term *recognition* is 'previously known', and Mandler (1980) has proposed two ways in which our memory system indicates this. His analysis is based on an experience that we all have from time to time. He notes that we often encounter someone or something and experience it as 'familiar', even though we cannot identify who or what it is. Thus we may meet someone in the street and be aware that he or she is familiar, even though we do not know just who the person is. In order to identify the person, a second process must be initiated, in which LTS is searched until the person's identity can be established. This process might well involve generating possibilities about the person's role (is he the milkman? or the dustman?).

The experience of familiarity is useful, since it tells us that our memory contains additional information about what we have just encountered. Conversely, the absence of familiarity indicates that there is no relevant information in memory and precludes a needless search of LTS. A related phenomenon is *feeling of knowing*. It describes situations in which we are unable to recall a fact but know that we have it in our memory somewhere. This rather annoying state can even reach a point where people can recall various related facts, but not the specific information required. Brown and McNeill (1966) demonstrated this 'tip-of-the-tongue' phenomenon by asking people to say which word corresponded to a particular definition. The words were rather unusual (e.g. 'sampan'), and subjects frequently failed to remember them. Nonetheless, they could state correctly facts such as the number of syllables and the word's stress pattern.

FORGETTING

If someone asks you what you have just been reading, it is likely that you will be able to tell them quite a lot. However, if you are asked sometime later, your recollection will not be as good. This indicates that forgetting is a time-dependent process; but at what rate does it actually occur? The first systematic investigation of this problem was carried out by Hermann Ebbinghaus (1885), who is regarded as the founder of experimental research on memory. Ebbinghaus's approach to experimentation was extremely thorough, with every effort made to exclude the influence of extraneous factors. His techniques have been considered artificial by some, but the rigours he practised are still present in much recent research. The experiments, which he conducted on himself, involved learning lists of nonsense syllables until he could recall them perfectly. To measure his forgetting rate, he would record the number of repetitions needed to learn a list and then retest himself after a delay. At retest he recorded the number of repetitions he needed to relearn the list. Forgetting was measured in terms of the difference between the number of repetitions originally required to learn the list and the number required when retested. Figure 3.2 shows the amount of 'savings' in relearning after different delays; this pattern is now known to be typical of forgetting in general. At first, forgetting is rather rapid, with a 60 per cent saving in learning time after 20 minutes reduced to a 45 per cent after an hour. After this, forgetting occurs much more slowly, with only a 5 per cent difference between 2 and 31 days.

The next and more difficult question concerns how forgetting occurs. One theory is the 'Law of Disuse' (Thorndike, 1913), which states that memories naturally deteriorate over time. This view held considerable popularity until McGeoch (1932) raised two impor-

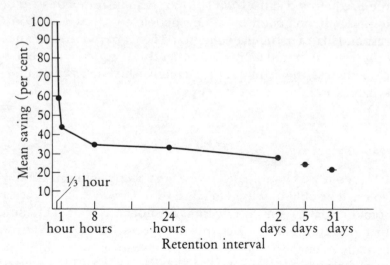

Figure 3.2   Forgetting rate, as measured by Ebbinghaus. (Note that forgetting is most rapid in the hour or so following learning.) (From Baddeley, 1976, p. 8)

tant objections. First, in many situations, disuse was shown to have no effect on retention. Second, and more important, even if disuse does lead to forgetting, this does not constitute an explanation. McGeoch drew an analogy with the fact that a nail becomes increasingly rusty over time. However, time is not the cause of the rust, but merely the logical prerequisite for the process of oxidation to occur. Similarly, if a memory fades through disuse, it is not time that has caused the forgetting, but something that has happened during that time.

McGeoch put forward an alternative explanation of forgetting, which led to the development of *interference theory*. The basis of this theory is that all learning involves the formation of associations (e.g. $A \rightarrow B$). As more learning takes place, some of the new associations will have elements in common with those already formed (e.g. $A \rightarrow C$), and this 'interference' wil give rise to forgetting. One extensively used technique for exploring inter-ference effects is that of *paired-associate learning*. The subject is first required to learn a series of arbitrary associations between, most commonly, pairs of words. Thus a subject would learn that the stimulus PIANO is associated with the response 'cigar' ($A \rightarrow B$). A second series of pairs is then presented, in which the stimulus terms remain the same, but the responses are changed. Now the subject has to learn that PIANO is associated with 'giraffe' ($A \rightarrow C$). Within this paradigm two forms of interference can be distinguished: *retroactive interference* (RI), in which subsequent learning ($A \rightarrow C$) impairs recall of older memories ($A \rightarrow B$), and *proactive interference* (PI), in which older memories impair subsequent learning.

The two forms of inteference have been demonstrated in a number of different ways, but in most cases the experiments have involved either lists of single words or simple binary associations. This has led to the criticism that interference theory lacks external validity because it is derived from experiments with learning tasks that are uncharacteristic of everyday life. This criticism is not altogether valid, for the common mistake of giving your previous address instead of the one to which you have just moved can be thought of in $A \rightarrow B$, $A \rightarrow C$ terms. However, most of what we learn and then forget is difficult to conceive of as patterns of simple association. Further, interference theory has yet to explain how forgetting occurs in simple tasks such as paired-associate learning. These difficulties lead us to consider forgetting from a different, less theoretical, perspective.

THE PENFIELD PHENOMENON

During the 1940s Wilder Penfield carried out many brain operations on epileptic patients in order to relieve their intractable seizures. Patients were first fully anaesthetized; the appropriate area of the skull was then removed, and the brain exposed. Consciousness was then restored, with only a local anaesthetic being maintained. During the operation it was necessary to stimulate the surface of the brain with an electrode. Penfield noted that stimulation in one particular region (the temporal lobe) resulted in patients recalling 'experiences'. One patient said: 'I just heard one of my children speaking ... it was Frank, and I could hear the neighbourhood noises,' and another: 'Something brings back a memory. I can see the Seven-Up bottling company ... Harrison Bakers' (Penfield, 1958). In general, these recollections were vivid, detailed, and concerned with seemingly insignificant past events. Penfield was deeply impressed by this phenomenon, and believed that he had located 'the stream of consciousness'. The apparent triviality of the patients' recollections led him to propose that 'nothing is lost [from memory], the record of man's experience is complete'. For Penfield, difficulties in remembering stemmed entirely from failure to gain access to memories.

Penfield's view of memory as a 'videorecorder' faithfully recording every detail of our lives has come under serious criticism. Loftus and Loftus (1980) took a close look at the evidence on which Penfield based his claims. Penfield reported that recollections occurred only when stimulation was applied to the temporal lobe region, a finding that is consistent with the known involvement of this area in memory function (see chapter 6). However, of the 520 patients stimulated in this way, only 40 showed the phenomenon, and of these, only 12 appeared to experience genuine recall. When these 12 were examined in more detail, their responses had more in common with the content of dreams than actual memories.

Students of memory no longer accept the data on which Penfield based his claims. However, his conclusions about the nature of forgetting are still widely accepted by many, in particular, by those who maintain that hypnosis can allow people to remember more than is possible in their normal conscious state. Such claims gain plausibility when presented in the context of Penfield's assertion that memory contains a perfect record of experience. In fact there is no reliable demonstration that hypnosis can aid people's memory (see below).

It seems both implausible and impractical that our memory system should be burdened with the storage of millions of trivial experiences that are no longer of any use to us. A more attractive hypothesis is that memory is a selective process in which only certain aspects of our experiences are committed to LTS. In this connection we should note that possession of an STS in which information can be held temporarily provides an ideal basis for sorting out what does and does not need to be remembered. Thus, far from being a disadvantage, the labile nature of short-term memory traces has permitted the development of a more effective memory system. What needs to be stored can undergo consolidation, while the rest will simply be lost when the period of active storage is over.

It must be stressed again that acquiring new memories does not depend on a conscious intention to do so. What is probably more important is interest level and the relevance of an event to an individual. Somebody interested in football, for example, would be far more likely to attend to the football results on the radio than someone who is not interested. Furthermore, his greater knowledge of the game would give him a more sophisticated and effective basis for remembering. Thus a result might be remembered because it runs counter to the form of the two sides involved.

STORAGE VERSUS RETRIEVAL FAILURE

By accepting that memory is a selective process, we can entertain two fundamental reasons for forgetting. The first is *storage failure*, in which the desired information failed to be transferred from STS to LTS, or once in LTS, became permanently unavailable for some reason. Unfortunately there are logical difficulties in trying to demonstrate that forgetting has occurred due to storage failure. Imagine an experiment in which you tell someone your address, and he or she is able to repeat it back accurately moments later. An hour later you meet that person again, and he or she cannot remember anything about it. You try a few cues such as the first letter of your street name, but none of these is effective. At this point you are tempted to conclude that information about your address is no longer in that person's memory. However, it might be that you have failed to provide the right kinds of retrieval cues. To prove unequivocally that failure to remember is due to storage failure, you would have to examine independently the contents of that person's memory, but this is impossible.

Storage failure is therefore an explanation of forgetting which we accept by default if the alternative account of *retrieval failure* fails to provide an answer. This second explanation proposes that forgetting occurs because of deficiencies in the retrieval process. It is much more attractive at the experimental level, because it can be verified empirically. All that is required is a demonstration that a subject can retrieve information under one set of circumstances but not under another. Forgetting due to retrieval failure can be shown in a number of different ways, which will now be briefly described.

CONTEXT EFFECTS

Work on the encoding specificity principle highlighted the importance of context in memory. Since then, many other experiments have shown that manipulations of context can have striking effects on both recall and recognition.

Effects of intrinsic context have been shown in a number of different ways. It has been demonstrated not only that disguises impair facial memory (Patterson and Baddeley, 1977), as one would expect, but that a mere change of clothing can make someone much less easy to recognize (Thomson et al., 1982). A change in expression on someone's face between learning and test can also reduce recognition accuracy (Parkin and Goodwin, 1983). Intrinsic context effects can likewise be shown in verbal learning experiments. Light and Carter-Sobell (1970) showed that subjects will often fail to recognize ambiguous words if they are presented for learning in one context (e.g. JAM as in 'traffic') and tested in an alternative context (JAM as in 'Strawberry').

Retrieval failure caused by changes in intrinsic context are to be expected on common-sense grounds. It is not surprising that a disguised face may go unrecognized because, in effect, the disguise constitutes a different stimulus to that already learnt. However, intuition does not allow us any easy conclusions about the possible effects of extrinsic context, because it is not easy to see why factors unrelated to the target material should affect how well it is remembered. Nonetheless, a considerable number of investigators have reported impaired memory due to changes in extrinsic context. Godden and Baddeley (1975) required subjects to learn information either on land or under water and found that recall was better when the learning and test environments were the same. However, in a subsequent study (Godden and Baddeley, 1980) they failed to find an effect when a recognition test was used. It is not necessary to go to the extremes used by Godden and Baddeley to obtain extrinsic context effects. Following the early observations of Abernathy (1940), several studies have shown that information learnt in one room is remembered more easily in the same environment than somewhere different (e.g. Smith, 1979; Metzger et al., 1979).

STATE-DEPENDENT LEARNING

There is a well-known story of a man who gets drunk at a party and hides his car keys so that he will not be tempted to drive home. Sobering up the next day, he discovers that he cannot remember where he put them, so needs to get drunk again to remember where they are. This anecdote illustrates the phenomenon of *state-dependent learning*. It is assumed that, under certain circumstances, the internal psychophysiological state of the body acts as a form of context, and thus influences retrieval. This effect has been shown a number of times. Eich (1980) found that word lists learnt under the influence of marijuana were recalled better when subjects were once again under the influence of the drug than when they were not. However, state-dependent learning is not a wide-spread phenomenon; it occurs only under specific conditions. Eich made a survey of 57 state-dependent learning studies, and found that significant effects were restricted almost exclusively to experiments that had used free recall as the means of testing memory. When cued recall or recognition was used, no state-dependent effects were found. This suggests that a person's physiological state can influence the retrieval system, but that the effects are very weak and are easily overriden when the subject is given specific information to aid remembering.

State-dependent learning is not easy to explain, but one possibility is that psychoactive states lead people to adopt unusual strategies when trying to learn and retrieve information. Thus information learnt in an intoxicated state will be incompatible with the type of retrieval strategy adopted when sober. Evidence for this idea is slight, although there are a number of studies indicating that marijuana intoxication causes people to make unusual associations to stimuli (e.g. Block and Wittenborn, 1985). In the context of a memory experiment, this could lead to the formation of unusual representations or promote atypical retrieval strategies. This would be fine when learning and retrieval occurred in the drugged state, but when they occurred in different states, retrieval would be more difficult.

HYPNOSIS AND MEMORY

The use of hypnosis to enhance memory has a long history. During the nineteenth century there were numerous reports of people recalling memories under hypnosis that they could not recall in their normal conscious state. In the last twenty years interest in hypnosis and memory has revived, principally on account of repeated claims that hypnotic procedures can improve the memory of witnesses.

Early practitioners were aware that hypnosis was an unreliable method of improving memory, but modern advocates have nonetheless promoted its use by police forces in various parts of the world. The case for hypnosis usually rests on anecdotal evidence; when objective experiments are carried out, there is little support for the view that hypnosis enhances memory.

Zelig and Beidelman (1981) showed subjects a distressing film depicting an industrial accident and then tested subjects' memory in either a hypnotic or a normal state. The hypnotic subjects were found to make more errors on leading questions, and their confidence in their answers was related to their degree of hypnotic susceptibility (how easy they were to hypnotize), not to the accuracy of their memories. Similarly, Sheehan and Tilder (1983) found that hypnosis did not enhance subjects' recall of a simulated wallet theft, even though they were significantly more confident in their answers than control subjects. These findings, along with many others, provide no evidence that hypnosis enhances memory (Wagstaff, 1984). What they do show is that hypnosis makes subjects more prone to make false positive errors, particularly in response to leading questions.

To understand why hypnotic interviews lead to such inaccuracies, we must look more closely at the nature of hypnosis. Wagstaff (1981) has argued that hypnosis involves a form of *compliance*, in which the hypnotized individual abdicates responsibility for his or her actions on the assumption that he or she is now under the 'control' of the hypnotist. In support of this notion are many examples of people engaging in apparently dangerous or antisocial behaviour while in a hypnotic trance. When asked to recall information under hypnosis, the subject's readiness to comply with the aim of the interview (by recalling more information) results in inaccurate statements, particularly in response to leading questions. Compliance can extend to the point where interviewers can 'plant' false memories in hypnotized subjects. Laurence and Perry (1983) report that 13 of 27 hypnotized subjects claimed to have heard some loud noises during their trance, when these had merely been suggested by the hypnotist.

Proponents of hypnosis argue that laboratory simulations of hypnotic procedures are invalid, because they do not reflect the real-life situations in which hypnosis is typically used. However, the unanimity of the experimental findings makes such a sweeping rejection difficult to accept. Furthermore, there have been a number of instances in which court decisions based on hypnotic evidence have been overturned using arguments similar to those derived from the experimental findings. The demonstrable unreliability of hypnosis has led to evidence obtained under hypnosis being ruled as inadmissible.

EMOTION AND MEMORY

The idea that the emotional content of memories can affect how accessible they are has a long history. Francis Bacon (1561–1626), for example, believed that events associated with strong emotions, positive or negative, were more easily remembered than those that aroused indifferent feelings.

Modern interest in emotion and memory stems from the work of Sigmund Freud (1856–1938), who proposed the concept of *repression* to explain why people forget certain things, but not others. According to Freud, an individual can repress the recall of memories that are likely to cause anxiety. In Freud's writings, examples of repression are usually drawn from psychoanalytical interviews with mentally disturbed people, but Freud believed that the concept applied to normal forgetting as well. In his book *The Psychopathology of Everyday Life* he cites many examples of repression in normal people, noting that 'the tendency to forget what is disagreable seems to me to be a quite universal one; the capacity to do so is doubtless developed with different degrees of strength in different people' (Freud, 1914).

During the first part of the twentieth century, large numbers of experiments were carried out to try to confirm the Freudian hypothesis, which became known as the *hedonic selectivity* or *Pollyanna* hypothesis (the latter designation deriving from a popular film featuring a girl who saw only good in the world). The basic idea was to show that unpleasant memories were harder to remember than pleasant ones. Unfortunately these experiments were plagued with methodological and interpretive difficulties. One problem is that the greater recall of pleasant experiences might reflect *response bias* rather than differences in the availability of memories. Thus the general tendency of people to remember pleasant rather than unpleasant experiences may be due to an unwillingness to report the latter, and not to a failure of memory. Another problem is that the effects of emotion on memory can often be attributed to other factors, such as the level of arousal induced by information varying in its emotional content (Parkin et al., 1982).

In chapter 10 we will see that the concept of repression is useful when considering certain kinds of memory disorder. In everyday life we may point to some instances of forgetting that can be interpreted as repression (e.g. failing to keep a dental appointment), but most of our forgetting has no such obvious motive and must be explained in other ways.

An alternative idea about the relationship between emotion and memory is that emotion exerts state-dependent effects on retrieval. In one study (Bower, 1981) subjects were asked to keep a diary for a week of events in their emotional lives. A week after they had completed their diaries, they returned to the laboratory and were put through a mood-induction procedure. This makes use of hypnosis, and its effect is to put the subject in either a pleasant or an unpleasant mood. The subjects were then required to recall the events recorded in their diaries. The most important finding was that subjects in a pleasant mood recalled more pleasant events, while those in an unpleasant mood remembered a greater proportion of unpleasant events. These results are inconsistent with the Pollyanna hypothesis, since this would predict superior recall of pleasant experiences regardless of mood.

Before considering explanations of this result, a second study by Bower and co-workers (1981) will be considered. Subjects listened to a story about two characters called 'Happy André' and 'Sad Jack'. The story was contrived so that only good things happened to André, whereas life was one disaster after another for Jack. Hypnosis was again used, with half the subjects listening to the story in a happy mood, the remainder in a sad mood. Most subjects were found to remember more facts about the character consistent with their mood while listening to the story (i.e. happy subjects remembered more about André). The experiment was subsequently repeated, except that subjects listened to the story in a neutral state, and a happy or sad mood was induced only at recall. Under these conditions, the subjects' moods did not affect the nature of recall.

The interpretation of these findings is that the mood experienced at the time of an event becomes part of the memory of that event. This being so, retrieval of the event is more likely if the person's current mood is similar to that associated with the events that he or she is trying to remember. Unlike repression, this allows for the possibility of selective recall of unpleasant experiences over pleasant ones. As with repression, however, it is difficult to accept that emotional state-dependence plays much of a role in normal forgetting. Furthermore, the kind of evidence used to demonstrate these effects is highly artificial and has the added drawback that it involves hypnosis.

Despite these reservations, the state-dependent theory may have application in the clinical setting. Depressed patients are known to recall more unpleasant than pleasant experiences. Lloyd and Lishman (1975) found that the time taken by depressed subjects to recall negative experiences decreased as they became more depressed. In a number of studies, summarized by Teasdale (1983), it has been shown that a normal individual's tendency to recall more pleasant than unpleasant experiences can be eliminated by inducing a depressed state. However, results such as this might be due to the demand characteristics of the experiment, from which the subject infers that certain mood states should produce certain kinds of memory. A more convincing study was carried out by Clark and Teasdale (1981). They exploited the natural swings in mood that depressed patients experience. When patients reported low levels of depression, more pleasant than unpleasant memories were retrieved, whereas the reverse was found when the patients' depression was deepest. This study suggests that state-dependent retrieval mechanisms may contribute to the maintenance of depression; that is, a depressed mood biases the patient towards recalling unpleasant experiences which, in turn, reinforces the depressed condition.

In a very recent clinical study, Williams and Broadbent (1986) examined how easily people who had attempted suicide would retrieve personal memories in response to negative and positive cue words. The patients, who were all clinically depressed, were no different from control subjects in terms of the speed at which they retrieved negative memories, a finding that runs contrary to a state-dependent theory of emotion and memory. However, the depressed subjects took longer to retrieve memories in response to positive words; moreover, the experiences recalled tended to be far less specific than those recalled in response to negative words. The authors suggest that depression may selectively 'block' the recall of pleasant experiences.

Retrieval takes three distinct forms: recall, cued recall, and recognition. The process of retrieval is a reconstructive act in which currently available information guides a search of LTS. Generation-recognition theory and encoding specificity represent contrasting approaches to explaining retrieval. The former views recall and recognition as separate processes, whereas the latter sees them as different aspects of one retrieval mechanism. The only general theory of forgetting so far developed is interference theory, but this has failed to provide a satisfactory explanation. An alternative approach is to consider factors that affect how well information is remembered. Experiments have shown that changes in intrinsic and extrinsic context can affect recall adversely. Furthermore, intoxication with psychoactive drugs can exert certain state-dependent effects on recall. The emotional content of memories can also influence how easily they are retrieved. This may arise from repression or by the association of memories with particular mood states during learning.

4

Improving Memory

Newspapers often carry advertisements for courses which claim to result in vastly improved powers of memory. In reality the ability of people to improve their memories is much more modest, and in this chapter we will explore the various scientifically validated techniques that exist. The study of memory improvement techniques has gained in importance with the realization that some of them are applicable to the remediation of memory disorders.

ATTENTION

It seems a truism to state that successful remembering depends on paying attention to what you are trying to learn. However, in the light of rather dubious claims that we can learn in our sleep, for example, it is probably worth reiterating. Attention can be measured in two ways: as the ability to avoid distraction or the capacity to sustain concentration over a period of time. Under normal circumstances, human beings are very good at directing their attention to one specific source of information. At a crowded party with many conversations going on, we can usually pay full attention to the one we are engaged in, without being distracted by the others. But we are not completely oblivious to everything else. If another conversation suddenly switches to the topic that you are discussing, your attention is immediately drawn to it. This phenomenon, which has been called the 'cocktail party effect', indicates that information which is not attended to is still analysed to quite a considerable degree. The attentional mechanism therefore operates by selecting one of a number of different information channels as that to which conscious processing should be addressed.

This 'single channel' theory of attention appears to suggest that we can do only one thing at a time. But this is not so. We can eat dinner while listening to the radio, or drive a car and talk at the same time. However, there are clear limits to the ways in which we can divide our attention. The critical factor appears to be the extent to which the two things depend on the same mental processes. In the above cases, not much overlap is involved, so the two things can be done with little difficulty. But when two tasks depend on the same processes – e.g. reading a book and listening to a story – both are severely disrupted.

Attentional capacity can vary enormously between individuals, and can be affected by many factors, including alertness, motivation, and age. Furthermore, certain brain lesions can produce selective impairments in the attentional mechanism. When assessing patients with memory difficulties, the presence of disturbed attention should not be overlooked.

ORGANIZATION AND MEMORY

One of the most effective ways to improve memory is to organize material so that it is easier both to learn and to retrieve. Many experiments have shown that subjects spontaneously organize material as they learn it. Jenkins and co-workers (1952), for example, gave subjects a list comprising 24 pairs of highly associated words (e.g. TABLE–CHAIR) to remember. The list was scrambled so that the associated words were not adjacent to each other; nevertheless, at recall, subjects tended to recall the words in associated pairs. This and similar studies have shown that subjects will exploit experimenter-imposed organization when remembering lists of words. But what happens when information has no inherent organization? A number of studies (e.g. Tulving 1962) have shown that people impose their own subjective organization on lists of words that have no obvious organization of their own. Thus, with repeated recalls of the same word list, subjects will tend to recall the items in the same order.

It is clear that organization also plays a vital role in everyday memory. Learning of any set of facts will be enhanced if we can establish some link between them, so that recall of one will serve as a cue for remembering others. Furthermore, our ability to absorb new facts is related to what we know about the subject already. Noting unusual links between something you are trying to learn and something you know already can also improve memory. Thus, remembering my surname may be easier if you know that it means 'gingerbread'. The importance of organization increases as the material to be remembered becomes more complex. Learning a list of words may not pose any great organizational problem, but attempting to internalize the contents of a chapter of a book certainly does. One approach is to devise a 'tree diagram' which covers the basic conceptual framework. This is relatively easy to remember, and provides a basis for accessing memory in more detail and understanding the relationship between the various topics (Buzan, 1972).

It would be impossible to list the many different ways in which people organize information in order to remember it more efficiently. However, two methods, imagery and mnemonics, have been particularly well researched, and their role in memory improvement will now be considered.

IMAGERY AND MEMORY, THE STRANGE CASE OF 'S'

In 1968 the Russian neuropsychologist A. R. Luria published a book called *The Mind of a Mnemonist*. In it he described the case of a man called S who possessed an almost perfect memory. Figure 4.1a shows a meaningless mathematical formula which S was able to reproduce exactly, after studying it for only a few minutes. More remarkably, S was able to reproduce it again *fifteen years* later without prior warning. Luria studied S's memory skills in great detail and discovered that his predominant means of remembering was to create elaborate visual images of the information he was trying to learn. In the above example the start of the formula was remembered using the following image: 'Neiman (N) came out and jabbed at the ground with his cane (.). He looked up at a tall tree which resembled the square root sign (/), and thought to himself: 'No wonder the tree has withered and begun to expose its roots. After all, it was here when I built these two houses (d) . . .' (p. 42).

Luria's account of S alerts us to the importance of visual imagery

a)

$$N.\sqrt{d^2 \times \frac{85}{vx}} \cdot \sqrt[3]{\frac{276^2 \cdot 86x}{n^2v \cdot \pi264}}\; n^2b = sv\,\frac{1624}{32^2} \cdot r^2s$$

b)

6	6	8	0
5	4	3	2
1	6	8	4
7	9	3	5
4	2	3	7
3	8	9	1
1	0	0	2
3	4	5	1
2	7	6	8
1	9	2	6
2	9	6	7
5	5	2	0
x	0	1	x

Figure 4.1   a) Meaningless equation; b) random table of numbers both learnt by S (from Luria, 1968, pp. 42 and 21, respectively)

as an aid to memory. However, we must qualify this by noting two additional aspects of S's phenomenal memory. First, it is clear that S's experience of imagery was extremely unusual. Figure 4.1b shows a table of numbers which S could accurately reproduce in many different ways after studying them for three minutes. It is interesting to note how S explained his performance:

He told us that he continued *to see* the table which had been written on a blackboard or a sheet of paper, that he merely had to 'read it off' successively enumerating the numbers.... Hence it generally made no difference whether he 'read' the table from the beginning or the end, whether he listed the elements that formed the vertical or the diagonal groups, or 'read off' the numbers of the horizontal rows. The task of converting the individual numbers into a single, multi-digit number appeared to be no more difficult for him than for others ... asked to perform this task visually. (p. 23)

When most of us experience mental images, we do not perceive them as something we are looking at directly. Images appear to be 'inside our head', visible only to our 'mind's eye'. By contrast, S's report has more in common with *eidetic imagery*, a rare phenomenon in which the individual seems able to form vivid and detailed images which are experienced as if they were actual percepts.

Another unusual quality of S's memory was *synaesthesia*, in which stimulation in one sensory modality produces a sensation in another. Whenever anyone spoke, the person's voice would cause S to experience visual images. This ability was used extensively by S to remember sounds, nonsense syllables, and words. However, his synaesthesia also had its drawbacks:

To this day I can't escape from seeing colours when I hear sounds. What first strikes me is the colour of someone's voice. Then it fades off . . . for it does interfere. If a person says something I see the word; but should another person's voice break in, blurs appear. These creep into the syllables of the words and I can't make out what's being said. (p. 26)

S's memory capacity also affected his life adversely. His tendency to remember everything in terms of mental images often prevented him from grasping abstract concepts. When remembering tables of numbers, for example, it made no difference to him whether the numbers were meaningfully organized. He was also hindered by his inability to forget. At one stage in his life, S was a professional mnemonist, giving several performances each night. Problems arose when he began to confuse the information he had just committed to memory with that from previous performances. He eventually solved this problem by devising a forgetting strategy which, although effective, was never properly understood.

IMAGERY AND NORMAL MEMORY

The experience of imagery is something that is common to all of us, although not as pronounced as with S. Images appear to play a central role in mental experience. Much of our memory takes this form, and we experience imagery when solving problems and planning actions. Thus it is surprising that mental imagery has been investigated seriously only during the last twenty years. The reason for this omission once again lies with the behaviourists. Prior to the rise of behaviourism, the predominant movement in psychology was *introspectionism*, in which the nature of psychological processes was inferred from the subjective impressions of observers. Not surprisingly, the characteristics of images featured strongly in these accounts. But Watson (1914), the founder of behaviourism, was vehemently opposed to this approach:

Psychology, as the behaviourist views it, is a purely objective, experimental branch of natural science, which needs introspection as little as do the sciences of chemistry and physics. . . . It is possible to define as 'the science of behaviour' and never to go back upon the definition: never to use the terms consciousness, mental states, mind, content, will, imagery, and the like. (pp. 9, 27)

There is no doubt that Watson's view is extreme. Bolles (1975) has speculated that Watson's dismissal of mentalistic concepts stemmed from 'his own peculiar subjective world', the claim being that Watson did not have visual imagery. Nonetheless, the behaviourist doctrine came to dominate experimental psychology, ensuring that mental imagery was hardly investigated before its rediscovery in the mid-1960s.

Renewed interest in the topic arose from the work of Paivio, who argued that mental imagery was susceptible to serious experimental analysis (see Paivio, 1971, for an extensive account). Initially, experiments on mental imagery made use of existing experimental techniques such as paired-associate learning (see chapter 3), which required subjects to learn arbitrary associations between single words (e.g. PIANO–'cigar'). Using this paradigm, it was an easy step to investigating how instructions to form images during learning might affect the learning of associations. Bower (1970) required subjects to learn lists of thirty word-pairs under one of three kinds of instruction. Group A had to repeat the word-pairs aloud as they appeared (rote learning); group B had to form an image of the two items interacting in some way (e.g. a piano smoking a cigar); and group C had to form separate images of the two words (e.g. imagine a piano, then a space, then a cigar). They were first given a recognition test for the first member of each word-pair. If successful, they were then asked to recall the word that had been paired with it. The groups performed similarly on recognition, but group B showed a marked superiority on recall. This shows that forming mental images is superior to rote learning, but only when the instructions require the subject to imagine elements of the two items interacting in some way.

Interacting images might produce better recall because this type of instruction leads subjects to create bizarre images (such as a piano smoking a cigar), and it is this that underlies superior memory. This view is certainly held in the classical and anonymous work *Ad Herennium*, which suggests rules for the use of imagery. We remember what is 'exceptionally base, dishonourable, unusual, great, unbelievable, or ridiculous', whereas 'ordinary things easily slip from memory' (cited by Paivio, 1971, p. 160). Wollen and co-workers (1972) investigated whether experimental demonstrations of enhanced recall using interactive images did in fact stem from their tendency to encourage bizarre imagery. Like Bower, they found that interactive imagery was better than separate images, but that bizarreness had no additional effect. They concluded that it is primarily the interactional quality of images that determines their effectiveness.

It is now accepted that imagery is a powerful aid to memory under certain circumstances. There are problems, however, in specifying the processes that are responsible for our subjective experience of mental imagery. Some argue that images are a distinct form of internal representation (Kosslyn, 1983), whereas others view images as an 'epiphenomenon' stemming from the operation of 'propositional knowledge' (Pylyshyn, 1979). The debate is complex and unlikely to affect the conclusions about mental imagery reached here. The interested reader is thus referred to the suggestions for further reading.

MNEMONICS

Mnemonics are specific devices for improving memory and have been used since classical times. It is unlikely that any of us have come through life without relying on a mnemonic at some time or another. At school or college, we may well have used *first-letter mnemonics* to remember facts in the correct order. The phrases 'Richard Of York Gained Battles In Vain', or 'Real Old Yokels Guzzle Beer In Volume' both enable us to remember the order of colours in the spectrum (red, orange, yellow, green, blue, indigo, violet). Rhymes are also useful, such as this one for diluting acid:

May his rest be long and placid,
He added water to the acid!
The other boy did what he oughter:
He added acid to the water.

There are large numbers of verbal mnemonics dealing with all kinds of technical information, and they can be found in various dictionaries of mnemonics (e.g. *Mnemonics*, 1972): However, psychologists have been most interested in mnemonic systems that employ imagery as the principle ingredient.

One of the best-known imagery mnemonics is the *Method of Loci*. Its invention is attributed to the Greek poet Simonides, who lived around 500 BC. According to Cicero, Simonides was invited to recite at a dinner given by a local nobleman called Scopas. His poem was supposed to be entirely in praise of Scopas's recent achievements, but half of it concerned the twin gods Castor and Pollux. Scopas was angry and paid Simonides only half his fee. Later, Simonides was called away from the table to speak to two young men (Castor and Pollux), at which point the roof of the building collapsed on the guests, crushing them into an unrecognizable pulp. When the relatives arrived, there was confusion because the various remains could not be identified. However, the problem was solved by Simonides, who could remember where everyone had been sitting during the dinner.

From this grisly experience, Simonides gained the following insight as to how to improve memory. He reasoned that the clarity of his memory of the guests arose because each one had been seated in a separate location. He went on to suggest that memory in general could be made more effective if the things to be remembered were placed at different locations in the same imaginary space. The method is very simple. First, imagine a suitable setting, such as a room, with enough different locations for the items you want to remember. Next, use mental imagery to link each item with a location. If you are trying to memorize a shopping list and the first item is milk, you might imagine a milk bottle on a window-ledge. Finally, when all the items are in place, you can 'walk' through the room naming each in turn.

Another related method involves the peg-word device. Some quite complex peg-word systems have been devised (Higbee,

1977), but to illustrate the point we will describe a simple example. The method involves learning a list of 'pegs'; these are easily learnt words which can be used as mental locations for remembering other items of information. The pegs are generated using the rhyming principle, 'One is a bun, two is a shoe, three is a tree', and so on. Each item you wish to learn can then be associated with one of the pegs by forming a composite image. Using the shopping list example again, we could remember milk as the first item on the list by imagining a bun cut in half with a milk bottle sandwiched in between.

So far, the imagery techniques described have been quite simple. However, there are other, more sophisticated techniques in which the generation of effective images requires considerable ingenuity. A good example is the face-name mnemonic devised by Lorayne and Lucas (1975). The idea is to link a person's face with a distinctive interacting image which can be decoded to give the person's name. There are three steps to this process:

1 Choose the most prominent feature of the person's face.
2 Select a word or phrase that sounds similar to the name (name transformation). This word or phrase must denote something that easily gives rise to an image.
3 Create an image in which the objects denoted by the phrase interact with the chosen facial feature.

McCarty (1980) gives the example of someone called *Conrad*, whose most prominent facial feature is his nose. The name transformation is *con* and *rat*, and the visual image involves a prisoner (*con*) riding on a *rat* that is sliding down a nose. When that person is encountered again, the prominent feature acts as a retrieval cue for the image, and the name transformation is derived from the image and decoded to give the name. This may sound rather complicated, but McCarty found that with college students this strategy produced better performance than simple face-name association learning.

There are many other mnemonics which use mental imagery as an essential ingredient (see Paivio, 1971, and Yates, 1966). However, a difficulty arises with regard to the practical application of these discoveries. For example, when the method of loci first evolved, it was of considerable value to orators as a means of remembering the points in their speeches. But modern speakers would be highly unlikely to use such a method, and would rely instead on either notes or an 'autocue' machine. Furthermore, Hunter (1977) has argued that the method is 'useless for all practical purposes', because the conditions needed for it to be effective are rarely encountered in real life. The face-name mnemonic has more potential, but, as McCarty himself notes, 'It is conceivable that in practice, the face-name mnemonic would be so complicated and time consuming that most people would not use it' (p. 155).

MEMORY AND PRACTICE

Much of what we learn requires some form of practice before memory is firmly established. A fundamental question is whether practice is most effective when concentrated in short periods of time, or if learning is more efficient when practice is spread over a longer period. The effects of 'massed' versus 'distributed' practice have been studied ever since experimental studies of memory began. On the basis of his classic studies of memory, Ebbinghaus was in no doubt that learning was more efficient when practice was distributed. Studies of motor-skill learning also show a clear advantage for distributed practice. Figure 4.2 shows the results of an experiment in which subjects practised the *pursuit rotor* task under massed or distributed conditions. The task requires that the subject maintain contact with a revolving target by means of a hand-held stylus, and performance is measured as percentage of time on the target. In the massed condition, subjects were allowed only 2 seconds between each trial, whereas in the distributed condition, subjects were given 1.5 minutes rest between trials. With distributed practice there is a rapid improvement on day 1, an initial drop on day 2, followed by further improvement in performance. With massed practice there is little improvement on day 1 after the first few trials. However, on day 2 performance is at a more accurate level than that achieved by the end of day 1. This phenomenon is known as *reminiscence*, and suggests that some of the deleterious effects of massed practice can be avoided if a lengthy rest period is given.

In attempting to master new facts, we often repeat them. In our

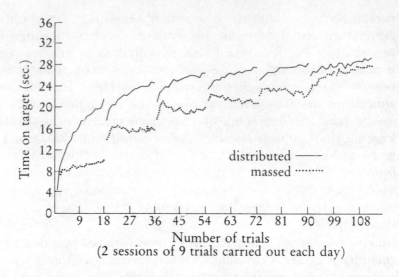

Figure 4.2   The effects of massed versus distributed practice on pursuit rotor learning (after Digman, 1959; taken from Holding, 1965)

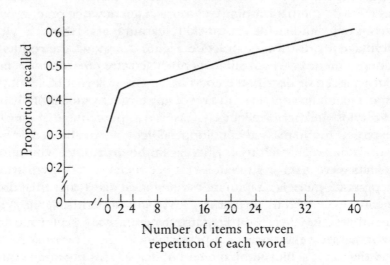

Figure 4.3   The effects of spacing repetition on recall. (Note that recall increases as the time between repetitions lengthens.) (After Madigan, 1969, p. 829 and Melton, 1967)

earlier discussion of rehearsal (chapter 1), we saw that repetition *per se* influences how well we remember something. Further research has now indicated the conditions under which repetition is most effective. Most of the research has been concerned with how the interval between repetitions of the same information affects how well it is remembered. A typical experiment was carried out by Madigan (1969), in which subjects were presented with a long series of individual words and required to learn them. Each word was repeated, but the interval between repetitions was varied from immediate up to 40 different intervening items. Figure 4.3 shows how well the subjects subsequently recalled the words as a function of the interval between repetitions. Two effects are clearly shown. First, recall of items repeated immediately (the 0 condition) is far worse than spaced repetitions *per se*. This is called the *spacing effect*. Second, the recall of items given spaced repetition increases as the interval between repetitions increases. This is known as the *lag effect*.

To some, it seems counter-intuitive that, within certain limits, repetitions should be more effective the further they are apart. However, the spacing effect is extremely strong and can be found in many different situations. Unfortunately, explaining it has proved a much more difficult matter, and no definite conclusion has been reached. One theory is that immediate and spaced repetition produce differently encoded memory traces. With immediate repetition, the recency of the first presentation may lead subjects to perform exactly the same encoding operations when the information is repeated, whereas, when the repetition is delayed, the first presentation is less accessible, and the second encoding is likely to be different. This is known as the *encoding variability* hypothesis, and has much in common with the elaboration hypothesis discussed in chapter 2. Both these theories stress that the more variably information is encoded, the more easily it can be remembered, because there are more potential ways in which it can be contacted in the retrieval process.

A variant of the lag effect has been applied in a practical setting by Landauer and Bjork (1978). They investigated how the interval between learning and testing affected memory for names. Subjects were presented with a continuous series of names to learn. At various intervals, these learning trials were replaced by a test trial in which the first name of a previous target was presented and the subject was asked to recall the appropriate surname. Retention of all the names was tested a number of times, but the intervals between these tests were varied systematically. At the end of the experiment subjects were given a final recall test. Of most interest was the comparison between 'uniform' testing, in which the interval between successive tests was constant, and 'expanding' testing, in which the intervals were gradually lengthened. The results showed that the expanding pattern produced much better retention of the names. In practice this suggests that learning will be facilitated if the interval between sucessful recall trials is extended gradually.

An efficient memory depends on normal attentional capacity. Memory can be improved by means of mnemonics. Most widespread are mnemonics based on mental imagery, but techniques using other factors such as rhyme can also be effective. Practice is another important variable in memory improvement, with distributed practice giving better results than massed practice.

Part II

Memory Disorders

5

Assessment of Memory Disorders

The assessment, study, and treatment of memory disorders is part of *neuropsychology*, the subdiscipline of psychology concerned with the relationship between brain damage and psychological processes. The term is sometimes used more broadly to include any scientific investigation of the nervous system's role in controlling behaviour. In this book, however, the term will be used in its more restrictive sense.

Neuropsychological assessment was first used as a means of distinguishing between patients whose abnormal behaviour stemmed from brain dysfunction and those whose illness was caused by psychological factors. Disorders due to brain dysfunction are described as *organic*, those with no apparent physical cause as *functional*, or *psychogenic*. Early tests were based on the assumption that there was some common element in all organic impairments. These procedures gave only a general assessment of 'organicity', rather than information about the status of different mental functions (Walsh, 1985). The concept of organicity lingers on in some circles, but the vast majority of neuropsychologists recognize that a patient's status can be assessed accurately only by examining specific psychological functions such as memory, language, and perception. In this chapter, we will focus on the various tests and procedures that can be used to evaluate memory impairments.

Presented with a patient with a memory disorder, the neuropsychologist's first task is to establish whether the disorder is organic or psychogenic in nature. This can usually be inferred from the patient's medical record. Thus, there would be little doubt that a concussion victim's poor memory had an organic basis. Similarly, a psychogenic loss of memory would be suspected if the patient had no history of brain injury. Unfortunately, distinguishing between these two kinds of memory loss is not always as easy as this, because psychogenic factors may 'overlay' an organic impairment, making accurate assessment of the disorder problematic. Similarly, a psychogenic disorder may be complicated by disorders such as epilepsy.

Organic memory disorders can be divided into two basic types: *global* and *specific*. In the former, a large component of memory is affected, whereas in the latter, the loss of memory is localized. Examples of specific memory deficits will be considered briefly later in the chapter.

TERMINOLOGY

Case reports of memory disorders have employed many different descriptive terms. Thus a patient may be described as having an impaired 'short-term' or 'recent' memory, or as having difficulty in accessing 'remote memory'. These terms are confusing because they lack specificity. Take 'short-term' memory, for instance; does this refer to information retained for a few seconds, minutes, hours, or days? Similarly, 'recent' memory might refer to events that have occurred subsequent to some injury, but could also include events prior to this. It is therefore necessary to adopt a terminology that can be interpreted unambiguously. The following two terms are now used by most workers: *anterograde amnesia*, which refers to difficulty in acquiring new information after some trauma or illness, and *retrograde amnesia* (RA) in which the patient cannot remember things he or she knew prior to the precipitating illness or trauma. Note also that the period of the patient's life before the onset of amnesia is referred to as 'pre-morbid' and that following it as the 'post-morbid' period.

CLINICAL ASSESSMENT

Isolated defects of memory following brain damage are relatively uncommon, and most patients with memory disorders are likely to exhibit other psychological deficits as well. Prior to making any detailed assessment of memory, it is essential to get information about the patient's general neuropsychological status. Many disabilities can be associated with a memory disorder. There may be motivational problems, personality disturbance, or attentional problems, all of which would impair memory performance. There may also be perceptual and motor impairments as well as both receptive and expressive language disorders.

When assessing a patient with memory problems, the clinician's first aim is to find out how extensive the deficit is. In chapters 1–4 we have considered a number of different memory tests, but these are not suitable for clinical assessment, because they were devised to test particular theories, rather than measure differences between individual people. What we require is a *standardized test* in which the score achieved by the patient can be compared with a norm for the population so as to provide an accurate measure of the degree of impairment. The need for standardized clinical memory tests was recognized as early as 1920, but the first attempts to devise a satisfactory procedure were generally unsuccessful (see Erikson and Scott, 1977). However, in 1945 David Wechsler published the *Wechsler Memory Scale* (WMS), and this rapidly gained acceptance. The test is composed of seven components, which are outlined in table 5.1. The scores on each of these subtests are combined to give an age corrected 'Memory Quotient' (MQ) which is measured like IQ on a scale in which 100 indicates average performance.

Although it is now more than forty years since it was devised, the WMS is still the most widely used clinical memory test. Nevertheless, its value as an assessment procedure has been seriously questioned on a number of counts. Table 5.1 shows that all but one of the subtests involve verbal memory of some kind. Because of this bias, the test may overestimate memory disorders in patients whose deficits are primarily verbal, or, conversely, underestimate memory impairments in those who have problems with non-verbal information. The WMS has also been shown to correlate highly with measures of overall intelligence, such as the Wechsler Adult Intelligence Scale (WAIS). This is a major disadvantage, because it suggests that MQ reflects a patient's general intelligence rather than his or her memory capability. This deficiency is nicely demonstrated in a case reported by

Table 5.1   Wechsler Memory Scale

Test	Procedure
Personal and current information	Questions about age, date of birth, name of Prime Minister.
Orientation	Questions about date and where patient is.
Mental control	Count backwards in 1s from 20. Recite the alphabet. Count forwards in 3s.
Logical memory	Patient is read a story (approx. 60 words) and must recall as much as possible. Two stories are given.
Digit span	Patient is read a short sequence of numbers and asked to repeat them back in correct order. Size of sequence is increased until subject fails or maximum of 8 is reached. Procedure is then repeated, but patient must report numbers in the reverse order to that read out.
Visual reproduction	Patient is shown a figure and asked to draw it from memory. Four figures are given.
Paired-associate learning	Patient is read 10 pairs of words; 6 are 'easy' associations (e.g. metal–iron), and 4 are difficult (e.g. crush–dark). Patient is then given the first word of each pair and asked to recall the second. Patient has three trials to learn associations.

Wilson (1982). Her patient produced a WAIS score of 130 and an MQ of 96, which would suggest someone with only a mild memory problem; but the patient was found to be highly amnesic when tested by other procedures.

That the WMS continues to be used is probably because of its value as a quick screening procedure, rather than any belief that it provides an accurate assessment of memory ability. The confounding of MQ with IQ can be overcome to some extent by including delayed testing of the logical memory, paired-associate learning, and visual reproduction components. Thus a patient of high intelligence may perform well under the standard immediate testing conditions but, if amnesia is present, will be unable to retain the information for more than a few minutes (Russell, 1975).

Other attempts at devising a clinical memory test have concentrated on assessing a broader range of memory functions than those measured by the WMS. One example is the *Williams Scale for the Measurement of Memory* (Williams, 1968). This contains a verbal learning component, but places more emphasis on non-verbal memory. Another feature of the test is its assessment of the patient's memory for past personal events. The WMS screens patients only for anterograde amnesia and disorientation. By asking the patient questions about personal events, the Williams Scale can also give a preliminary indication of any retrograde deficit that may be present. A more recent test battery is the *Recognition Memory Test* (Warrington, 1985), which was devised to detect minor deficits in the retention of verbal and visual information. It is particularly useful in distinguishing between right- and left-hemisphere damage.

As an alternative to a test battery, the clinician may select a number of different tests, each of which addresses a specific aspect of memory function. These tests may come from existing test batteries or may be ones that have been devised to assess some particular form of memory. This approach has the advantage of being comprehensive and flexible. In particular, it allows the clinician more scope in taking account of any specific impairment(s) (e.g. a speech deficit) that may distort memory assessment. The disadvantage is that it does not produce a unified measure of memory impairment, because different tests have been standardized with respect to different populations, and their results cannot be compared directly. However, on balance, the advantages of employing a range of tests seems to outweigh the disadvantages. Interest in the rehabilitation of memory-disordered patients has increased considerably in the last few years (see chapter 11). In devising a rehabilitation program, it is important that the therapist has as much information as possible about the patient's memory problems. Thus it is better to test a patient on a wide variety of tasks rather than be restricted to those in one particular battery.

The clinical memory tests described so far all involve the

retention of novel experimental material, such as paired associates or meaningless designs. There are at least two drawbacks to this. First, the tests may not reflect accurately the demands made on memory in everyday life and hence may give an inaccurate picture of the patient's problems. Second, many memory tests lack 'face validity' because of the artificial tasks involved, and patients may fail to take them seriously. In an attempt to devise a more realistic memory assessment, Wilson and co-workers (1985) developed the *Rivermead Behavioural Memory Test* (RBMT). The various subtests are shown in table 5.2, and were chosen on the basis of a survey of the type of memory impairments encountered in head-injured patients (Sunderland et al., 1983). It has been found that the RBMT only correlates mildly with the WAIS, but correlates strongly with components of the WMS and Warrington's battery. The RBMT

Table 5.2   Outline of the Rivermead Behavioural Memory Test

Test	Procedure
Remembering a name	Patient is shown photograph of a named person and told to remember it. Retention is tested 20–25 mins later.
Remembering a hidden belonging	One of the patient's possessions is hidden. Retention of location is tested 20–5 mins later.
Remembering an appointment	Alarm clock is set to ring 20 mins later. Patient has to ask a specified question when bell rings.
Picture recognition	10 line-drawings of common objects are shown to patient. 5 mins later, patient must pick out target pictures from sequence of 20 pictures.
Immediate prose recall[a]	Similar to logical memory component of WMS.
Face recognition	Patient views 5 faces. 5 mins later, subjects pick out targets from sequence of 10 faces.
Remembering a route and delivering a message[a]	Interviewer traces a route around a room and leaves a message at one particular point. Patient then tries to repeat the route.
Orientation	Similar to WMS.

[a] A delayed test for these items also given.

thus seems sensitive to the deficits identified by other tests; in addition, it measures more everyday aspects of forgetting.

MEASURING RETROGRADE AMNESIA (RA)

As we have seen, the development of clinical memory tests has centred on means of assessing anterograde amnesia, with relatively little attention paid to the measurement of retrograde deficits. This stems, in part, from the fact that RA, although disturbing, may be of less consequence in terms of the immediate problems of a memory-disordered patient. An additional factor is that satisfactory tests for RA are intrinsically much more difficult to devise. In the next chapter we will see that RA manifests itself in the inability to remember personal and public events, rather than in loss of language, conceptual knowledge, and skills. Assessment of RA has therefore been in terms of a patient's memory for previous events.

In someone with RA, loss of memory appears to be most pronounced for the period immediately preceding the onset of amnesia, more remote memories being less disrupted. Thus a patient may be able to recount events from schooldays, but have no recollection of the job he or she was doing when their illness started. This phenomenon was first reported by Ribot (1882) who formulated his 'law of regression' to account for it. He suggested that older memories were more 'stable', and that 'the progressive destruction of memory follows a logical order ... from the unstable to the stable'. Awareness of Ribot's law has led psychologists to construct RA tests which can systematically measure the *temporal gradient* of a patient's memory for events. One way of doing this might be to acquire a detailed life history of the patient from relatives and friends, and from this formulate a series of questions about each period of the patient's life. However, this is both time-consuming and impractical under most circumstances. An alternative is the *autobiographical cueing procedure*, in which the patient is asked to recall personal events in response to particular words (Robinson, 1976). This may be indicative of RA by showing that patients recall events only from particular time periods. However, it is difficult to establish the authenticity of the patient's recollections, and the procedure is thus unreliable.

The alternative is to assess RA by measuring a patient's ability to remember public events, the assumption being that public-and personal-event memory have a common basis. Devising a test of this kind presents considerable methodological problems, however. A particular difficulty is ensuring that the questions asked about each time period are of equal difficulty, so that any temporal gradient observed is not an artefact of asking more difficult questions about recent events. Another problem is to avoid, or at least control for, the degree to which certain events are *publicly rehearsed* (see Weiskrantz, 1985). Most events are quickly forgotten, but more important ones such as Kennedy's assassination, Watergate, and the Falklands War become part of general knowledge, and are therefore known to people of all generations. As a result, the ability to remember these events does not imply that the person has specific memory for those time periods. In devising an RA test, it is therefore necessary to select events that are low in public rehearsal. One approach is to select a large number of events and see how well people who were not alive when they took place can answer questions about them. By selecting only events that younger people know little about, it is possible to minimize the effects of public rehearsal on performance (Warrington and Sanders, 1971).

The most extensive test for RA is the *Boston Remote Memory Battery* (table 5.3) devised by Marilyn Albert (Albert et al., 1979) from an earlier test by Seltzer and Benson (1974). It has three components, and each has 'easy' and 'hard' questions, the former reflecting information that might well be answered on the basis of general (publicly rehearsed) knowledge, the latter reflecting information whose recollection relies much more on remembering a particular time period. The difficulty with this test is that it is culture-specific, and in its existing form cannot be applied to populations outside the USA.

Although the nature of RA in British populations has been explored a number of times (e.g. Sanders and Warrington, 1971; Stevens, 1979; Meudell et al., 1980), a standardized test has only just appeared (Wilson and Baddeley, in press). Rather than explore event memory, this questionnaire assesses RA by asking subjects to

Table 5.3   Outline of the Boston Remote Memory Battery

Test	Procedure
Faces	Patient shown a series of faces of people famous in different decades (e.g. Charlie Chaplin, Mussolini, Lyndon Johnson). If patient cannot identify them, cues are then given (e.g. starred in *The Gold Rush*).
Recall	Patient asked questions about events in different decades (e.g. Kermit the Frog, Miss Piggy, and Fozzie Bear are characters in what popular TV show? Answer: The Muppet Show). Cues are given if patient cannot answer (e.g. creator was Jim Henson).
Recognition	Patient asked questions about events in different decades. Has to select one of three alternatives as the answer (e.g. Bernard Montgomery: a) wrote *For Whom the Bell Tolls*, b) was a British general (correct), c) was president of the AFL).

estimate the prices of common commodities such as a pint of milk and pair of shoes. It is assumed that the patient can answer the questions only by referring to the most recent time period available in memory; results of this test show that amnesic patients often provide estimates based on prices many years ago. Although it needs constant updating, this test is an attractive alternative, since it is less likely to be influenced by intelligence, and concerns knowledge that all people might be expected to have.

MEMORY QUESTIONNAIRES

A useful adjunct to clinical memory testing is the use of question-naires addressed both to the patient and to relatives. A number of these have been developed, all of which aim to evaluate the impact of a patient's memory disorder on everyday life (Bennett-Levy and Powell, 1980; Hermann and Neisser, 1978). Sunderland and co-workers (1983) devised a questionnaire covering five categories of everyday forgetting. These categories are illustrated in table 5.4, along with the scoring procedure. The questionnaire is given to both patients and relatives, so that the patient's own assessment of his or her memory disorder can be matched with the observations of a relative, which are generally more accurate. Experiments have shown that the severity of a memory disorder as assessed by

Table 5.4   The Memory Questionnaire of Sunderland and co-workers (sample)

Speech
Forgetting the names of friends or relatives or calling them by the wrong names.
Feeling that a word is on the tip of your tongue.

Reading and writing
Forgetting the meanings of unusual words.
Unable to follow a story.

Faces and places
Forgetting where you put something. Losing things around the house.
Failing to recognize friends.

Actions
Discovering that you have done a routine thing twice by mistake.
Being absent-minded.

Learning new things
Unable to pick up a new skill or game.
Unable to cope with a change in routine.

Instruction: Please indicate how often you do these things by circling the appropriate numbers:

4	several times a day
3	about once each day
2	once or twice a week
1	less than once a week
0	never.

For instance, if you find that you are forgetting the names of friends and relatives very frequently, circle 4. If, on the other hand, you do so only rarely, circle 1.

relatives using this questionnaire correlate with a patient's abilities on paired-associate learning and the WMS logical memory test, indicating that the questionnaires are measuring the same kind of memory function as these laboratory tests.

By measuring the discrepancy between the patient's assessment and that of relatives, questionnaires also indicate the degree of *insight* that a patient has about his or her memory problem, a factor of considerable importance in determining the potential for rehabilitation. In addition, questionnaires provide therapists with information about those aspects of a patient's life that are most disrupted by memory failure, which can then be targeted for remediation. They can also highlight the social consequences of a patient's memory problem.

SPECIFIC DISORDERS OF MEMORY

There are a large number of specific impairments to memory. What follows is a very brief outline of some of the more common ones and the terms used to describe them. Readers interested in following up on these disorders are referred to the textbooks of clinical neuropsychology listed in the Suggestions for Further Reading.

The most commonly encountered specific impairments to memory involve language. *Aphasia* is a general term covering loss of language ability, but there are many different ways of classifying the various forms that it can take. One distinction accepted in most classifications is that between *Broca's* and *Wernicke's aphasia*. In the former, the patient has very disturbed speech and will often experience some difficulties in comprehension. In the latter, speech is fluent, but its content is often meaningless. However, as in Broca's aphasia, there is usually some deficit in comprehension. A more detailed classification can be found in Heilman and Valenstein, 1985.

Alexia refers to a loss of the ability to read, and *agraphia* to a loss of the ability to write. Often these abilities are only partially affected, and in such cases the relative terms are *dyslexia* and *dysgraphia*. *Acalculia* is a specific impairment of dealing with arithmetical concepts, and patients with *amusia* have lost the ability to comprehend music.

Agnosia is a failure to recognize something when the patient shows no signs of sensory impairment. In *visual agnosia* the patient is unable to identify visual material, even though he or she may be able to indicate recognition of it by other means such as gestures. Agnosia is often restricted to particular classes of stimuli, such as colours and objects. *Auditory agnosia*, in which there is a deficit in the identification of sounds, takes a number of forms. *Pure word deafness* is the inability to recognize spoken words, even though the patient can read, write, and speak. A more general disorder is *cortical deafness*, in which the patient has difficulty discriminating all kinds of sounds. Finally, we can identify *somatosensory agnosia*, in which patients are unable to recognize objects by shape and size.

Prosopagnosia is defined as a selective impairment in recognizing faces. However, there is some doubt as to whether this definition is satisfactory, since prosopagnosic patients also appear to have difficulty in identifying other classes of stimuli that are confusable, such as makes of cars and species of birds (Damasio et al., 1986).

Reduplicative paramnesia can be defined as the syndrome of 'doubles'. Patients with this rare disorder fail to recognize people and places well known to them, claiming instead that doubles have replaced them. This disorder has often been assumed to have a purely psychogenic origin and, considered thus, is referred to as *Capgrass Syndrome*. However, recent research has indicated that the disorder has, at least in some cases, an organic origin (Staton et al., 1982).

Memory disorders can be either organic or psychogenic in origin. Within the class of organic disorders, memory deficits can be either global or specific. The neuropsychologist is faced with a wide range of tests and procedures for evaluating a patient's memory deficit. Although there is no optimal combination, certain recommendations can be made. All patients should receive a preliminary screening for memory impairment using WMS. In addition, a test such as the RBMT should be administered, to obtain a more general impression of the patient's difficulties. These tests should give some qualitative indication of the patient's memory disorder, and can be backed up by more detailed tests aimed at specific memory functions. Finally, within the broader therapeutic setting, question-naire techniques can often prove useful in evaluating the impact of the disorder on the patient and his or her relatives.

6

The Amnesic Syndrome

In fiction, amnesics are typically portrayed as wandering the streets, unable to say who they are or how they come to be there. Amnesia of this sort does occur (see chapter 10), but in neuropsychology, the term *amnesic* is most commonly used to describe a patient suffering from the *amnesic syndrome*. This can be defined as a permanent global disorder of memory following brain damage. Historically, interest in the amnesic syndrome lagged behind interest in other neurological conditions. Among the Greeks, Hippocrates (460–370 BC) correctly diagnosed epilepsy as a disease of the brain, and also noted that damage to one side of the brain produced paralysis and convulsions on the opposite side of the body. However, neither Hippocrates nor any other Greek scholar appears to have linked disorders of memory with the brain. Indeed some Greeks, such as Aristotle, considered that memory was located in the heart.

Medicine in the first millennium was dominated by the writings of Galen (AD 131–201), who wrote more than four hundred different treatises, many of them on neurological illness, but never made any mention of amnesia. This is rather surprising, given that one of Galen's duties was to attend injured gladiators, many of whom must have exhibited post-concussional syndrome, including loss of memory. By the time the first anatomical drawings of the brain appeared in the Middle Ages, the existence of memory as one of several specific mental abilities located in the brain had been recognized. Recognition of different mental functions led scholars to consider how these functions might be distributed within the brain. One theory allocated each mental ability to a different cerebral ventricle. Figure 6.1 shows the famous woodcut by Gregor Reisch (1467–1525) in which the faculty of 'memorativa' is

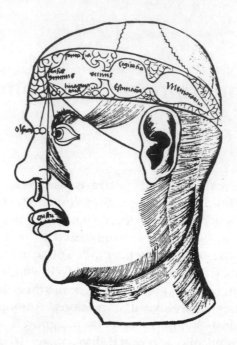

Figure 6.1   Woodcut by Gregor Reisch illustrating the 'ventricular localization theory' of psychological functions

located in the fourth ventricle. The alternative and correct view, that functions are localized within the tissue of the brain itself, also had its proponents. Notable among them was Descartes, although he suggested erroneously that the pineal gland was the centre of memory.

Further developments concerning the relationship between memory and the brain did not occur until the latter part of the nineteenth century, when a number of neurologists began to take an interest in memory disorders. This, coupled with improved anatomical accounts of the brain and neuropathological techniques, provided the starting-point for modern interest in the amnesic syndrome. A number of important figures can be identified, including Ribot (see chapter 5) and Hughlings Jackson. However, present-day interest in the amnesic syndrome stems most directly to the work of Carl Wernicke and Sergei Korsakoff. In 1881

Wernicke described an acute neurological condition which included among its symptoms ataxia, optic abnormalities, and gross confusion. According to the traditions of naming in neurology, this condition was named *Wernicke's Encephalopathy*. At the same time, Korsakoff was studying the long-term recovery of patients who had survived a neurological illness usually associated with long-term alcohol abuse. Korsakoff noted that the major symptom of his patients was a profound memory disorder in which they seemed almost totally incapable of learning any new information. It is now established that what Korsakoff was studying was the long-term effects of Wernicke's Encephalopathy; patients in this condition are diagnosed as having the *Wernicke-Korsakoff Syndrome*, but we will follow common practice and abbreviate this to *Korsakoff's Syndrome*.

Because of the enduring prevalence of alcoholism, Korsakoff patients have been the most readily available subjects for students of the amnesic syndrome, and most of the literature has been concerned with them. Talland's notable monograph *Deranged Memory* (1965), for example, is exclusively devoted to patients with Korsakoff's Syndrome. However, the amnesic syndrome can arise for a number of reasons, and interest in patients in whom the syndrome has developed for other reasons is growing. Thus, Korsakoff's Syndrome must not be considered synonymous with the amnesic syndrome.

GENERAL CHARACTERISTICS OF THE AMNESIC SYNDROME

Although there are variations, the amnesic syndrome has a number of characteristics that are found in all patients. These patients score very badly on clinical memory tests, such as the WMS, but perform normally on intelligence tests such as WAIS. In practice, this means that an amnesic patient will have an MQ which is between 20 and 40 points below his or her IQ. Patients score very poorly on tests involving the retention of novel information, such as paired-associate learning, free recall, and recognition of unfamiliar faces. But they show a normal memory span as measured by the digit span subtest of the WMS. Thus amnesics have no trouble understanding a normal length sentence; their problem is remembering it for any significant time. Skills acquired prior to the onset of illness, such as driving and musical ability are unaffected. Finally, there will almost always be some RA, but this may vary considerably from patient to patient, with Korsakoff patients usually showing severe RA (see figure 6.2), but other amnesics sometimes having a small deficit.

THE NEUROPATHOLOGY OF THE AMNESIC SYNDROME

By studying the neuropathology of the amnesic syndrome, it is possible to get some idea of which brain structures are implicated in memory. The oldest form of neuropathology is the post-mortem, in which the brain is examined either macro- or microscopically for tissue damage (see figure 6.3). Methods have now improved

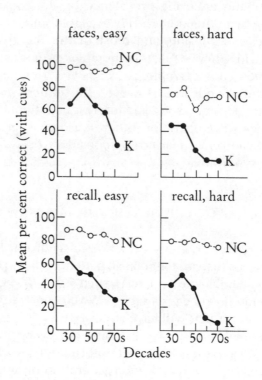

Figure 6.2   Performance of Korsakoff patients (K) and normal controls (NC) on components of the Boston Remote Memory Test (from Albert et al., 1979)

enough to allow identification of brain lesions in the living brain. An early technique was *air encephalography*, in which X-rays of the brain were enhanced by passing air into the cerebro-spinal fluid. Another widely used technique is *angiography*, in which the blood vessels of the brain are filled with a radioactive medium. This allows the detection of circulatory abnormalities by X-ray. *Electro-encephalograms* (EEGs), which show the electrical activity of the brain as monitored by electrodes attached to the scalp, can also indicate brain abnormality, because each brain region has its own characteristic pattern of electrophysiological activity. EEGs average the electrical activity from a large area of the brain, and are therefore of limited use in locating specific areas of damage; but they are valuable in some circumstances, especially in the diagnosis of epilepsy.

Within the last twenty years, there have been major advances in medical-*imaging* techniques. The most widespread is *computerized axial tomography*, often called CAT. This also makes use of X-rays, but involves a scanning device which assesses the density of brain tissue at numerous points and produces from this information a three-dimensional image. Areas of damage show up as darker areas; figure 6.3 shows a typical CAT scan in which a damaged area can be detected. Other more accurate medical imaging techniques are slowly being introduced. *Positron emission tomography* (PET) can provide better information about brain damage than CAT, and can even measure metabolic changes and blood flow in the brain. Another important method is *nuclear magnetic resonance* (NMR), which can provide high-resolution images of brain structure without using the potentially harmful radiation required by other techniques.

The amnesic syndrome can arise from lesions in a number of different parts of the brain, either singly or in combination. Figure 6.4 shows the various brain structures which, when damaged, produce the amnesic syndrome. These structures occur in two distinct areas of the brain, a subcortical region known as the *diencephalon* and the *medial temporal lobe* of the cortex. Damage can result from disease, neurosurgery, intracranial injury, brain tumours, cerebro-vascular accidents (CVAs or 'strokes'), closed-head injury, and anoxia (deprivation of oxygen).

Disease-related amnesic syndromes tend always to affect the

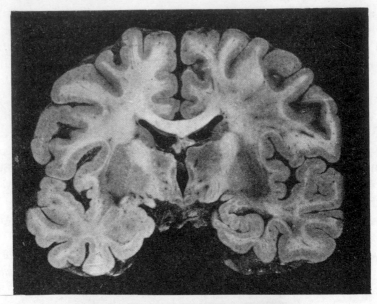

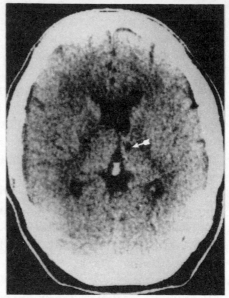

Figure 6.3   a) Section through the brain of a Korsakoff patient showing diseased mamillary bodies (from Victor et al., 1971). b) CAT scan showing lesion in the left dorsomedial thalamic nucleus (from Speedie and Heilman, 1982)

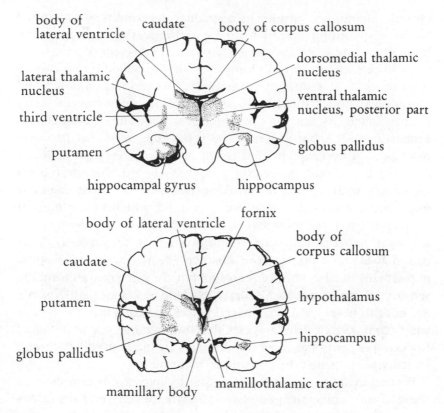

Figure 6.4   Two sections through the human brain (from Butters and Cermak, 1980, p. 12)

same areas of the brain. Studies of Korsakoff's Syndrome indicate that brain damage in these patients is centred on the diencephalon, with the mamillary bodies and dorso-medial thalamic nucleus being principally affected (Mair et al., 1979; Victor et al., 1971). Initial accounts de-emphasized any cortical involvement in Korsakoff's Syndrome, but modern techniques have shown that Korsakoff patients often have considerable atrophy of the frontal cortex, as well as diencephalic damage (e.g. Lishman, 1981; Wilkinson and Carlen, 1982).

There are two theories about the cause of brain damage in Korsakoff's Syndrome. According to the *continuity hypothesis*, chronic alcoholism results in a gradual deterioration of mental function, stemming directly from the toxic effects of alcohol on the brain; the amnesic syndrome is simply the end result of a memory impairment that started long before Korsakoff's Syndrome developed. If the continuity hypothesis is correct, then detoxified chronic alcoholics should also show memory impairments. Early studies failed to find any evidence of this (e.g. Parsons and Prigatano, 1977), but Butters (1985) has suggested that this may have been a consequence of using insensitive test procedures. Along with several co-workers, he has shown that detoxified alcoholics with extensive drinking histories do have memory impairments, but that these are very mild and have a different character from the memory deficits of Korsakoff's Syndrome. Korsakoff patients, for example, are extremely sensitive to PI on paired-associate learning (see chapter 3). Alcoholics also show impairment on this kind of learning, but they are not abnormally sensitive to interference. Similarly, chronic alcoholics show some RA, but this is very mild compared with Korsakoff patients (Squire and Cohen, 1982). This suggests that the memory impairments of Korsakoff patients and chronic alcoholics are qualitatively different, which argues against the continuity hypothesis.

Further evidence against the continuity hypothesis comes from the study of a university professor (PZ) who developed Korsakoff's Syndrome at the age of 65. He had been an alcoholic for many years, but had nonetheless succeeded in writing several hundred articles and many books, including a detailed autobiography completed only two years before the onset of amnesia. It was found that PZ was very poor at recalling the events described in his autobiography, especially those from later periods of his life. Since PZ had obviously been able to recall those facts when he wrote his autobiography, his present amnesia could not be the end result of memory that had deteriorated gradually over many years (Butters, 1984).

The alternative, widely accepted theory is that brain damage in Korsakoff's Syndrome stems from *thiamine deficiency* brought on by the poor diet typical of chronic alcoholics. Experiments show that animals deprived of thiamine begin to develop the symptoms of Wernicke's Encephalopathy, and that this can be relieved by thiamine administration. The link between thiamine deficiency and

Korsakoff's Syndrome was reinforced in a unique study carried out by De Wardener and Lennox (1947). These army doctors were among many British soldiers held captive by the Japanese in Burma. They lived on 'a grossly unbalanced diet consisting mainly of polished rice", under appalling conditions in which diseases such as dysentery were endemic. Because of the resulting malnutrition, the doctors noted Wernicke's Encephalopathy in over fifty men, many of whom reported memory problems. Although conditions were extremely primitive, some post-mortem investigations were carried out, and these confirmed diencephalic brain damage. Furthermore, a number of the patients were cured through administration of thiamine. These findings provide strong support for the thiamine deficiency theory, but some workers have cautioned against accepting it as the sole cause of Korsakoff's Syndrome. Malnutrition is extremely widespread, but there are few other reports of permanent memory impairment in badly under-nourished populations other than chronic alcoholics. Brain damage in Korsakoff's Syndrome may therefore depend on the interaction between thiamine deficiency and excessive alcohol consumption (for further discussion see Mayes and Meudell, 1983).

Another cause of the amnesic syndrome is *Herpes Simplex Encephalitis*, a highly contagious and frequently fatal disease which leaves its survivors with extensive brain damage. Neuro-pathological studies have shown that this damage is located in the medial temporal lobes, where it affects the hippocampus, amygdala, and uncus, but leaves diencephalic structures relatively intact. Some patients may also suffer frontal lobe damage and, in extreme cases, the *Kluver-Bucy Syndrome* may result. Patients with this condition exhibit a number of symptoms including amnesia, hyperorality, visual agnosia, and altered sexual behaviour (see Lilly et al., 1983). More frequently the patient's deficit will be restricted to a pronounced amnesic syndrome. Rose and Symonds (1960) were the first to draw attention to the post-encephalitic (PE) amnesic syndrome, but since then a number of other reports have appeared, most notably the detailed study of patient SS (Cermak, 1976; Cermak and O'Connor, 1983).

PE amnesia implicates the medial temporal lobe structures in memory function. More direct evidence comes from neurosurgical procedures in which parts of the temporal lobe have been removed as a means of relieving epilepsy. Scoville and Milner (1957) reported 10 cases in which regions of the medial temporal lobe had been excised bilaterally to alleviate intractable epileptic seizures. The operations had been successful, but pronounced memory deficits had appeared as side-effects in eight of the patients. Within this group was a young man known as HM, whose amnesic syndrome is considered to be among the 'purest' ever studied. He has been described as living in the 'eternal present' unable to remember more than a handful of events since the time of his operation. Examination of the operative procedures used on these patients indicated that amnesia was present only in those where both the hippocampus and the amygdala had been removed. Removal of the amygdala alone did not produce amnesia, a fact supported by more recent findings (e.g. Sarter and Markowitsch, 1985). Thus, we can conclude that temporal lobe amnesia depends on a bilateral lesion in the hippocampus, either alone or in combination with amygdala damage. Where a lesion to this area is unilateral, the most common outcome is a material specific memory deficit, with left-hemisphere damage impairing the retention of verbal information and right-hemisphere damage affecting non-verbal memory (see Bradshaw and Nettleton, 1983, for an account of human hemispheric asymmetries).

Brain tumours are abnormal growths which both destroy tissue and put pressure on adjacent brain structures. Thus, when the presence of a tumour causes some form of cognitive impairment, it may be difficult to establish the exact region of the brain responsible for the malfunction. Nonetheless, evidence from tumour cases in particular has corroborated the view that diencephalic structures are implicated in the memory process. The floor of the third ventricle is adjacent to diencephalic structures, and tumours in this region are known to produce amnesia resembling Korsakoff's Syndrome (Williams and Pennybacker, 1954). Korsakoff's Syndrome has also been reported following the excision of tumours in the region of the mamillary bodies (Kahn and Crosby, 1972). It is difficult to specify the precise region affected by a CVA, but what evidence there is concurs with that obtained from other sources. Several authors have reported amnesia following occlusion of the posterior cerebral artery, a blood vessel that supplies the hippocampal region (e.g. Benson et al., 1974). Less commonly, CVAs cause damage to diencephalic structures, resulting in amnesia (Graff-Radford et al., 1984). A more extensive account of amnesia following CVAs and tumours can be found in Parkin (1984b).

Over the years, neurosurgeons have reported a considerable number of 'unusual intracranial injuries' caused by foreign bodies other than bullets. Through accidents or suicide attempts, people have introduced into their brains an astonishing variety of objects, including sewing needles, paintbrushes, keys, knives, and even a chopstick. These cases have generally been of purely medical interest, but one patient, NA, has generated enormous interest amongst neuropsychologists because of his amnesia (Teuber et al., 1968). What is unusual about NA is that he shows only a small amount of RA and can describe his accident very clearly:

I was working at my desk.... My room-mate had come in [and] he had taken one of my small fencing foils off the wall and I guess he was making like Cerano de Bergerac behind me.... I just felt a tap on the back.... I swung around ... at the same time he was making the lunge. I took it right in the left nostril, went up and punctured the cribiform area of my brain.

NA has been studied extensively by Squire and his colleagues (e.g. Squire and Moore, 1979). Descriptions of his brain damage have consistently located it in the diencephalon centred on the left dorsomedial thalamic nucleus, and his case has been assumed to present a pure 'diencephalic amnesia' (Squire, 1982b). Weiskrantz (1985) has recently questioned the interpretation of NA's brain damage, pointing out that the fencing foil could not have reached the assumed lesion area without passing through other structures on the way, including, he suggests, the mamillary bodies. In a macabre postscript to this debate, Zola-Morgan and Squire (1985) obtained an intact cadaver and attempted to simulate NA's injury with a surgical instrument. Three attempts failed to produce a lesion in the mamillary bodies but came close to the presumed site of NA's lesion.

THEORETICAL INTERPRETATION OF THE AMNESIC SYNDROME

The general characteristics of the amnesic syndrome indicate that it is not some general deterioration of memory function, but a selective impairment in which some functions such as learning novel information, are severely impaired, while others, including memory span and language, remain normal. This has two important implications. First, the consistent nature of the amnesic syndrome means that our models of memory must be structured so as to account for the pattern of impairment it produces. Second, the pattern of impairment may provide important evidence about the organization of memory – the assumption being that amnesia is not some random decay of the memory system, but a selective impairment of some component(s), leaving others intact.

In chapter 1 we noted a major conceptual distinction in memory models between STS and LTS. STS is assumed to rely on temporary active storage processes which initiate, but are nonetheless independent of, those processes underlying the formation of permanent memory traces in LTS. This allows for the possibility that STS might continue functioning normally even if the processes responsible for permanent trace formation were defective. A defining feature of the amnesic syndrome is a normal memory span, indicating that STS function is preserved. From this it follows that the amnesic syndrome must be a deficit in the function of LTS.

The apparent sparing of STS in the amnesic syndrome is well illustrated by an observation of HM reported by Milner (1971). She noticed that he 'was able to retain the number 584 for at least 15 minutes, by continuously working out elaborate mnemonic schemes. When asked how he replied: 'It's easy. You just remember 8. You see 5, 8 and 4 add to 17. You remember 8, subtract it from 17 and it leaves 9. Divide 9 in half and you get 5 and 4, and there you are: 584. Easy.' A minute or so later, HM could not remember the number or any of his complex mnemonic and did not even know that he had been asked to remember a number.

A major line of experimental evidence supporting the STS/LTS distinction is the free recall paradigm (see chapter 1). If the amnesic syndrome does represent a sparing of STS, then certain predictions about the performance of amnesics on this task can be made. The recency effect is assumed to represent the output of STS, so one would expect amnesics to show similar recall to normals for the last few items on the list, but poorer recall for items earlier on the list, which depend on LTS. Figure 6.5 shows that this is exactly what happens. These results have led most psychologists to accept that in the amnesic syndrome STS function is preserved but LTS function is impaired. Indeed, evidence from the amnesic syndrome is seen as one of the major reasons for accepting the STS/LTS distinction. Atkinson and Shiffrin (1968), who were early proponents of the multistore model, saw the amnesic syndrome exhibited by HM as 'perhaps the single most convincing demonstration of a dichotomy in the memory system'.

Having localized the deficit to LTS, it is now necessary to be more specific about how this structure has been impaired. HM's normal performance on intelligence tests indicates that some aspects of LTS must have been spared. Thus the patient retains language and conceptual knowledge, as well as the ability to perform previously

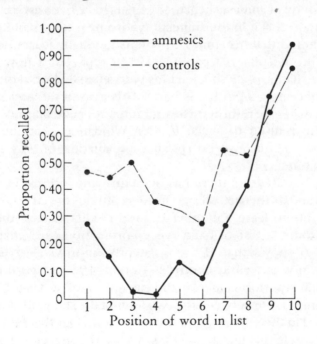

Figure 6.5   Serial position curves of amnesic and control subjects (after Baddeley and Warrington, 1970)

acquired skills. By contrast, he has immense difficulty in recalling personal events, both before and after the onset of amnesic symptoms. This is apparent in his account of his day-to-day activities and his failure on memory tests such as free recall and paired-associate learning.

As we have seen, LTS is considered to be a tripartite structure composed of episodic, semantic, and procedural memory. The pattern of impairment in the amnesic syndrome seems to fit nicely with this division of LTS. Preservation of language and general intellectual function suggests an intact semantic memory, and the ability to make use of previously acquired skills indicates that procedural memory is also unaffected. By contrast, the almost complete failure to recall or recognize novel information and the difficulty in remembering past personal events suggests a selective failure of episodic memory.

The above interpretation of the amnesic syndrome gains support from the phenomenon of *residual learning capability*. Since the serious study of amnesia began, scientists have been aware that the anterograde deficit in the amnesic syndrome is not total. Korsakoff himself noted that his amnesic patients gradually learnt their way around the hospital. Claparede (1911) reported a now famous anecdote that he once shook hands with a female Korsakoff patient while concealing a pin in his hand. This caused the patient some pain, and when he returned a few minutes later and offered his hand again, she refused to shake it. Her avoidance continued, even though she could give no specific explanation of why she was avoiding him.

In the last 20 years there has been growing interest in residual learning and its theoretical significance. Studies of HM showed that he was able to learn a number of motor skills. One of these was pursuit rotor, a test of hand-eye co-ordination (see chapter 4). Figure 6.6 shows that HM consistently improved on the task, although not as well as controls (Corkin, 1968). Figure 6.6 also shows HM's performance on the mirror drawing task. Here the subject must trace between the two lines of the star while looking at their hand in the mirror. From the graph it is clear that HM learned this task, but in this and all other tasks which he succeeded in doing, he consistently denied knowledge of having done them before. Pursuit rotor was one of a number of new motor skills that HM was able to acquire normally, and this gave rise to the suggestion that 'motor memory' was selectively preserved in amnesia. However, more recent research has shown that amnesic patients also show residual learning capability on non-motor tasks.

Amnesic patients also show *perceptual learning*. In a typical experiment the patient is first presented with a stimulus and then asked to make some kind of response to it. Following an interval, the stimulus is presented again, and the subject is asked to make the same response. In addition, the patient is asked whether he has ever seen the stimulus before. Crovitz and colleagues (1981) showed amnesic subjects 'picture puzzles' such as that shown in figure 6.7, and measured the time they took to identify them correctly. The pictures were presented again the next day, and the patient was asked to identify them. On the second presentation, the patients' ability to remember seeing the pictures was very unreliable, but they identified them more quickly than on day 1. The picture shown in figure 6.7, for example, took an average of 163 seconds to identify on day 1, but only 17 seconds on day 2. This was not due to a 'practice effect', because new pictures presented on day 2 were identified much more slowly. This result, along with results of many similar studies (e.g. Meudell and Mayes, 1981), shows that amnesics can retain information about the perceptual organization of a stimulus, even though they have no conscious recollection of it.

Many readers will be familiar with Pavlov's dogs, who learnt to salivate when a bell sounded because this had previously been associated with food. This is an example of *classical conditioning*, in which a previously neutral stimulus (the bell) now elicits one of the animal's existing responses (salivation). Classical conditioning has also been shown in amnesics. Warrington and Weiskrantz (1979) showed that two amnesic patients could acquire a conditioned eye-blink response. At the outset a buzzer was paired with a puff of air, which caused a reflexive eye-blink. This pairing was continued until the patients blinked in response to the buzzer alone. Despite having acquired this response, the patients' commentaries showed no recollection of the conditioning procedure.

An impressive example of residual learning involves the 'Tower of Hanoi', a problem-solving task in which the subject must move a series of blocks from the start to the finish peg, only one block can

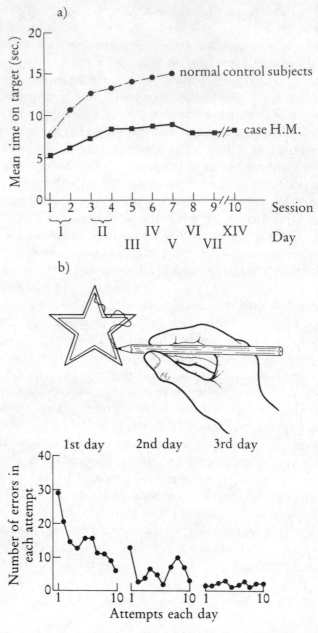

*Figure 6.6   a) Graph showing HM's performance on pursuit rotor.
b) The mirror drawing task and HM's performance (from Blakemore,
1977)*

*Figure 6.7   One of the 'picture puzzles' used by Crovitz and co-workers
(Crovitz et al., 1971, p. 273)*

be moved at a time, and a larger block can never be placed on a
smaller one (see figure 6.8). The minimum number of moves
required for successful solution is 31. Cohen (1984) has recently
compared the performance of amnesic and normal subjects in
learning this task and claimed that the groups do not differ in the
rate at which they reach an optimum solution. Cohen also reports
that HM was able to learn and retain the solution over a year long
period. However, it must be noted that other workers have failed to
replicate these results (for example, Beatty et al., in press; Butters et
al., in press).

The range of tasks on which amnesics show residual learning
capability is very broad (see Parkin, 1982, for a fuller account). It
therefore seems implausible that a different type of memory is
preserved for each of these types of learning, so a more general
explanation must be sought. Moscovitch (1984) has pointed out
that, despite their diversity, all tasks on which amnesics succeed are
united by three common elements: the tasks are structured so that
the patient can immediately understand what is required; the
response called for is part of the subject's existing repertoire; and
finally, and perhaps most important, the goal of the task is attainable

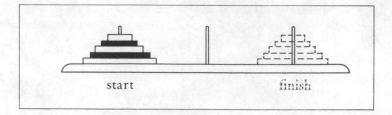

Figure 6.8   The 'Tower of Hanoi'

without reference to a specific past event.

Motor skills seem to come closest to these criteria. They are well structured, involve simple responses already available to the subject, and do not require reference to the patient's previous experience of the task. In fact, with these kinds of tasks, no benefit is derived from remembering the last occasion on which you did it. Pursuit rotor learning, for example, is essentially a procedural memory task, because what is being assimilated cannot be verbalized or inspected consciously. Thus, a normal person able to recollect previous attempts at the task would gain only a minimal advantage from being able to do so. It is not so surprising, therefore, that amnesics should have been shown to acquire motor skills such as this as rapidly as normal people.

Moscovitch's 'task analysis' approach also helps us understand some apparently anomalous findings. We saw above that HM was able to learn the Tower of Hanoi, a task that would be a challenge to most normal people. However, the same patient was unable to learn the stepping stone maze illustrated in figure 6.9a, despite 125 trials. When it was shortened to four points (figure 6.9b), he was successful, but he needed 155 trials to learn it. SS (Cermak, 1976) managed to learn an eight-point maze, but to do this he broke the maze down into two four-point parts. If we analyze the demands of these two tasks, the greater difficulty of the maze task becomes easier to understand. Remembering the solution of a maze requires that the subject learn an arbitrary sequence of movements; thus, remembering that the first move was 'up' does not constrain the direction to be taken at the next point. Faced with such a task, remembering what the first four steps were would be a valuable aid, enabling learning resources to be devoted to later parts of the maze. The amnesic, unable to recollect this sort of information, must proceed by the more basic process of repetition. The fact that amnesics can learn only short mazes or solve longer ones only by linking shorter sequences together suggests that their maze-learning ability may be constrained by how much information they can rehearse in STS. Thus the failure to learn longer mazes may indicate that STS can only hold information about four moves (e.g. 'up', 'left'. 'left again', 'right').

The Tower of Hanoi is different because the sequence of moves is not arbitrary, but is governed by the overall goal of the task. Because of this, a potential move can be evaluated by considering its consequences for subsequent moves. It seems unlikely that a solution will be achieved by remembering a long sequence of moves. Instead, solving the problem may depend on the acquisition of guiding principles which constrain possible moves at different stages. Intuitively, it seems that remembering past encounters with the Tower of Hanoi would aid solution. However, the claim that some amnesics can learn it suggests that the guiding principles might be implicit rather than explicit. For this reason the ability to remember past attempts at the task may not be particularly beneficial because much of what is carried over from one session to

a) finish

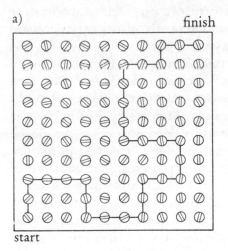

start

b)

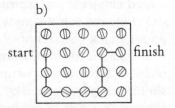

start / finish

Mazes are constructed from metal bolts screwed into wood. Black line indicates correct route.

Figure 6.9   Mazes attempted by patient HM (from Milner et al., 1968)

another cannot be recollected consciously.

The task analysis approach thus allows us to specify the conditions required to show residual learning in amnesia. The next question we must consider is whether these conditions allow us to identify which component or components of LTS have ceased to function. We have concluded already that amnesic performance indicates an impairment in episodic memory, and this is confirmed by the observation that amnesics find it hard to learn any task which requires them to remember specific past events. But, what can we conclude about semantic and procedural memory? It can be argued that the tasks on which amnesics show residual learning capability are predominantly procedural in nature – that is, they involve acquisition of knowledge that cannot be verbalized and is unavailable for conscious inspection. We have already noted this in relation to skill learning, and this is also true of perceptual learning. To understand this point, look again at the perceptual closure figure shown in figure 6.7. As soon as you look at it, you are able to identify it, but you are not aware of the processes that allow this to happen; these occur prior to awareness and cannot be described.

We must now consider the status of semantic memory in the amnesic syndrome. A number of researchers have proposed that semantic memory remains intact in amnesia (e.g. Kinsbourne and Wood, 1975; Parkin, 1982; Tulving, 1983), and they cite unimpaired language and normal performance on intelligence tests as the principal supporting evidence. Recently, this view has come under attack for a number of reasons.

If semantic memory remains intact in amnesics, then it should be possible for them to acquire new general knowledge. This possibility was investigated by asking HM to define common words and phrases that had come into use only since his operation. He did show some ability to do this, correctly defining 'rock and roll', for example, but his success was relatively slight. In a recent experiment, HM tried to learn the meaning of 10 unfamiliar words. After extensive training over 10 days, he was hardly able to match any of the words with their definitions (Gabreli et al., 1983).

Wood and co-workers (1982) report the case of a 9-year-old girl who developed PE amnesic syndrome. Since her illness, she has returned to school and shown normal progress in acquiring various academic skills despite having severe anterograde amnesia. Wood

and his colleagues consider this to be 'an unambiguous demonstration of the dissociation between episodic and semantic memory
in the amnesic syndrome'. However, their evidence is not entirely
consistent with this conclusion. The girl continued to show poor
performance on vocabulary tests and the Weschler Intelligence
Scale for Children (WISC), both of which could indicate impaired
semantic memory. Recently, Ostergaard (in preparation) studied a
10-year-old boy who became amnesic after an anoxic episode. Not
only did he have severe anterograde amnesia, but his reading age
failed to increase significantly after his accident, and he performed
poorly on various tests of semantic memory. By contrast, his
procedural memory appeared to function normally, in that he
learnt how to use computer-based games as easily as his peers.

In chapter 1 it was proposed that episodic and semantic memory
constitute a highly interactive system. More specifically, the
acquisition of new semantic memory may depend, at least in part,
on normal episodic function. Thus, in the initial stages, learning a
new word will be dependent on remembering previous encounters
with it. We should therefore not be surprised that amnesics find it
difficult to learn new words and facts. Nonetheless, proponents of
the episodic/semantic distinction would feel more comfortable if
amnesics performed better than they do when trying to acquire
new semantic memory.

Another difficulty is the kind of evidence usually cited in support
of semantic memory being preserved in amnesia: normal language
function and standard levels of performance on intelligence tests.
However, it has been pointed out that these tasks primarily deal
with information acquired early in life. Episodic impairment is
inferred, however, from the patient's inability to recall post-morbid
events and a varying degree of failure in remembering pre-morbid
events, particularly those occurring in the time period immediately
before the onset of amnesia. Thus, one could redescribe the
amnesic syndrome as an inability to remember more recently
acquired information.

This issue can be addressed by examining the nature of semantic
memory in amnesics more carefully, to establish whether knowledge acquired more recently is as available as that learnt earlier in
life. An early study by Nyssen (1956) suggested that Korsakoff
patients were less able to define words that had come into use in the

period immediately prior to their illness than those from earlier stages of their lives. PZ, the amnesic professor we discussed earlier, was not only handicapped in the recall of personal events, but he was also unable to remember technical terms introduced during the later stages of his academic career. Since his use of these terms was not dependent on episodic memory before he became ill, we can only conclude that semantic and episodic information have both been affected, thus weakening the view that the former is selectively preserved. Finally, Ostergaard's child-amnesic showed a temporal gradient in his vocabulary, in that he had more difficulty defining words he had acquired just prior to his illness than those learnt earlier.

At first sight, the nature of RA in the amnesic syndrome would seem to be consistent with a selective deficit in episodic memory, in that amnesics, especially Korsakoff patients, have considerable difficulty in remembering past events. However, we can accept this only if we are sure that responses on the RA test rely solely on episodic memory. Introspection suggests that this is probably not the case. Try answering the question 'Which British Prime Minister introduced the three-day week?' If you get the right answer (Edward Heath), are you reliving your experiences in 1973? Probably not, although, on occasion, one might well be helped by remembering a specific personal experience. RA tests probably measure both general knowledge and personal memory, and one cannot attribute failure to an exclusive loss of either episodic or semantic memory.

ALTERNATIVE THEORETICAL FRAMEWORKS

The above difficulties have led some authors to consider alternative theoretical interpretations of the amnesic syndrome. Cohen and Squire (1980) have come up with an interpretation based on Gilbert Ryle's celebrated distinction between *knowing how* and *knowing that* (Ryle, 1949). Ryle noted that one form of memory enables us to do things – e.g. ride a bicycle, jump a fence – even though we cannot say what form this information takes. By contrast, we also have memory that we can consciously inspect – thus we can state that grass is green, or that we went to Greece for a holiday. Cohen and Squire use the terms *procedural* and *declarative* to describe these two types of memory. As you can see, procedural memory is defined in much the same way as it is in Tulving's system. Declarative memory is defined as concerning knowledge that can be consciously inspected, and no distinction is made between memory for episodes and memory for facts; they are just different forms of declarative knowledge.

In line with our previous theory, Cohen and Squire maintain that procedural memory remains unaffected in the amnesic syndrome. However, the amnesic deficit is seen as a general impairment of declarative memory, rather than one restricted to memory for episodes. This account, without any additional assumptions, can accommodate retrograde and anterograde amnesia for events, failure to acquire new general knowledge, and the loss of pre-morbid semantic memory.

Unfortunately the procedural-declarative theory is not without its problems. A major difficulty is that not all amnesic residual learning is procedurally based. For example, Cermak and O'Connor (1983) taught their amnesic SS a large number of specific instructions and facts. Schacter and colleagues (1984) showed that amnesic patients could learn a considerable number of fictitious statements about well-known people, even though they could not remember when and where they had heard them. More recently still, Glisky and co-workers (1986; in press) have shown that amnesics can learn computer terminology. Moreover, as we shall see in chapter 11, memory remediation programs provide many other instances of amnesics acquiring declarative knowledge.

There have been a number of other attempts to characterize the amnesic deficit. Warrington and Weiskrantz (1982), for example, have proposed that amnesics cannot acquire information that requires some form of *cognitive mediation system* for its retention. Such a system is described as one 'in which memoranda can be manipulated, inter-related, and stored in a continually changing record of events. It may be by recourse to this mediational memory system that normal subjects recall or recognize events' (p. 242). They cite a number of findings consistent with this view. For example, amnesics find it very difficult to learn paired associates when the two words are unrelated, but can succeed when there is some relationship between them (e.g. rhymes or strong semantic associations). In the former case, some 'mediation' is required before a successful association can be formed, whereas this is already embodied in the latter. The cognitive mediation theory has much in common with the other approaches we have considered and, like them, can accommodate most of the data. However, there are also difficulties. First, there is no easy way of dividing tasks into those that do and those that do not require cognitive mediation for their performance. As a result, the theory has a rather circular feel to it, in that all tasks that amnesics fail on are assumed to require mediation, whereas those on which they succeed are said not to require it. This can be remedied only by providing a more specific account of what cognitive mediation actually involves. Another problem is that the theory leans heavily on the claim that amnesics cannot make use of mental imagery, since this is thought to require cognitive mediation. In putting forward this argument, Warrington and Weiskrantz (1982) cite only instances in which amnesics have failed to benefit from imagery instructions (Baddeley and Warrington, 1973; Jones, 1974). They do not consider positive examples (Cermak, 1976) and the many successful implementations of mental imagery techniques in memory remediation programs (see chapter 11).

At present, none of the theoretical approaches provides an adequate characterization of the amnesic syndrome. However, before we get too excited about this, we should recognize that none of these approaches constitute *explanatory* theories. Rather, they are different means of providing a *description* of the deficit, on which explanations of the deficit can then be imposed. In the rest of this book, we will describe the amnesic syndrome as primarily a deficit in episodic memory. Such a view does not presuppose that episodic memory is a distinct entity within LTS; it merely acknowledges that the primary difficulty experienced by amnesics is a failure to retrieve information about events.

SELECTIVE DEFICITS IN STS

Before going on to the next chapter, it is necessary to digress for a moment and consider impairments in STS. Because STS is assumed to be the locus of conscious control, it is not possible to observe a patient with a global deficit of STS, since, by definition, the individual would be unconscious. However, in chapter 2 we considered the working memory model, in which STS is divided into a central executive, which represents the locus of conscious control, and subsystems responsible for processing information in specific ways. With models of this kind it is possible to envisage selective deficits due to impairments in the subsystems, without any general disturbance of consciousness.

Warrington and Shallice (1969) reported the case of KF, a man who suffered a lesion in the left cerebral hemisphere. He exhibited a number of residual impairments, the most striking of which was that his auditory digit span, a measure of STS capacity, was only one item. Since then, there have been reports of several other patients showing severely impaired auditory digit span (e.g. Saffran and Marin, 1975). By contrast, these patients' digit spans following visual presentation are consistently better. These patients are not amnesic, and the deficits cannot be attributed to auditory perception problems or defective speech. Instead they are assumed to have a deficit in the immediate storage of phonological information (Shallice and Butterworth, 1977).

The working memory model provides one way of explaining this selective deficit. As we saw, the model includes an articulatory loop, a structure of limited capacity capable of storing a limited amount of phonological information. It seems reasonable to suppose that a selective deficit in the immediate recall of information presented auditorily could arise if the articulatory loop were inoperative. Although an explanation in these general terms seems possible, however, it is first necessary to complicate matters considerably by proposing separate articulatory and storage components (Vallar and Baddeley, 1984a). If one accepts this modification to the model, then patients with a defective STS should allow us to evaluate the role of this phonological subsystem in processes such as comprehension. The evidence suggests that such patients are largely unimpaired, indicating that this subsystem does not play a particularly vital role in everyday mental processes. However, Vallar and Baddeley's (1984b) patient PV, who had a grossly defective auditory memory span, did have trouble understanding longer sentences when comprehension required that the verbatim content of the sentences be retained. This concurs with our earlier conclusion that the temporary storage of phonological information during reading is necessary only when dealing with more complex sentences.

Patients with the amnesic syndrome exhibit severe anterograde amnesia and a degree of RA. Their intelligence, language, motor skills, and immediate apprehension appear to be normal. The syndrome can arise from focal lesions in the mid-line dience-phalon or the medial temporal lobes. Experimental evidence shows that amnesics have an intact STS and an impaired LTS. The nature of the LTS impairment is a matter of some debate, although it is agreed that amnesics show preserved procedural memory, as indicated by their ability to learn things such as motor skills effectively. One view is that episodic memory is selectively impaired, but alternative explanations have been suggested. Selective deficits in STS function have also been observed, although the only difficulties so far identified concern the immediate retention of auditorily presented material.

7

Explaining Amnesia

Chapter 6 identified the amnesic syndrome as a selective impairment of LTS, with a sparing of STS. Furthermore, the LTS deficit was shown to involve episodic memory predominantly. This is a useful framework for describing the behavioural characteristics of patients suffering from the amnesic syndrome, but it does not explain why memory has ceased to operate normally. To do this, we must entertain theories regarding why memory no longer functions. Two approaches to this problem can be taken. First, we can try to explain amnesia at the physiological level. Evidence presented in chapter 11 shows that some progress has been made in this area, but the research does not enable us to identify the psychological deficits underlying amnesia. Accordingly, this chapter will be concerned with the second possible approach, that is with psychological explanations of the amnesic syndrome.

There have been many attempts to explain the amnesic syndrome, and to cover them all would be beyond the scope of this book. Our discussion will be restricted to psychological theories proposed during the last 20 years. The most straightforward explanation of amnesia is that it is a *storage deficit* due to disruption of the consolidation mechanism. This theory, proposed by Milner in 1966, was quickly discounted in favour of other theoretical approaches (but see below). One suggestion, now refuted, was that amnesia was essentially a *retrieval deficit*. Thus, amnesics were thought to be capable of storing new information, but unable to retrieve it. If correct, this theory would predict that anterograde and retrograde amnesia would be equally extensive, since retrieval of pre- and post-morbid memories would presumably rely on the same defective retrieval system. However, the literature shows that amnesics can often remember substantial amounts of pre-morbid information, while having a severe anterograde deficit; and the reverse has also been observed (Andrews et al., 1982; Kapur et al., 1986), albeit more rarely. This, and other evidence, argues against a general retrieval deficit hypothesis.

Explanations of the amnesic syndrome have concentrated on the origin of anterograde amnesia. One theoretical approach attributes the syndrome to a *specific encoding deficit*, whereby some deficiency in the initial processing of information gives rise to defective memory. The effects of this could be experienced at storage or retrieval: a poorly encoded memory trace might be less durable or, because of its deficient content, more difficult to locate at time of retrieval. These theories have been concerned with identifying the nature of the deficit, rather than specifying the stage of memory that is disrupted. The first of these theories emerged from the levels of processing approach to memory (see chapter 2). The major finding of this research was that semantic processing of information produced better retention than non-semantic processing. Butters and Cermak (1980) conducted many experiments which confirmed that, under certain circumstances, Korsakoff patients failed to encode information semantically; they argued that this might represent the fundamental deficit in amnesia.

One of their main findings came from a phenomenon known as *release from PI*. Demonstration of this involves the presentation of three items which are related in some way – e.g. RED, MAUVE, BROWN – and which the subject is instructed to remember. Next, the subject is shown a three-digit number and is required to subtract from it in threes for about 15 seconds. Following this distraction, the subject is asked to recall the three words. In successive trials involving words drawn from the same category (in this case, colours), recall on each new trial becomes increasingly poor. After three trials, one of two things is done: either a fourth set of words from the same category is presented, or a set of words from a different category appears. Category shifts can be either semantic – e.g. colour names to vegetable names – or non-semantic – e.g. a change in rhyming principle (e.g. BED, HEAD, RED, → SOME, HUM, RUM). Normal subjects showed 'release' either way, in that recall on the fourth trial was enhanced following both types of shifts; but Korsakoff patients showed release only with the non-semantic shift. The reasons underlying release from PI have not been fully explained, but we can at least conclude that subjects take some account of the dimension being manipulated. It appears, therefore, that normal subjects can utilize both semantic and non-semantic dimensions, whereas Korsakoff amnesics can make use of the latter only.

The idea that amnesics make less use of semantic information when trying to remember has been explored by investigating whether their memory deficit can be ameliorated by forcing them to use semantic processing strategies during learning. It is known that memory for unfamiliar faces can be improved if subjects make semantically based judgements about faces (see chapter 2). Biber and co-workers (1981) examined how this manipulation affected the recognition memory of Korsakoff patients and normal people, and found that, proportionally, the former gained more benefit than the latter when using a semantic processing strategy.

This supports the semantic encoding deficit theory, although there are a number of drawbacks to it as a general explanation of amnesia. First, several studies have shown that amnesics gain no selective advantage from instructions to use semantic strategies during learning (e.g. Mayes et al., 1980; Wetzel and Squire, 1980; Cermak and O'Connor, 1983). Second, where such advantages have been found, they may be due to motivational factors. Korsakoff patients typically lack spontaneity, and the effect of forcing them to use an unusual processing strategy may be to cause a general increase in task motivation, rather than the adoption of a more efficient learning strategy. This proposal is supported by Davidoff and his colleagues (1984), who demonstrated that the inclusion of a single sexual reference in a story greatly enhanced the recall of Korsakoff patients, while this had no effect on the overall recall of normal subjects.

Another problem is that encoding deficits, as reflected in failure to release from PI, may reflect a deficit unconnected with amnesia (see below). Finally, the encoding deficit theory seems counter-intuitive. Observations of amnesics show that they are perfectly capable of semantic processing, since they can read normally and understand conversation. Thus, to maintain the encoding deficit theory would require a rather artificial distinction between the semantic processing underlying conscious mental activity and that required for memory formation.

An alternative approach is to explain the amnesic syndrome as a *contextual memory deficit* (e.g. Huppert and Piercy, 1976; Stern, 1981; Hirst, 1982; Winocur, 1982). Evidence reviewed in chapter 3 showed that the retrieval of novel information, as measured by recall or recognition, can be disrupted substantially if the context in which testing takes place is different from that during learning. This indicates that, under normal conditions, the memory of an event includes information about the circumstances under which it occurred. The encoding of context is vital to the normal functioning of memory, because it is the basis by which individual memories are distinguished from each other. It follows, therefore, that a memory system unable to encode context would be extremely inefficient, because information about events stored in it would be highly likely to be confused.

There are a number of studies that support this theory. Winocur and Kinsbourne (1978) examined the performance of Korsakoff amnesics on the A → B, A → C, paired-associate paradigm (see chapter 3). Typically, amnesics show many 'intrusions' on this test, in that in the A → C phase they tend to recall many of the A → B associations. It was found that when the A → C phase took place in an environment that was very different from that in which the A → B phase occurred, the number of intrusions was significantly reduced. It was presumed that the new context in the A → C phase allowed association with sufficient new contextual information for effective discrimination from pairs learned in the A → B phase. Thus, amnesics may be poor at encoding extrinsic context under normal conditions, but be able to utilize it provided it is sufficiently distinctive.

A study by Schacter and co-workers (1984) likewise suggests that amnesics may be particularly bad at storing contextual information. It explored the phenomenon of *source amnesia*, in which a person is often able to remember a fact but not where he or she heard it. One of two experimenters read fictional statements about well-known people (e.g. 'Bob Hope's father was a fireman') to eight amnesic subjects. It was found that the patients could often remember the facts when asked to recall them after a few minutes, even though they could not recall who told them or where they heard them.

The temporal dimension of context is particularly important for the efficient operation of episodic memory. Huppert and Piercy (1978a) investigated the performance of Korsakoff amnesics and normal people on a task involving temporal discrimination. The subjects saw 80 pictures on one day, followed by a different set of 80 pictures on the following day. Half the pictures of each set were shown once, and the remainder were shown three times. Ten minutes after the day 2 presentation ended, subjects were shown a sample of pictures from days 1 and 2. Their task was to indicate whether each picture had been seen 'today'. As one would expect, both groups usually placed pictures seen three times on day 2 in the 'today' category and rejected pictures shown only once on day 1. However, amnesics were just as likely to put pictures seen three times on day 1 in the 'today' category as those seen once on day 2. By contrast, control subjects placed very few of the repeated day 1 pictures in the 'today' category but correctly categorized more than two-thirds of the pictures seen only once on day 2.

Recognition memory involves two stages: an assessment of *familiarity*, followed by a *search* process to establish the identity of a target (see chapter 3). This provides a useful framework for understanding Huppert and Piercy's result. On the assumption that familiarity fades with time, the performance of amnesics indicates that their assessment of recency was determined entirely by the overall familiarity of each picture. Thus pictures presented three times on day 1 seemed as recent as those presented once on day 2, because similar amounts of familiarity were involved. By contrast, the performance of normal subjects seems to be determined by both factors. The more accurate identification of pictures presented three times on day 2 compared with those presented once might suggest that familiarity also plays a role. However, the fact that normal subjects accurately distinguished pictures presented once on day 2 from those presented three times on day 1 indicates that their responses involved an additional search stage, in which each picture was linked to a specific temporal context – namely, day 1 or day 2. The fact that the amnesics could not do this implies that they had no record of temporal context.

One problem with the above study was that amnesic and normal subjects were tested over the same time interval. Thus, not only were amnesics poorer on temporal discrimination, but they also performed worse overall. This allows for the possibility that the temporal discrimination deficit might characterize poor memory in general and not reflect a specific impairment in the amnesic syndrome. To test for this, Meudell and co-workers (1985) replicated Huppert and Piercy's finding but, in addition, carried out the same experiment on normal subjects using much longer retention intervals. The effect of this was to reduce the memory of normal people to that of the Korsakoff patients. Despite this, the normal subjects were far more able to discriminate temporally among events, which suggests that Korsakoff amnesia is qualitatively different from poor normal memory.

The contextual deficit theory provides a plausible explanation of amnesia, but has the major drawback that the evidence on which it is based derives almost exclusively from studies of Korsakoff's Syndrome. Thus the theory can be considered as a general explanation of amnesia only if all amnesics suffer from the same kind of memory deficits.

AMNESIC SYNDROME OR SYNDROMES?

In chapter 6 it was shown that the amnesic syndrome can arise from lesions in two different anatomical regions of the brain, the diencephalon and the medial temporal cortex (see figure 6.3). To recap, diencephalic amnesia arises mainly from Korsakoff's Syndrome, whereas temporal lobe amnesia has a variety of causes, including temporal lobectomy and encephalitis. The existence of at least two separate sites has given rise to the idea that amnesia may take more than one form. However, one possible argument against this proposal is that the structures damaged in these different brain regions are part of the *limbic system*. From figure 7.1, which shows this system, it can be seen that the hippocampus projects to the mamillary bodies via the fornix, thus providing a link between the medial temporal lobes and the diencephalon. This has led some workers to suggest that the limbic system constitutes a memory 'circuit'. If so, damage to the fornix should also produce the amnesic syndrome. Evidence on fornix lesions in humans is rather sketchy, but I have reviewed what there is (Parkin, 1984b). A number of studies report asymptomatic lesions of the fornix, but only one case has been described in detail (Heilman and Sypert, 1977), and there, amnesia is attributed to a lesion localized in the fornix. However, the authors add a note of caution by suggesting that there may also have been some hippocampal damage.

The absence of any definite indication that fornix lesions cause amnesia in humans allows us to consider an alternative possibility: that there may be qualitative differences between the amnesic syndromes produced by diencephalic and medial temporal lobe lesions. This idea was first proposed by L'Hermitte and Signoret (1972), following a comparison of Korsakoff patients with PE patients on four different tasks. One of these involved trying to learn the names and positions of nine objects. All the Korsakoff patients managed to learn the array eventually, but only one of the PE amnesics succeeded. Subsequent testing showed that even after four days the Korsakoff patients were reasonably capable of arranging the nine objects correctly. However, the one PE amnesic who learnt the array forgot it within a few minutes.

This finding led some workers to propose that diencephalic and medial temporal lobe amnesia differ in terms of *forgetting rate*. It has been claimed that Korsakoff patients, given enough learning trials, can retain information as well as controls for considerable periods of time. The results of one of these studies (Huppert and Piercy, 1977) are shown in figure 7.2; it involved a comparison of

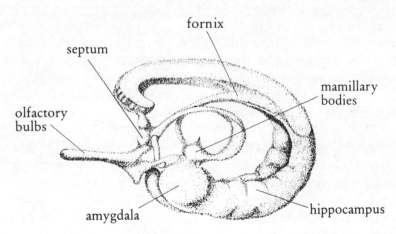

Figure 7.1   Model of the human limbic system (from B. Kolb and I.Q. Whishaw, Fundamentals of Human Neuropsychology, *2nd edn, 1985, New York: Freeman, p. 24)*

Korsakoff with normal subjects on a recognition memory test. Although Korsakoff patients needed many more trials to learn the test material, they forgot it at the same rate as the controls. Similar findings have been reported by Huppert and Piercy (1978a), Squire (1981), and Kopelman (1985).

The investigation of forgetting rate in medial temporal lobe amnesia has been less extensive. Huppert and Piercy (1979) attempted to compare HM with their Korsakoff group reported above, but there is some doubt as to whether HM's initial level of learning was as good as that of the Korsakoff group, thus invalidating any comparison of forgetting rate (see also Weiskrantz, 1985). Other evidence provides better support for differences in forgetting rate. In one study, Mattis and co-workers (1978) presented PE and Korsakoff amnesics with various types of word lists. Both groups performed very poorly on free recall, but on recognition testing an interesting difference was found. PE amnesics always performed at chance rates, suggesting that they rapidly forgot the stimuli, whereas the Korsakoff group performed significantly better. Earlier, we looked at a study by Huppert and Piercy (1978a) which showed that Korsakoff subjects base their recognition decisions on the familiarity of a stimulus, rather than an ability to remember the context in which it occurred. The results of the

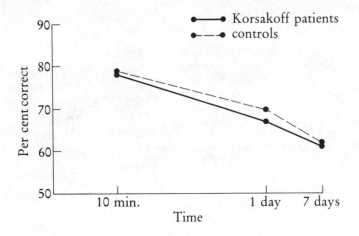

Figure 7.2   Forgetting rates of Korsakoff and control subjects on a recognition test (from Huppert and Piercy, 1978a)

Mattis study are consistent with this, in that successful recognition performance occurred only when responses could be made on the basis of familiarity. Once a correct response required the recollection of a discrete event, Korsakoff performance was reduced to chance levels.

Recently, Parkin and Leng (in press) compared the forgetting rate of a group of Korsakoff patients with that of patients whose amnesic syndrome was caused by bilateral medial temporal lobe damage. Patients were presented with 4 target pictures which they were asked to memorize. The criteria for establishing that the patients had memorized the stimuli at the outset were correct verbal recall immediately after the targets were withdrawn and correct identification of the targets from an array of 16 pictures 1 minute later. The ability of the patients to recognize the 4 targets was tested over intervals ranging from 1 minute to 1 week. As figure 7.3 shows, Korsakoff patients forgot the stimuli less rapidly than the medial temporal lobe group, even though the groups needed similar numbers of trials to memorize the pictures during the learning stage.

It has also been proposed that diencephalic and temporal lobe

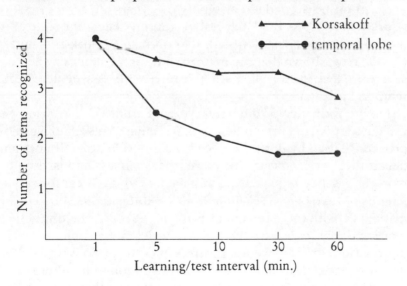

Figure 7.3   Comparative forgetting rates of Korsakoff and temporal lobe amnesics (from Parkin and Leng, in press)

amnesia are associated with different patterns of RA. Studies of Korsakoff patients have shown a consistent severe impairment extending back for periods of up to 30 years. Furthermore, this RA exhibits a marked temporal gradient, with recall being worst for events immediately prior to the onset of amnesia (e.g. Albert et al., 1979). Although less reliable, case histories of patients with diencephalic tumours suggests that damage in this region is associated with substantial RA (Parkin, 1984b). An exception to this pattern is found in patients whose amnesia seems attributable to lesions of the dorsomedial thalamic nucleus (Squire and Moore, 1979; Winocur et al., 1984).

The amount of RA arising from medial temporal lobe damage appears to depend on the manner in which the damage occurred. In early assessments of patients who had undergone bilateral temporal lobectomy, Milner (1966) reported that they had a relatively limited RA, extending over only a few years, compared with the twenty years or so typically encountered in Korsakoff's Syndrome. In particular, HM was thought to have an RA extending back no more than three years (Marslen-Wilson and Teuber, 1975). It has recently been claimed that HM's RA covers a longer period, but this is based on tests conducted twenty-five years after his operation (Corkin et al., 1981) and may not accurately reflect the state of his memory when originally tested. By contrast, Cermak and Butters (1980) have shown that the pattern of RA in PE amnesia can be as severe as that in Korsakoff's Syndrome, with less evidence of a temporal gradient.

The performance of different types of amnesics has also been evaluated using the Brown-Peterson paradigm. This is similar to the procedure used by Butters and Cermak to evaluate their encoding deficit theory of amnesia. The patient is given a stimulus, usually a word, and is then required to count backwards in threes for varying lengths of time before recalling it. Korsakoff patients showed very marked PI, with recall declining as the length of distracting activity increased. By contrast, the PE amnesics were able to retain information almost as well as controls over the periods tested. Poor performance of Korsakoff patients has been found in other studies (e.g. Cermak and Butters, 1980), and three other studies have produced results similar to those of Butters and Cermak when making direct comparisons between Korsakoff patients and amnesics with a temporal lobe pathology (Cermak, 1976; Leng, in preparation; Starr and Phillips, 1970).

Unfortunately, the suggestion that Korsakoff patients are abnormally sensitive to interference, at least in the Brown-Peterson paradigm, is not fully supported. Mair and co-workers (1979) reported no difference between Korsakoff patients and controls on this test, and the same result has been found in a much larger study by Kopelman (1985). Until the discrepancies between these various studies can be accounted for, the possibility of distinguishing amnesic syndromes in terms of PI effects in short-term memory will remain uncertain.

There is now substantial evidence that Korsakoff patients have frontal lobe impairments. The frontal lobes are somewhat enigmatic brain structures, but neuropsychologists have gradually established that certain behavioural problems can be attributed to damage in this region. Frontal lobe damage can lead to an impairment in memory, but this is qualitatively different and milder than that found in the amnesic syndrome (Stuss and Benson, 1984).

One of the most commonly used tests for assessing frontal lobe damage is the *Wisconsin Card-Sorting Test* (WCST). The subject is presented with a deck of cards, each bearing a pattern which varies with respect to symbol shape, number, and colour. The subject is given a rule to start sorting them by, such as placing all the cards with red symbols in one pile, all with yellow ones in another, and so on. After ten correct trials, the subject must generate a new rule for sorting the cards by, for example, using symbol shape as the critical dimension. At this stage the patient may make a *perseveration error* by continuing to sort by the first rule. This kind of error is symptomatic of frontal lobe damage (Nelson, 1976), and has also been found extensively in Korsakoff patients, not only with the WCST, but also on problem-solving tasks and *word fluency* tests which require the subject to write down as many words as possible beginning with a certain letter. There are no reports that medial temporal lobe amnesics produce abnormal levels of perseverative responding. Finally, failure of release from PI with a semantic shift, which was earlier described as a characteristic of Korsakoff's Syndrome, also appears to be a sign of frontal lobe damage, since it has been demonstrated in patients whose brain damage is restricted to the frontal lobes (Winocur et al., 1981).

Confabulation is another frontal symptom encountered in the amnesic syndrome. This term is used rather loosely in the clinical literature, but can be defined as fabricating an answer to cover up a memory deficit. It takes at least two forms. First, there is 'fantastic' confabulation (Berlyne, 1972), in which the patient's answers bear no relation to his or her past history; this seems restricted to patients with frontal lobe damage (Stuss et al., 1978; Kapur and Coughlan, 1980). Accounts of Korsakoff's Syndrome reveal a milder form of confabulation, in which patients' responses are often plausible and can sometimes reveal, indirectly, that the patient has remembered something of his experiences since becoming amnesic. An interesting example of this is provided by Warrington and Weiskrantz (1979), whose eye-blink-conditioning experiment with two amnesics was discussed earlier. One interesting feature of this study was the recollection of each of the two amnesic patients about what had occurred in the experiment. The first patient, a Korsakoff, could not remember any specific details about the conditioning procedure but offered a number of suggestions based on the plausible theme of psychological testing. However, as an aside, he said that he 'had a weak right eye because someone had once blown some air into it' (note that the conditioning procedure made use of an air puffer). This observation is reminiscent of Claparede's Korsakoff patient who, following the handshake involving the hidden pin, refused to shake hands again, claiming that 'sometimes pins are hidden in hands'.

Confabulation is very uncommon in medial temporal lobe amnesia once the acute stages of illness have passed (Parkin, 1984). Returning to the Warrington and Weiskrantz study, the other patient was a PE amnesic who answered most questions by saying that he just could not remember. Even when encouraged to guess what had taken place, his answers showed no evidence of remembering the conditioning procedure.

Amnesics seem to vary systematically in their demeanour. Some researchers have reported that Korsakoff patients lack insight into their predicament and deny any impairment. In practice, this seems to be relatively rare, and a more general characteristic is that Korsakoff patients lack concern about their disorder. Patients with medial temporal lobe amnesia, on the other hand, are usually highly aware of their disorder and show appropriate concern, which occasionally produces 'catastrophic reactions' (Rose and Symonds, 1960). This difference is probably tangential to our discussion of possible differences in the amnesic syndrome, but a patient's approach to his disorder has important implications for the success of treatment.

There appear to be a number of differences between diencephalic and medial temporal lobe amnesics. We must now decide whether the available evidence argues for or against the existence of two distinct amnesic syndromes. First, let us consider the presence of frontal symptoms only in diencephalic amnesia. There are two views one can take of this: first, that the various frontal deficits shown by amnesic patients are incidental to a 'core amnesia' which is similar in all patients suffering from the amnesic syndrome; second, that malfunction of frontal lobe structures is implicated in the amnesic syndrome associated with diencephalic damage.

The strengths of these two views can be evaluated by establishing whether there is a correlation between the extent of amnesia and the extent of frontal lobe deficits found. If frontal impairments are merely incidental to amnesia, their extent should be independent of the patient's degree of memory impairment. Conversely, if the extent of amnesia in Korsakoff's Syndrome is proportional to the degree of frontal impairment, it would suggest but not prove that the frontal lobe function contributes to the memory disorder.

Squire (1982b) replicated the result of earlier studies by showing that Korsakoff patients did not show release from PI under certain conditions. Furthermore, in line with Huppert and Piercy (1978b), he found that Korsakoff patients performed poorly on a temporal discrimination task. The latter involved presentation of two lists of sentences which the patients had to remember, also which list they appeared in. Memory was tested by measuring how well the patients could discriminate between sentences they had seen and ones they had not seen, and whether they could remember which list any sentence they recognized occurred in. Squire examined the correlation between the Korsakoff patients' performance on WCST and two other tests of frontal lobe dysfunction with their performance on the release from PI and the temporal discrimination tasks. Performance on the latter two tasks correlated significantly with the patients' frontal impairment. However, similar correlations between the frontal test results and overall memory performance were not significant. It was thus concluded that impaired judgements of temporal order and failure to release from PI may stem from frontal lobe damage superimposed on the basic diencephalic lesions of Korsakoff patients, whereas their basic memory impairment was unrelated to this.

Earlier we considered a study by Schacter and colleagues (1984) in which amnesics showed substantial source amnesia. In a follow-up analysis, the authors tested for a correlation between the degree of source amnesia and the extent of patients' frontal lobe impairment as measured by WCST and the Benton word fluency test. The correlation was found to be quite large, indicating that the degree of source amnesia was related to the degree of frontal lobe impairment in the patients. This study and that of Squire both suggest, therefore, that the contextual deficits exhibited by Korsakoff patients originate, at least in part, in some frontal lobe dysfunction.

The strongest case for two amnesic syndromes is provided by the forgetting-rate studies of Mattis and co-workers, Leng, and to a lesser extent L'Hermitte and Signoret. All these suggest that medial temporal lobe amnesics forget information rather rapidly. By contrast Korsakoff patients forget much more slowly, often at a rate comparable with normal control subjects.

THEORIES AND SYNDROMES – A RESOLUTION?

Despite the relatively small amount of evidence in its favour, the idea that diencephalic and medial temporal amnesia are different syndromes has gained considerable currency (e.g. Butters et al., 1983; Squire et al., 1984). But there are those, notably Weiskrantz (1985), who have argued that the evidence is more consistent with a single amnesic syndrome. In this section we will examine both sides of the argument.

The existence of two distinct amnesic syndromes has been advocated most strongly by Squire and his associates. In advancing their arguments, they have returned to the idea that consolidation failure contributes to the amnesic deficit. Consolidation theory was originally dismissed because of various residual learning phenomena (described in chapter 6) which showed amnesics capable of storing new information. However, our analysis has shown that these phenomena reflect the continuing modification of procedural or, less commonly, semantic memory in the absence of any new episodic memory. This reopens the possibility that a fundamental cause of amnesia could be an inability to consolidate new episodic memories. Squire and co-workers (1984) have argued that amnesia following lesions of the medial temporal lobe is caused by a deficit in consolidation. Their argument is consistent with the evidence gained from medial temporal lobe amnesics. The rapid forgetting shown by these patients is to be expected if their memory systems are no longer capable of consolidating new episodic memories. Furthermore, their insensitivity to PI effects from previous learning is also consistent with this theory. In order for PI to occur, some record of previous learning must be maintained. If, as a result of faulty consolidation processes, previous events fail to form durable traces, there can be no basis for interference.

Squire and his colleagues have not been so specific in their explanation of diencephalic amnesia, but, on the basis of evidence discussed earlier, a plausible hypothesis can be put forward. Forgetting-rate studies suggest that Korsakoff patients are capable of retaining some new information over considerable periods of time, but only when retention is measured by recognition testing. We have noted several studies showing that the recognition response of Korsakoff patients is based on the overall familiarity of the target, rather than on an ability to remember the context in which it was presented. This suggests that their memory systems are capable of storing sufficient information for making judgements of familiarity. Deficits are most pronounced where events have to be discriminated from one another. We could thus argue that the deficit in Korsakoff's Syndrome lies in a failure to encode sufficient contextual information. This theory explains why Korsakoff patients, although superior on recognition, do no better than PE amnesics on free recall. The latter task depends, initially, on locating a specific event – namely, the previous exposure of the word list. Without context, this cannot occur, and so recall is very poor.

This line of reasoning can also be applied to the pattern of RA found in Korsakoff's Syndrome. As we noted earlier, Korsakoff patients always exhibit a substantial retrograde impairment. It can be argued that the part of the memory system responsible for encoding new temporal context also mediates the retrieval system. Thus, not only does it ensure that sufficient contextual information is associated with an event; it also maintains a network of retrieval routes which allow specific events to be recalled in response to particular cues. The finding that RA is worse for more recent pre-morbid events can be explained by assuming that each memory retrieval is itself a new event; the record of this thus provides extra access to the original information. Older memories are therefore less vulnerable, because more potential retrieval routes are available.

So far so good, but problems arise when we try to be more specific about how contextual coding has been affected. One possibility which has been proposed a number of times is that the fundamental deficit lies in the encoding of temporal context (Huppert and Piercy, 1977; Van der Horst, 1932). Furthermore, it has been shown that Korsakoff patients are very poor at temporal discriminations. But can we assume that a temporal coding deficit is the basis of the disorder? The answer would appear to be no, because failure on temporal discrimination tasks correlates with the degree of frontal damage found in Korsakoff patients (see above). Furthermore, studies of patients in whom damage is exclusively in the frontal lobes can also be markedly impaired on temporal discrimination (Milner, 1971; Parkin and Wilson, in preparation). The correlation between source amnesia and frontal symptoms found by Schacter and associates (1984) also raises problems for an explanation of the amnesic syndrome based on a selective contextual deficit.

Because of these interpretive difficulties, it might be more profitable to examine patients whose amnesia is entirely dience-phalic in origin; however, such patients are remarkably uncommon. Patient NA is claimed to be such a case (Squire, 1982b), but, as we saw earlier (chapter 6), there is uncertainty about the site of his lesion. Moreover, his amnesia does not appear to be as dense; the unilateral nature of his disorder means that he is more impaired on verbal than non-verbal learning; he does not exhibit RA; and he shows more knowledge than one would typically expect about events occurring since his illness. Winocur and co-workers (1984) provide data on a man with amnesia following mid-line thalamic damage. Their patient showed release from PI and was not abnormally sensitive to interference in short-term memory tasks, but the authors are unable to offer any strong conclusion about the origins of his amnesia beyond suggesting that it is a disruption of encoding.

A further problem for the 'two amnesias' view is how to explain RA in temporal lobe amnesia in terms of consolidation theory. If a patient is amnesic because he cannot consolidate, why should there be any problem in retrieving pre-morbid memories, since these were formed before the onset of amnesia. Estimates of HM's RA suggest that his memory is impaired for the events of at least three years preceding his operation. To account for this, Squire and associates argue somewhat implausibly that the process of consolidation takes a number of years to complete. Such an assertion would be fine if there were independent evidence supporting it, but the only motivation for this claim appears to be the need to accommodate all HM's amnesia within a consolidation theory. Furthermore, PE amnesia, which also has a temporal lobe pathology, produces RA which can be more severe than that encountered in Korsakoff's Syndrome. An alternative explanation is that the medial temporal region is also the storage site for episodic memory (Butters and Miliotis, 1985). The greater severity of PE amnesia relative to that of HM is then explained by making two further assertions: first, that encephalitis produces more extensive lesions, thereby disrupting more of the storage area, and second, on the basis of brain stimulation work by Fedio and Van Buren (1974), that the more posterior lesions associated with encephalitis are more likely to produce RA than the medial lesion suffered by HM.

Weiskrantz (1985) has argued against the two amnesias theory on two grounds. Contrary to the majority view, he argues that there is no strong evidence that the amnesic syndrome can arise from more than one type of lesion. He acknowledges that Korsakoff's Syndrome can occur without medial temporal lobe pathology, but he disputes the claim that temporal lobe amnesia stems from a lesion that is qualitatively different from that underlying Korsakoff's Syndrome and other cases of diencephalic amnesia. He suggests that HM, the patient who has provided most evidence about temporal lobe amnesia, may also have damage in the diencephalon, although no evidence is given to support this. However,

Weiskrantz's point is strengthened by neuropathological studies of encephalitis which show that diencephalic structures can be affected by this disease. Patient SS (Cermak, 1976), for example, is known to have some diencephalic damage.

Turning to the behavioural data, Weiskrantz argues that differences between temporal lobe and diencephalic amnesics, which cannot be explained by the additional frontal damage of the latter, are an artefact of subject selection. He suggests that evidence of long-term retention in Korsakoff's Syndrome reflects a milder amnesic deficit than that in temporal lobe cases, in which amnesia is so severe that it precludes any ability to remember new events. This approach accounts for the faster forgetting rate that we have observed in temporal lobe cases and the more extensive RA in PE amnesics. However, it does not account for HM's amnesia so well, unless, of course, one assumes that Milner's original assessment of his RA was a gross underestimate.

The severity hypothesis seems a nice simple alternative, but again there are problems. First, there has to be some independent means of assessing the severity of amnesia, for if a patient's performance on experimental tasks is the only basis, the argument becomes circular. Acknowledging the problems of assessing severity, Weiskrantz suggests that the best available option is to measure amnesia in terms of the discrepancy between the WMS quotient and IQ as measured by WAIS. However, for the group of amnesic patients studied by Parkin and Leng (in press), there does not appear to be any relationship between this discrepancy and the degree of impairment shown on other tests of memory. One man, for example, had a 37-point WMS/WAIS discrepancy, but when given the WMS again several weeks later, he remembered hearing the passages before and could correctly name the psychologist who had previously administered the test. Another difficulty is to explain why damage centred on the temporal lobes produces a more severe deficit than damage to the diencephalon, without invoking some functional difference between the regions. One possibility is that temporal lobe cases, because of the nature of their precipitating illness, tend to have more extensive lesions than those encountered in Korsakoff's Syndrome. However, good neuropathological evidence for this has yet to be produced.

One attraction of the severity hypothesis is that it does not make many assumptions. By contrast, the two amnesias theory rests on a number of assertions in need of more substantial support. However, the simplicity of the severity hypothesis belies the fact that it is really no explanation at all. If all amnesics forget for basically the same reason, we need to know what that reason is. Proponents of the severity view must therefore be more specific about the nature of the underlying deficit.

In order to establish whether amnesia takes more than one form, certain methodological shortcomings need to be addressed. First, as we have already noted, more appropriate means of assessing the severity of a patient's memory disorder must be found. Second, the number of patients studied needs to be increased. At present, there is a tendency to base theories on the performance of just one or two patients. Much of the theorizing about temporal lobe amnesia, for example, has been based on HM. Reliance on single cases runs the risk that the patient may be atypical of patients with damage in that particular brain region. Kopelman (1985) has demonstrated that, within a relatively large group of Korsakoff patients, there are substantial individual differences in forgetting rate. It is reasonable to suppose that patients with temporal lobe pathology may show similar variation. This problem can be overcome only by studying large enough samples of patients, so that individual differences can be ruled out. Finally, there is the problem of establishing that amnesics with different aetiologies differ qualitatively with regard to the nature of their critical lesions. Most studies merely assume this on the basis of pathological studies done on other patients of the same kind, and there is a remarkable lack of experimental studies in which the pattern of amnesia can be directly related to detailed pathological findings, the exception being the two Korsakoff patients studied by Mair and his associates (1979).

Neuropsychologists must also come to terms with the role of the frontal lobes in memory. There is abundant evidence that Korsakoff's Syndrome is associated with varying degrees of frontal impairment, but there is a tendency to treat the symptoms of this as a 'contamination' which interferes with the study of amnesia itself (although, see Warrington and Weiskrantz, 1982, for an account of amnesia incorporating frontal lobe dysfunction). Deficits attributed to frontal damage include impairment of temporal discrimination and contextual memory. This suggests that some components of the memory process may be subserved by frontal lobe structures. It will therefore be important to establish which aspects of memory function rely on frontal involvement and which do not. One approach would be to investigate more closely the relationship between frontal symptoms and forgetting in Korsakoff's Syndrome, but an alternative might be to compare amnesics without frontal damage with patients whose memory impairment is entirely frontal in origin.

FUTURE RESEARCH ON AMNESIA

Although our understanding of amnesia has increased considerably, we are still a long way from being able to offer a complete psychological explanation. At present there are at least two major difficulties that must be overcome before a significant breakthrough can occur. First, it must be established whether the amnesic syndrome is a heterogeneous disorder as many claim. Until we know whether amnesia varies qualitatively as a function of lesion site, our explanations will be weak, because we cannot be clear about what it is we are trying to explain.

In the preceding section we acknowledged that comparisons between different forms of amnesia are problematic, because it is difficult to be certain about the location of a patient's lesion. One answer might be to do research on animals. Here it is possible to make very precise brain lesions and to test the behavioural consequences in highly controlled environments. But, aside from possible ethical objections, there are pragmatic reasons for being cautious. One difficulty is that the memory of animals, even primates, may be organized differently from that of humans. As a result, the various dissociative deficits revealed by such studies may be difficult to relate to disorder in humans. Some progress has been made towards uniting research on humans and animals (e.g. Weiskrantz, 1982; Squire and Zola-Morgan, 1983; Zola-Morgan and Squire, 1985), but many still argue that models of human amnesia based on studies of animals are likely to be unproductive (Morris, 1985).

A particular difficulty in using animal studies in this way is the characteristics of the amnesic deficit itself. Whether we characterize it as a deficit in episodic or declarative knowledge, we are specifying a deficit in conscious memory and an inability to reflect on our own past. Jaynes (1976) has suggested that self-reflection is an essentially human quality which has emerged during historic times. This is no place to discuss Jaynes's controversial view, but the fact remains that man is the only animal in which we can be confident that consciousness exists. This being so, there are a priori reasons for doubting the validity of animal research as a means of confirming or developing our theories of amnesia and normal memory.

The second difficulty lies in the inadequacy of current theories of forgetting. In this chapter we have seen that recent attempts to explain amnesia have been derived from our account of normal forgetting. If we maintain this approach, our success at explaining amnesia will be entirely dependent on the progress made towards explaining forgetting in normal people. As we saw in chapter 3, forgetting can be caused by a change in context, state-dependence, or emotional factors. The paradigm used to support these ideas provide valid explanations of some instances of everyday forgetting, but they cannot account for the bulk of what we fail to remember. Thus, changes in intrinsic context, such as removing someone's spectacles, may account for some failures of facial recognition, but most forgetting of faces and names occurs for different, unexplained reasons. We have frequently alluded to the idea that successful memory storage depends on the association of target information with sufficient context. However, aside from showing that gross changes in context cause forgetting, we have done little to characterize and investigate context in its more perasive role as the basic organizing principle of long-term storage. What we need, therefore, is a general theory of forgetting. Interference theory was one such attempt, but this failed even within the confines of the paired-associate learning paradigm.

The dependence of amnesia research on theories of normal forgetting also illustrates a more general point about research into memory disorders. At both the descriptive and the explanatory levels, there is total dependence on models and theories based on research on normal people. Patients with memory disorders have thus become a 'test-bed' for theories of normal memory function; neuropsychologists therefore study brain-damaged patients with the aim of evaluating some preconceived theory of normal memory function. This research can reinforce existing ideas by showing that memory breaks down in a manner that is consistent with current theoretical ideas. Thus, amnesics have an intact STS but impaired LTS, and their residual learning capability supports a distinction between procedural memory and memory of knowledge that can be consciously inspected.

Although there is obvious value in attempting to confirm our ideas through the observation of brain-damaged patients, there are drawbacks. If we approach memory disorders with the aim of testing our existing theories of memory, we take a very selective view of the patient's disorder – that is, we tend to emphasize those aspects of the disorder that are relevant to our concern and to either ignore or devalue others. Memory disorders are not, therefore, a source of new ideas about how memory works, but merely a means of testing what we already assume to be the case. As Crowder (1982) notes: 'Who knows, if there were Greek physicians interested in amnesia they might well have conjectured that these patients suffer from insufficient plasticity in their cerebral wax' (p. 38). In order to break this one-way traffic between amnesic and normal memory research, Crowder argues for a more observational approach, in which the characteristics of amnesia are investigated free of the constraints of a particular theoretical standpoint. A more precise description of the syndrome might then emerge. This, in turn, might suggest theoretical explanations which would not emerge from continually imposing theories of normal memory on abnormal memory. In particular, it might suggest new ways of understanding the nature of forgetting.

In this chapter we have considered various psychological theories about the cause of the amnesic syndrome. The specific encoding deficit theory suggests that amnesics have difficulty in performing certain kinds of learning tasks, but this seems not to be a sufficient explanation. A more general theory based on a contextual encoding deficit is more promising, although this too is not without problems. Explanations of amnesia are complicated by claims that the amnesic syndrome may take more than one form, and that Korsakoff's Syndrome (the major source of evidence about the amnesic syndrome) owes many of its symptoms to incidental frontal lobe damage. A possible resolution is the proposal that amnesia associated with temporal lobe damage is due to a storage deficit, whereas diencephalic amnesia is due to a contextual encoding deficit. However, this theory has been counterd by the suggestion that apparent differences between amnesics are due to variations in the severity of a common underlying disorder.

8

Ageing and Dementia

The amnesic syndrome has attracted so much interest because it is a relatively pure disorder, in which certain components of memory continue to function normally, while others are markedly impaired. Furthermore, the stability of the amnesic syndrome allows an experimenter to study the same patient over a considerable period, confident that no significant changes in memory function have taken place. The considerable scientific interest in the amnesic syndrome belies the fact that its occurrence is extremely rare within the neurological population. Far more common are *progressive* disorders, in which memory deficits arise as a consequence of some gradual deterioration of the brain. We are all aware that loss of memory appears to be a natural consequence of ageing, and we tend to consider it as inconvenient, rather than pathological. However, in many elderly people, memory deteriorates more rapidly than usual, because some form of *dementia* has set in. In this chapter we will consider the nature of memory loss in both normal ageing and dementia.

MEMORY IN NORMAL AGEING

There have been many experimental demonstrations that old people have poorer memories than young people, but explaining why this is so is difficult. Some general factors unconnected with memory may explain some of the difference. In practice, comparison of memory performance across different age-groups involves using different subjects. This *cross-sectional* design can be compared with the alternative *longitudinal* design, in which the same subject is tested on a number of separate occasions. For practical reasons, most studies of age differences in memory involve cross-sectional designs; thus, apparent differences in memory capability may reflect group differences unrelated to memory. Comparisons of older people with undergraduates, for example, could be confounded by differences in the amount of formal education received by each group (Zivian and Darjes, 1983). Despite problems such as this, the conclusion seems inescapable that memory does deteriorate with age, and one task of psychology is to explain why.

To understand memory deficits in old age, we must first establish which aspects of memory have been affected. As with the amnesic syndrome, we will attempt to do this by seeing how the characteristics of memory in the ageing map onto the memory model developed in chapters 1 and 2. Craik (1968) compared young and old subjects on the free recall task, and found that older people recalled less from early list positions but showed a normal recency effect. This suggests that the impairment is restricted to LTS, a conclusion supported by the observation that ageing does not appear to affect digit span (Drachman and Leavitt, 1972). Botwinick (1978) has identified a 'classic ageing pattern' in the LTS deficit of older people. There is little or no decline on standardized clinical tests such as WAIS, particularly in components of the test concerned with language and general information. The fact that language skills seem to deteriorate less rapidly than other aspects of memory has helped psychologists solve a rather difficult problem. When assessing a patient with brain damage, it is often useful to have some objective measure of their pre-morbid intelligence, but only in rare cases will previous test data be available. Nelson and O'Connor (1978) studied a group of patients with dementia and found that their ability to pronounce unusually spelled words (e.g. 'ache') remained constant, despite gradual deterioration in other intellectual spheres. On the basis of this observation, they devised the *New Adult Reading Test* (NART), a list of 50 words which become increasingly difficult. The score obtained on this test is considered to be a good predictor of pre-morbid intelligence in individuals of high-average or superior intelligence (Lezak, 1985).

Although language function seems to be unaffected in the elderly, deficits are revealed under certain circumstances. Schaie (1980) reports a marked decline in verbal fluency with age, even though the older subjects in his study had significantly better vocabulary scores than their younger counterparts. Elderly subjects also take longer to respond in word-association tests. Thomas and co-workers (1977) showed an age-related increase in picture- and object-naming times, but no difference in accuracy. Pezdek and Miceli (1982) have shown that the ability to detect that a sentence and a picture are meaningfully related is no poorer in older people than in younger subjects, provided that sufficient time is allowed for study. Together these findings suggest that semantic memory impairments in elderly people are greater when speed, rather than accuracy, is tested.

While there may be some impairment in semantic memory, the major deficit in old age is in episodic memory. We have already noted how old people perform on the free recall task, and there are many demonstrations of age differences in remembering novel information (Craik, 1977b). Kausler and Hakami (1983), for example, showed that older people are less likely to remember what they have just been doing than younger people. They gave subjects 12 different tasks to perform, ranging in complexity from simple motor activities to problem solving. A recall test showed that old and young subjects differed only slightly in their ability to remember the more complex tasks, but older people remembered significantly less about the less demanding tasks.

There have been a number of theories about why memory fails with increasing age, and they bear considerable resemblance to explanations of the amnesic syndrome. They must be viewed, therefore, within the constraints discussed in the final section of chapter 7. One proposal is that ageing impairs the retrieval system; thus older people have no problem in storing information, but more difficulty than younger people when trying to retrieve it.

The retrieval deficit hypothesis is supported by claims that older people are usually impaired on recall tasks, but perform at the same level as younger people when recognition is tested (Schonfield and Robertson, 1966). There are two difficulties with this theory: first, that several experiments have shown a milder, but significant decline in recognition performance with age (Craik, 1977b), and second, that absence of age differences in recognition would not restrict us to an explanation based on faulty retrieval processes. Under normal circumstances, recognition tests provide individuals with more information about what they are trying to remember than recall tests. This being so, a memory system in which there were some deficiencies in the way information was stored might still produce traces containing sufficient information for a recognition response, but not for successful recall.

An alternative approach is to explain memory difficulties in old age as some form of *encoding deficit*, although in the literature, the term *production deficiency* has been used (Kausler, 1970). Learning of most kinds of information is facilitated by organization. Thus a word list containing words drawn from only a few categories (e.g. flowers and colours) will be easier to remember than a random list because the category names provide retrieval cues. In this case organization of the list is imposed by the experimenter; but subjects can impose their own organization on information they are trying to remember. A number of studies have shown that older people make less use of both kinds of organization when learning lists of words (e.g. Denney, 1974). Older people also seem less likely to employ imagery as a learning strategy. Hulicka and Grossman (1967) compared young and old people on paired-associate learning, and found that the younger group performed better. Subsequent questioning showed that this group reported more use of mediating images than the older group.

These findings suggest that the memory deficit in normal ageing stems from an organizational deficiency. This theory predicts that memory deficits in older people should be less when they are given highly organized material to learn, or specific instructions to organize material in an effective way. This possibility has been explored in a variety of situations, but the general conclusion is that organizational manipulations increase the performance of both young and old subjects, but that age differences remain. Older people can improve their memories by applying strategies and exploiting organizational factors, but this does not eliminate their memory problems (Burke and Light, 1981).

Ageing and memory have also been explored within the levels of processing framework, in which age-related memory deficits are seen as stemming from some deficiency in the ability to employ semantic processing. However, the evidence for this idea is not convincing. Mitchell and Perlmutter (1986) presented young and old subjects with target words and required them to make either a semantic or a non-semantic decision about each one. Each target was accompanied by a 'flanker' word, but subjects were told to ignore these and concentrate on the targets. Half of each age group knew their memory for the targets would be tested; the remaining subjects had an incidental recall test. Measurements taken during the initial learning indicated that the tasks evoked similar processing strategies in both age-groups, and this was reflected in the incidental learning results, which showed no significant age differences. Intentional learning produced better recall in both old and young groups, but the effect was more marked in the younger subjects, particularly in the recall of flanker words.

Older people tend to be poorer at recalling stories, and Zelinski and his associates (1984) hypothesized that this is because old people make less use of story structure as a retrieval aid. However, their experiment showed that young and old made equal use of structure in their story recall, even though the older subjects remembered less. Hess (1985) required young and old subjects to read passages concerning everyday activities such as eating in a restaurant. In each passage, most of the events described were typical (e.g. paying the bill), whereas a few were atypical (e.g. picking up a napkin off the floor). It was found that old and young subjects did not differ greatly on recognition of typical actions from the passages, indicating that both groups made equal use of the underlying structure to help them to remember. However, older subjects were considerably poorer at recognizing atypical actions, which suggests that they relied more on the predictive aspect of story structure than the younger subjects.

These studies suggest that older people do not have a basic deficiency in semantic processing. They show the normal advantage of semantic over non-semantic orienting tasks, and seem as able as younger people to appreciate the structural qualities of prose. However, the findings of Mitchell and Perlmutter and Hess suggest that older people are poorer at picking up more peripheral information (e.g. flanker words, atypical actions). A similar finding is reported by Light and Zelinski (1983). Young and old subjects were shown a tourist map depicting a number of structures (e.g. a church). Half of both age-groups were told to remember each structure and its location, while the others were told to remember only the structures. Despite the instructions, all the subjects were subsequently asked to remember both the structures and their locations. Subjects instructed to remember the structures and locations performed better than those instructed to remember the structures only. However, the difference was more marked in the older group, who were much less able to remember the locations.

The failure of older people to remember more peripheral information can be attributed to a deficit in *processing capacity* (e.g. Craik and Simon, 1980). Put another way, older people simply have fewer resources available to learn new information. Thus they can perform as effectively as younger people on the main task, but have less capacity left over for taking in non-essential information. Rabbitt (1982), for example, has shown that older people are poorer at describing a familiar route, even though they have no more difficulty than younger people in finding their way around it. This suggests that older people may encode less context; such information may not be necessary when finding one's way around because of the cues provided by the immediate surroundings. However, when attempting to recall the route contextual information associated with route memory may provide an important means of distinguishing that memory from similar kinds of stored information (see also Simon, 1979).

A number of researchers have attempted to delineate this deficit in processing capacity in more detail by adopting Hasher and Zacks's (1979) distinction between *automatic* and *effortful* processes. As their names suggest, the former refers to psychological processes that occur without conscious intention, the latter to those that require some form of conscious effort. Furthermore, it has been proposed that automatic processes are age-invariant, whereas those requiring effort decline with age. Several studies have tried to demonstrate that older people do not show impairments on tasks requiring only automatic processing, but they have not succeeded (Lehman and Mellinger, 1984; Light and Zelinski, 1983; Pezdek, 1983). The general notion of a processing capacity deficit may still be useful in studying age-related memory loss, but the exact nature of the deficit still eludes us.

MEMORY IN DEMENTIA

The name *dementia* refers to a class of degenerative brain disorders, all of which produce a gradual decline in intellectual function. Loss of memory is usually the first sign, a patient may begin to ask the same question repeatedly, forget to switch things off, or fail to keep appointments. As the dementia progresses, confused episodes and more drastic impairments such as language dysfunction may develop. Because of similarities, there are difficulties in diagnosing particular forms of dementia. However, a number of distinct forms have been recognized, and we will start by considering the most prevalent.

In 1907 Alois Alzheimer reported the case of a 51-year-old woman whose illness began with lapses of memory and progressed to a state of profound dementia. The woman died five years later, and examination of her brain revealed some distinctive neuropathological features. Macroscopically, the brain had clearly shrunk, and under the microscope there were clear signs of abnormality. Within the cortex were a large number of *senile plaques*, ovoid structures much bigger than neurones that arise as a result of neural degeneration. Within the neurones, Alzheimer observed abnormal accumulations of filamentary material, which he called *neurofibrillary tangles*. Senile plaques had been observed before, and in smaller numbers were known to be a feature of the normal ageing brain. Neurofibrillary tangles had never been detected before, however, and this suggested to Alzheimer that he had discovered a new disease, now known as *Alzheimer's Disease* (AD).

AD has often been referred to as *pre-senile dementia*, to distinguish it from *senile dementia*, which affects elderly people. However, most workers now accept that this division is based arbitrarily on age, and that the two forms of dementia both reflect the same disease. The amnesia observed in AD has been the focus of considerable recent interest, but, in assessing the evidence, it is important to remember that it relates to the early stages of the illness; patients at a more advanced stage are too impaired intellectually to cope with the demands of experiments.

Memory loss in AD has been investigated by comparing AD patients and controls on the free recall task. Miller (1975) found that AD patients recalled fewer words from the early parts of a list, indicating impairment of LTS. However, he also found that the recency effect for AD patients was smaller than that for normal subjects, indicating a deficit in STS. This is an important difference from other organic disorders we have considered so far, because in the latter, STS appears to function normally. The STS deficit has been confirmed in a comparative study by Corkin (1982), who found reduced verbal and non-verbal memory span in AD patients as compared with both Korsakoff patients and controls, whose performances did not differ significantly. Morris (1984) studied AD patients in terms of the working memory model, thinking that the reduced STS capacity might reflect an impaired articulatory loop. However, his results failed to support this hypothesis.

Impaired STS in AD suggests that these patients may have an attentional deficit, which could, in turn, be responsible for their poor memory performance. Miller explored this possibility, again using the free recall task. The experiment by Rundus (1971; see chapter 1) showed that the primacy effect is directly related to the amount of rehearsal that each item receives. If AD patients have reduced attentional capacity, this may reduce the number of times they can rehearse items during the learning phase. Miller repeated his experiment, but allowed both the AD patients and the controls longer to study the items. As one might expect from the data shown in figure 1.4a, this substantially increased the primacy effect for controls, but had no influence on the AD patients' level of recall, thus indicating that the apparent memory deficit stemmed from some malfunction of LTS rather than reduced rehearsal capacity.

Free recall is a test of episodic memory, because it requires retrieval of information from a specific time. The above results suggest that AD, like the amnesic syndrome, is primarily a deficit in episodic memory. Schacter (1983) chose the unlikely setting of a golf course to confirm this view. He played a round with an AD patient, and reports that the man had considerable difficulty in remembering where he had just hit his ball (especially if he teed off), but had no trouble defining a wide range of golfing terms.

In the laboratory, a number of studies have compared the memory deficit in AD with other amnesic disorders. Kopelman (1985) compared AD patients with Korsakoff patients and controls, using the same technique as Huppert and Piercy (1978a; see chapter 7). The two patient groups needed more trials to learn the material at the outset, but, once acquired, the two groups forgot the information at a rate comparable to that of the controls. Another similarity between AD and Korsakoff amnesia has been reported by Butters and colleagues (1983). They required subjects to listen to four short stories. After each one, the patients were asked to recall it. Performance was very poor for both groups, but both showed a tendency to make intrusion errors – to recall facts from a previous story. Intrusion errors are a known characteristic of Korsakoff's Syndrome, and their equally common appearance in AD patients suggests a common memory deficit.

RA is also a prominent feature of AD, but may differ qualitatively from that found in amnesic patients. Wilson and co-workers (1981) tested AD patients on a version of the BRMT (see chapter 5). An overall analysis showed that the AD group performed much worse than the controls, but neither group showed evidence of a temporal gradient. More detailed analyses were carried out to see if the absence of a gradient was due to the poorer performance on harder test items, but this was not the case. This result indicates that RA in AD patients may differ from that in the amnesic syndrome, where temporal gradients are commonly found.

The absence of a temporal gradient on RA tests seems at odds with the general clinical impression given by AD patients. Typically, patients seem able to talk quite easily about events from the earlier parts of their lives, and only run into difficulty when trying to recount events from later periods. Two points may shed light on this discrepancy. First, as we noted in chapter 5, RA tests may not be tests solely of episodic memory. Failure to remember early public events does not necessarily mean that the patient is unable to remember early personal events. Second, recall of early memories may be based on a different form of memory from that used in the recall of later experiences. In our discussion of semantic memory (chapter 2), it was noted that part of its content was information about ourselves. A plausible assumption is that it takes time for this kind of self-knowledge to be constructed. Thus we may have a general knowledge about earlier stages of our lives (e.g. what happened to us as children), but be more reliant on the recall of specific experiences when recounting more recent events.

The idea that recall of events from different periods involves different kinds of memory is supported by a study by Nigro and Neisser (1983). They have proposed that

in some memories one seems to have the position of an onlooker or observer, looking at the situation from an external vantage point and seeing oneself 'from the outside'. In other memories the scene appears from one's own position; one seems to have roughly the field of vision that was available in the original situation and one does not 'see oneself'. (pp. 467–8)

The authors term these *observer* and *field* memories, respectively. Field memories seem to correspond to the recall of specific experiences, whereas observer memories are reconstructions which can come to be represented independently of the original experiences that gave rise to them. Thus an old soldier able to recount his early experiences may not be relying on the recall of specific events. His apparently vivid memory may be the product of much story telling, which has enabled him to build up a substantial observer memory for that time period. This is in line with the idea presented above, that personal memories may be episodically or semantically based; in this connection it is interesting to note Nigro and Neisser's report that recall of more recent experiences tends to be based more on field memories – a finding consistent with the view that recall of later periods of life is more dependent on episodic memory than recall of more remote events.

Given evidence that old people normally have some degree of semantic memory impairment (see above), it is hardly surprising that patients with AD also show deficiencies on tasks such as object naming and word finding (e.g. Bayles, 1982). These results suggest a severely disrupted semantic memory, but Nebes and associates (1984) have queried this interpretation. They argue that most demonstrations of impaired semantic memory in AD involve tasks which stress speed of responding; they have shown that when time pressure is removed, AD patients perform semantic tasks such as word naming just as well as controls. On the basis of this, they conclude that the semantic deficit in AD is best thought of as a retrieval problem, rather than a deficit in the structure of semantic memory itself. However, this conclusion needs to be modified in the light of Albert and Moss's (1984) demonstration that naming deficits in AD depend on the age of the patient.

The memory deficits associated with *Huntingdon's Chorea* (HC) have begun to attract interest. Butters and co-workers compared HC patients with Korsakoff patients on a battery of tests, and found that they had similar MQs but differed considerably in the manner in which memory was affected. Unlike Korsakoff patients, who are good at acquiring new procedural memory, HC patients were impaired. However, on recognition tests HC patients scored much better than Korsakoff patients. HC patients were also examined on the story recall task used by Butters and associates (see above) and were found to produce far fewer intrusions than either AD or Korsakoff amnesics. These data suggest a different pattern of memory impairment in HC amnesia, and further data are awaited with interest (see also Brandt and Butters, 1986).

Memory disorders associated with other dementias – *multiple infarct dementia, Pick's Disease, neurosyphilis, normal pressure hydrocephalus*, and *Jakob-Creutzfeld's Disease* – have yet to be investigated systematically. *Parkinson's Disease* is sometimes accompanied by a dementia which Boller and co-workers (1980) consider to be similar to that found in AD. As yet there are no objective accounts of memory disorders in Parkinson's Disease, but a moving personal account can be found in *A World Away* (Gilmore, 1970), a biography of Mervyn Peake, the novelist and illustrator whose attempts to continue working under the strains of the disease continued until the last few years of his life (see also Dakof and Mendelsohn, 1986). Finally, as the Acquired Immune Deficiency Syndrome (AIDS) epidemic continues to spread, there is growing evidence that this illness causes a dementia which includes loss of memory.

Normal ageing is associated with a consistent pattern of memory impairment. STS appears to function normally, but both the episodic and semantic components of LTS undergo some deterioration. This cannot be explained in terms of an encoding deficit, but seems to be a contextual deficit due to some loss in processing capacity. Dementia produces a profound loss of memory. Studies of AD patients show that both STS and LTS function are disrupted, with episodic memory being far more affected than semantic memory. Other dementias are beginning to be studied, and some qualitative differences have already emerged.

9

Transient Memory Disorders

So far we have considered only memory disorders that arise from some permanent deterioration of the brain. There are a number of *transient* memory disorders, however, in which a patient's memory ceases to function normally for a certain period of time. This may be due to some form of vascular disorder or a closed-head injury, or it may be drug-induced or an after-effect of electroconvulsive therapy (ECT). Psychogenic disorders are also transient, and these will be considered in the next chapter.

TRANSIENT GLOBAL AMNESIA

Regard and Landis (1984) have reported the case of a healthy 40-year-old policeman who, while exercising in a gymnasium, suddenly became confused. Returning to work, he repeated the same questions many times in an attempt to orient himself. His doctor could find no signs of neurological illness, but the man, convinced that something was wrong, drove through heavy traffic to a hospital. CAT scans and other neurological tests showed no signs of abnormality, but psychological testing revealed a profound memory impairment. The patient knew who and where he was, but was completely confused about the time and had an RA concerning the previous few months of his life. He showed concern about his disorder and did not engage in confabulation. Formal testing revealed a severe anterograde amnesia. He was unable to remember anything about a 15-word list 40 minutes after hearing it, and performed little better on a similar test of visual memory. By contrast, his digit span was within the normal range, and all his other mental abilities were unaffected. Nine hours after onset, his

RA had receded to the point where only his memory for the last two days was impaired, but there was little improvement in his anterograde deficit. However, this subsequently improved, and after 72 hours his performance on memory tests was within the normal range. One month after the episode, there was no sign of memory impairment.

This case is typical of a disorder known as *transient global amnesia* (TGA). Its major features are: a sudden onset of antero-grade amnesia, coupled with RA for more recent events in the patient's life; disorientation in time, but no loss of personal identity; insight into the memory disorder; no impairment of any other psychological function; duration of attack ranging from minutes to days.

A considerable amount is known about the aetiology of TGA. Victims usually have a record of good health, and are typically over fifty (Markowitsch, 1983). Its occurrence, which seems equally frequent in men and women, is rare, and it accounts for less than 2 per cent of a typical population of neurological patients. It can be precipitated by many things, including sudden changes in temperature (e.g. taking a cold shower), physical stress, eating a large meal, and even sexual intercourse. Several toxins have been associated with TGA, most notably clioquinol, an active component of many anti-diarrhoea drugs until it was banned. In 1966, widespread flooding in Japan led to extensive distribution of clioquinol to combat dysentery. Following this, more than a hundred people reported symptoms similar to those of TGA. In 1979 Mumenthaler and colleagues reported several cases in Europe, including one of a student who developed diarrhoea during a trip to Paris. She took only the prescribed dose of clioquinol-containing tablets, but, on returning home, found that she could remember nothing about her holiday.

There seems to be general agreement that the physiological dysfunction underlying TGA is triggered by a *transient cerebral ischemia* – that is, a temporary reduction in blood supply to regions of the brain concerned with memory function. The ischemic theory of TGA gains support from the observation that migraine is more than twice as common in victims of TGA than in the general population (Frank, 1981). Migraine is considered to be of ischemic origin, so its association with TGA would suggest that the two disorders have a common underlying cause. The age distribution of TGA victims also supports the ischemic theory, since this is the age at which the development of arteriosclerosis, which can give rise to ischemic attacks, first becomes a serious possibility. Specifying the region of the brain affected during an attack of TGA is problematic, because most victims appear to be neurologically normal. However, some studies have detected constrictions in blood vessels supplying the temporal lobe region, suggesting that TGA may have a hippocampal origin. Furthermore, clioquinol has been shown to induce hippocampal damage in animals.

POST-TRAUMATIC AMNESIA

Closed-head injuries involve a blow to the skull that does not expose the brain. Most victims of closed-head injury suffer only a temporary impairment of memory, but for some, the outcome is a permanent loss. Amnesia following head injury can be as severe as that found in the amnesic syndrome, but such patients have rarely been incorporated in experimental studies of this syndrome. This is because severe memory loss following closed-head injury invariably appears alongside deficits in other functions. In order to make inferences about normal memory from pathological data, the neuropsychologist assumes that amnesia arises directly from a malfunction of memory and not as a consequence of some other problem. The amnesia found in Korsakoff's Syndrome, for example, or encephalitis meets this requirement because the deficit is restricted primarily to memory. With a severely head-injured patient, however, amnesia may be complicated by severe language difficulties, attentional problems, and impaired intelligence. This makes any failure of memory much more difficult to interpret.

Severe memory loss occurs in about 10 per cent of patients admitted to hospital following closed-head injury, but our concern will be confined to those who undergo complete or near-complete recovery. Concussion has dramatic and usually immediate effects on an individual. If the blow is sufficiently powerful, the person will collapse, and respiration may even cease for a moment or two. As consciousness is regained, the victim will start to move, make noises, and eventually speak. There will be signs of restlessness, and the victim may be irritable or even abusive. Although fully conscious, the patient will be confused, disoriented, and show marked anterograde and retrograde memory deficits. The memory loss experienced in this period is termed *post-traumatic amnesia* (PTA), and varies in duration from a few seconds to several months (Russell, 1971).

The inability of PTA victims to remember events immediately preceding their trauma is consistent with the existence of an STS in which information is retained in a temporary and labile trace, the assumption being that the trauma has interfered in some way with the normal process of transfer. This disruption could occur in two ways: concussion could disrupt maintenance of the temporary trace or interfere with the consolidation process. Two lines of evidence support the latter explanation. First, Brooks (1975), along with other clinicians, reports that digit span is normal during the PTA phase. Normal performance of this task reflects an intact STS; so PTA victims would seem to be unimpaired in this respect. The second, rather unusual source of evidence is a study by Yarnell and Lynch (1973). They examined PTA in American football-players immediately after they had suffered concussion. In this game, players have to remember a set of instructions about the 'play' they must follow. At the time of concussion, therefore, a player is keeping in mind a certain amount of information about what he should be doing. In one case, a player was hit while being 'gang-tackled' during a '91 curl pattern play'. On immediate questioning, he could name the play, but, on removal to the touch-line, he was no longer able to do so. This phenomenon was observed frequently, suggesting that STS continues to function during PTA, but that concussion disrupts transfer to LTS.

Levin and associates (1985) have examined the pattern of RA, both during and after PTA. In their first study, young head-injured patients were tested on the 'titles for television programs' test developed by Squire and Slater (1975). In this test the subject must select from a choice of four titles the one that corresponds to a real TV program. The programs are drawn from different times during the period 1968–1981 with a view to detecting any temporal gradient that might be present. During the PTA phase, victims were equally poor at identifying programs from all time periods. Afterwards, performance improved, but accuracy remained the same across all time periods. The absence of a temporal gradient on the TV program test runs contrary to clinical accounts of PTA, which suggest that more remote memories are less affeceted during the PTA phase. Levin and his colleagues therefore conducted a second study in which patients were interviewed about major events in their lives, using information supplied by relatives. Four periods were identified: 'primary school', 'junior high school', 'high school', and 'young adult life'. During PTA there was a clear temporal gradient, with early memories being recalled much better than later ones; but when PTA cleared, this gradient disappeared.

The discrepancy can be accounted for on the assumption that the two types of RA test address different forms of memory. In chapter 8 it was suggested that recall of early personal experiences, as opposed to later events, may depend less on remembering specific occurrences. This is because people build up a general reconstruction of their earlier years, which exists independently of memory for the original events. The temporal gradient in recalling personal experiences may reflect patients' reliance on this form of memory. By contrast, knowledge of TV programs may depend more on remembering particular experiences, and the patients' uniform inability to remember them suggests that episodic memory is impaired during PTA.

The assessment of RA during PTA can be complicated by a phenomenon known as 'shrinking RA', as demonstrated in the case reported by Benson and Geschwind in 1967. A 33-year-old American was admitted to hospital after a head injury which initially rendered him stuporous but not unconscious. He was known to be separated from his wife and family (who lived in Washington) and had lived in Boston for the last two years. In Washington he had worked as a bus driver, but in Boston he had held two different jobs, as a messenger and a labourer. During the first week a number of mental impairments were apparent, but within a month these had disappeared except for a severe amnesia. He was very disoriented and thought he was still living in Washington. This continued for about three months, when he suddenly became concerned about his memory disorder and his memory for new information showed signs of improvement. His RA also began to lessen; first, he remembered the breakup of his marriage, then the first job he had held in Boston. A few days later, memory of the second job returned, and by the time the patient was discharged, he had amnesia only for the 24-hour period preceding his injury.

The phenomenon of shrinkage is consistent with the view that earlier memories can be derived from a different source from that needed for the recall of more recent experiences. At the outset, a victim of PTA may be wholly reliant on his general knowledge about himself, which, as we have noted, will be more extensive for earlier periods of life. As recovery occurs, the episodic record becomes increasingly available, and more recent experiences can be recounted. The temporal gradient in this recovery can be explained by suggesting that older experiences are more broadly distributed than newer experiences (which seems reasonable because older experiences will have been recounted more). It follows, therefore, that a gradual recovery process will restore some component of older memories before it restores more narrowly distributed newer memories.

The extent and nature of residual impairment following PTA have been subject to considerable investigation. Surveys have shown that a substantial number of PTA victims experience some permanent disorder of memory. Russell and Smith (1961), for example, found that only 10 per cent of patients with a brief PTA (less than one hour) showed memory difficulties at a later date, compared to 56 per cent of those whose PTA duration was more than seven days. More recently Van Zomeran and Van den Berg (1985) followed up 57 head-injured patients, and found that 80 per cent reported some form of residual deficit two years after injury. Over 50 per cent of the sample still regarded themselves as forgetful, and about 30 per cent reported irritability, poor concentration, and slowness. To determine how PTA duration related to subsequent impairment, correlations were made among PTA duration, subjective estimates of memory function, and whether the patient had returned to work. PTA duration correlated strongly with estimates of forgetfulness, and patients with shorter PTA duration were more likely to have returned to work. PTA duration therefore seems to be a reliable predictor of subsequent impairment, although there are complicating factors. Brooks (1974), for example, showed that for victims under 30, PTA duration did not reliably predict the occurrence of permanent disorder, while for subjects over 30, this appeared to be the case. Another complication is that the connection between PTA duration and subsequent impairment may lessen if longer follow-up intervals are used.

Permanent memory deficits following PTA seem restricted to episodic memory. Brooks (1975) tested free recall in a group of patients who were out of PTA, and found normal recency but impaired recall for earlier positions in tests using word lists. These data confirm that the impairment lies in LTS, rather than STS, but can we be more specific about the manner in which LTS has been disrupted? Evidence in chapter 4 emphasized the importance of imagery in memory. Richardson and Snape (1984) examined the possibility that poor memory in head-injured patients stems from some deficit in the use of mental imagery. Normal people recall high-imagery words (e.g. FLOWER) better than low-imagery words (e.g. FUNCTION); but they found that head-injured patients did not show this difference. Richardson and Barry (1985) confirmed this finding, and showed that head-injured patients did better with high-imagery words when given instructions to use interactive images. The authors concluded that the deficit in head-injured patients was an inability to use imagery spontaneously during learning. It remains to be seen how Richardson and Barry's theory relates to a comprehensive account of long-term memory deficits in PTA victims.

ECT AND MEMORY

Few medical treatments have stirred up as much controversy as ECT. Developed in Italy by Cerletti and Bini, ECT is often thought to have been inspired by the Roman tradition of applying electric eels to the head as a cure for madness. In fact, the origins of ECT go back only 60 years, to the Hungarian psychiatrist Meduna. He noted a number of studies reporting that schizophrenia and epilepsy did not occur in the same patient, and speculated that induction of a seizure similar to that experienced in epileptic fits might cure schizophrenia. Meduna induced seizures with camphor and by other pharmacological means, and claimed success in the treatment of schizophrenia. Cerletti and Bini extended Meduna's work by exploring whether seizures caused by brief electric shocks could achieve similar results. Their first patient was a chronic schizophrenic who received two shocks delivered from electrodes placed on either side of his head; the second caused him to burst into song, a sign of apparent success. A further seven treatments were given, and a two-year follow-up showed that the patient was leading a normal life.

Because of its simplicity and low cost, the use of ECT spread rapidly, and by the 1950s it was a major form of treatment for schizophrenia and other disorders including depression. The discovery of neuroleptic drugs has led to a substantial decline in the use of ECT, but it is still a widespread form of treatment. ECT is now very different from what it was in its heyday. When first developed, it was given while the patient was fully conscious. Given this way, as vividly depicted in the film *One Flew over the Cuckoo's Nest*, it produced violent *grand mal* seizures which often had unpleasant side-effects. Nowadays the patient is anaesthetized and then given a muscle relaxant to minimize the physical effects of the seizure. After seizure, oxygenation is used to facilitate the patient's immediate recovery. The seizure is induced by electrodes placed either bilaterally or unilaterally in the temporal lobe region, and the electrical wave form may be either sinusoidal or a brief pulse. Electrode placement and wave form are important variables in assessing the effects of ECT, including the resulting memory impairment (Daniel and Crovitz, 1983a, b).

Our concern will be with the effects of ECT on memory – the broader issue of its therapeutic effectiveness is beyond our present scope. ECT has an obvious, immediate, and highly disruptive effect on brain function. On regaining consciousness, patients who have received ECT are similar in many ways to victims of PTA (see above). They are disoriented, confused, and unable to respond in a coherent manner, and there is a dense anterograde amnesia. As time progresses, there is a gradual recovery of function. Typically, patients first regain their personal identity, next comes knowledge of where they are, followed finally, by correct orientation in time.

Tests of memory during the post-ECT recovery phase reveal substantial impairment. Various forms of recall task, such as paired-associate learning and memory for stories, show a clear anterograde amnesia. In one study, Squire (1981) showed a series of pictures to patients who had received bilateral ECT only two hours previously. Their memory for the pictures was tested again 2 hours and 32 hours later. During the ECT recovery phase, they showed very rapid forgetting, compared with their performance on the same test 4 months after treatment.

ECT patients invariably report amnesia for events immediately preceding treatment. Many studies have confirmed this experimentally by showing poor recall and poor recognition of novel information presented shortly before the seizure. Earlier memories are also disrupted by ECT. Squire and co-workers (1975) interviewed ECT patients about important events in their lives. These answers provided a basis for assessing the patients' episodic memory after ECT. Knowledge of public events was measured using the TV program test described earlier. One week after ECT there was evidence of considerable RA, but after seven months, all that remained was an amnesia for the days preceding the treatment and a suggestion of some impairment for events in the preceding year (the study was done around the time of 'Watergate', and many of the patients had difficulty recalling this very publicized event).

Practitioners of ECT agree that treatment results in a small amount of RA for events immediately before the seizure and a degree of amnesia for the treatment period. These deficits are assumed to reflect a transient derangement of memory processes, rather than a permanent disability. Opponents of ECT claim that it produces more substantial effects on memory. In assessing this argument, one can start by considering the effects of ECT on the physical nature of the brain, for, if ECT causes permanent memory loss, one might expect this to be evident in a neuropathological examination. Since its inception, there has been concern about possible neuropathological changes following ECT. Cerletti himself spent two years studying the brains of electrically stunned cattle before concluding that ECT was safe to use on humans. In fact, early ECT was a rather unsafe procedure and sometimes proved fatal. This allowed post-mortems to be carried out on people who had just undergone ECT. These patients typically exhibited brain damage, but it was concluded that this was a consequence of cardio-respiratory failure, and that the seizure itself had no structural effect. More recently pneumoencephalograms and CAT scans have been employed, but these have generally failed to show any evidence of damage. The effects of ECT on brain tissue have also been assessed in animal studies in which, following a series of electric shocks, the structure of the brain has been examined microscopically. Collectively, these studies indicate that ECT has detrimental, but largely reversible, effects on brain tissue (Weiner, 1984).

ECT has a widespread effect on the physiological processes of the brain. Before the introduction of safety measures, ECT was often accompanied by anoxia and a rise in brain acidity, but these adverse side-effects now seem to have been eliminated from the treatment. ECT disrupts protein synthesis, and this may contribute to the post-treatment memory deficit, but there is no strong evidence that this disruption is permanent. Some investigators have examined the after-effects of ECT by obtaining a 'baseline' measure of the patient's EEG prior to ECT and re-examining it at various intervals after the treatment has finished. Fukuda and Matsuda (1969) examined 53 patients, each of whom received 10 ECT treatments. Soon after treatment 42 per cent of the sample had an abnormal EEG, but this had dropped to 14 per cent within 30 days. Other studies report similar findings, and overall it would seem that ECT has a pronounced, but transient, influence on the electrophysiological activity of the brain.

Despite this, there are many who maintain that ECT causes permanent brain damage. One argument is that neuropathological techniques such as CAT scans may be insensitive to the kind of damage ECT produces. More sophisticated procedures such as NMR or PET given to ECT patients may decide the issue but alternatively, one could turn to the psychological literature for evidence of lasting impairment.

Opponents of ECT put great store in isolated reports of permanent loss of memory following treatment. However, these reports usually come from studies without controls, and are based mainly on subjective evidence. The question of whether ECT causes permanent memory failure can only be answered properly by experiments which disentangle lasting effects of the seizures from other contributory factors. One approach might be to find ECT patients who are complaining about their memory and see if their memories are impaired. Freeman and associates (1980) wrote a newspaper article entitled 'Is there any harm in shock treatment?'.

It ended by saying: 'if YOU have had ECT . . . and reckon it has had an adverse effect on you, the group would be grateful if you would help by allowing them to test your memory and ability to think quickly, and see how you compare with other people. It would only take an hour or so . . . and there are no shocks in store. That's a promise!' Memory tests showed that the recruits plus some additional ECT patients performed worse than control subjects. When the influence of residual depression and medication on memory performance was taken into account, the differences between the groups became smaller, but remained significant. Yet the researchers were still unable to conclude that ECT had a lasting effect on memory. First, it is possible that the ECT group had a lower-than-average memory capability before treatment. Before ECT, they may not have noticed this, but after treatment they may have monitored their memory more carefully in the belief that it might be permanently damaged. Thus, failure of memory prior to ECT would not have raised comment, but subsequent to ECT, it would have been regarded as a sign of impairment, leading them to volunteer for the study (see below). Moreover, the fact that subjects believed that their memories were affected might have produced poorer levels of task motivation in the ECT group compared with controls.

To get around these difficulties, Weeks and co-workers (1980) studied 51 depressed patients who received ECT and compared them with two control groups, a group of 51 depressed subjects who did not receive ECT but were carefully matched to the ECT group in terms of age, sex, class, education, and severity of depression, and a group of normal individuals matched in the same way apart from the depressive symptoms. The ECT group were tested at the outset of the study and then one week, three months, and six months after the termination of treatment (average number of treatments was 7.2). Control subjects were tested at similar intervals except that there was no test session corresponding to that given one week after ECT. At that time the experimental ECT group showed pronounced impairments, but at three months there was little difference between them and the two control groups, and after six months the only significant finding was slightly better recall by the ECT group on the logical memory component of the WMS.

The data from this study are consistent with those from a number of other studies in showing no permanent impairment of memory following ECT. However, failure to detect impairments may be because standard memory tests are insensitive to the particular impairments produced by ECT. A typical complaint from ECT patients is an inability to remember events from the time period immediately preceding treatment. Janis (1950) used an auto-biographical memory test similar to that used by Squire and colleagues (see above) and found evidence of substantial impairments three months after ECT. However, he concluded that motivational factors may have played a role, because amnesia was most evident for 'experiences which tend to arouse anxiety, guilt, or a lowering of self-esteem'. The strongest evidence for extensive permanent RA following ECT comes from the study of Squire and associates described earlier. They found an impairment in the retrieval of personal memories for the preceding year and for public events of that time. If forgetting was determined purely by the personal content of memories, it would not explain the poor performance on the second type of test, since this presumably involves emotionally neutral information.

The controversy surrounding ECT is likely to continue for some time, and the question of whether ECT affects memory permanently is likely to figure strongly in these arguments. We have considered only a small amount of the evidence, but some interim conclusions can be drawn. Studies which have examined the long-term effects of ECT and controlled for the influence of extraneous factors indicate that ECT does not have any extensive effect on permanent memory function. All patients show a degree of RA for events immediately preceding ECT and the treatment period itself. The only objective evidence for a more severe impairment is that of Squire and co-workers (1975), but, as Fink (1984) points out, the year preceding ECT represents the height of a patient's morbidity, and this may be the cause of the amnesia.

If ECT does not permanently affect memory, why are there so many complaints from patients, and individual case histories reporting long-term deficits? We have already noted that under-going ECT may cause patients to conclude falsely that their memory is impaired. Squire and Slater (1983) examined a group of ECT patients and found significant differences between patients who complained of memory difficulties and those who did not.

Complainers tended to believe that ECT had been ineffective in treating their depression; thus their own assessment of memory might have reflected their continuing illness rather than a true loss. Furthermore, complainers tested three years after ECT portrayed their memory problems as of an 'amnesic type', even though there were no objective signs of this. Squire and Slater suggest that these complaints are 'based on the experience of amnesia initially associated with ECT and reflect a persisting, and perhaps altogether natural, tendency to question whether memory functions have fully recovered' (p. 6).

Although such subjective factors may be the cause of many complaints following ECT, they seem insufficient to account for all such reports. A comprehensive answer must take into account other factors. The use of ECT on elderly depressives may accelerate decline if dementia is present. In addition, ECT can be abused as a treatment. Stenback and Viitamaki (1957) report the case of a schizophrenic who received 441 ECT treatments and was clearly impaired. Regenstein and colleagues (1975) studied a woman who underwent 16 ECT treatments in 4 months and then received 1 ECT every week for 2 years. Eleven months after treatment had stopped, she was still in very poor condition. The pattern of treatment in these two cases contrasts markedly with that in various controlled studies, in which the ECT patients usually received about 10 treatments. Claims in the latter that ECT does not affect memory are thus based on a small amount of treatment and do not reflect the cumulative effects of more extensive ECT. Calloway and co-workers (1981), for example, report significant frontal atrophy in a group of psychogeriatric patients who had a substantial history of ECT.

A final issue is the manner in which evidence relating to this problem is presented. Experimental studies almost always report their results in terms of group averages, with little or no information about the performance of particular individuals. Thus, within a large group of individuals receiving ECT, a small proportion may suffer permanent defects, a fact that will be masked when performance is reported as an average, since it is insufficient to show up statistically. Even proponents of ECT accept that there is a low incidence of adverse reaction to the treatment; but estimates of its extent seem to vary, and little is known about the predisposing factors (Weiner, 1984).

DRUG-INDUCED AMNESIA

A wide range of drugs are known to influence memory. The best known of these is ethanol, whose effects on human memory may be familiar to many of you reading this book! The effects of alcohol on memory were considered briefly in chapter 6, and there is further discussion in chapter 10. This section will be concerned with some other drugs known to have amnesic effects in humans.

Hallucinogenic drugs often impair memory, but it is not clear whether this is a genuine effect on memory or due to some more general cognitive derangement induced by the drug. Because of its widespread use, there has been considerable interest in the effects of marijuana on memory. Anecdotal reports suggest that there is an impairment of memory while under the influence of marijuana. Comments such as 'My memory span for conversation is shortened, so that I may forget what the start of a sentence was about even before the sentence is finished', and 'If I read while stoned, I remember less of what I've read hours later than if I had been straight' are commonplace among marijuana-users (Tart, 1972).

Experimental studies generally confirm these subjective views. Abel (1971), for example, examined subjects' performance on the free recall task when they were intoxicated and when they were not. He measured both immediate and delayed performance, and found that intoxicated subjects recalled less than normal subjects from the early parts of the list, but that there was no difference in the recency effect for the two groups. This suggests that LTS function has been disrupted by marijuana intoxication, but in what way? Darley and associates (1974) identified two groups of subjects, and gave each one a series of free recall trials in which the two groups produced similar results. One group was then given marijuana, and one hour later both groups were given recall and recognition tests for the first set of lists. The drug group performed as well as the control group on both kinds of test. While the drug group was still intoxicated, the experimental procedure was repeated with 10 new lists. In immediate testing, the marijuana group recalled less from the earlier list positions, but showed normal recency effects; and in delayed testing, the drug group recalled and recognized fewer words than the controls. Because the marijuana subjects were able to remember the first set of lists normally, even though they were intoxicated, but, in a similar state, showed impairments on the second list, it seems that marijuana affects the acquisition of new information rather than retrieval of old information. Wetzel and colleagues (1982) examined remote memory during marijuana intoxication using the TV program test described earlier. The marijuana subjects did not differ from a placebo group on this test, but were impaired on their ability to learn a word list. This result concurs with the results of Darley and co-workers in locating the deficit in the storage of new information rather than in the retrieval of existing memories. Finally, we should note that marijuana can exert state-dependent effects (chapter 3).

The *benzodiazepines* are an important class of psychoactive drug, the best-known of which are probably *lorazepam* (ativan) and *diazepam* (valium). They can be used either as hypnotics (to promote sleep) or anxiolytics (to reduce anxiety). Under normal conditions of use, they can impair mental function, including memory. Ativan taken as an overnight hypnotic, for example, produces a small memory impairment when subjects are tested the following morning (File and Bond, 1979). However, given under appropriate conditions, some benzodiazepines can induce a temporary amnesic state. Brown and co-workers (1983) administered doses of diazepam or lorazepam intravenously to a group of medical students. The drugs were found to have no appreciable effect on memory span but to produce a marked anterograde amnesia. Neither drug had any effect on the recall of information presented shortly before administration of the drug, indicating that the impairment had to do with some aspect of acquisition.

Benzodiazepine-induced amnesia recently made the news when several Parisian prostitutes were prosecuted for extortion. Their method was to lace their clients' drinks with valium, which resulted in temporary amnesia. In this condition the victims wrote cheques for large amounts of money, but when sobered up could remember nothing about the experience. Fortunately there are more constructive uses for this induced amnesia. Dentists now routinely use intravenous valium for patients who fear dental surgery. Not only does valium calm their nerves, but patients have difficulty remembering the surgery, which is viewed as an advantage, because the patient then has no unpleasant memories which might deter them from seeking further treatment. Surgeons also make use of benzodiazepine-induced amnesia in carrying out *endoscopy*, a procedure whereby optic fibres are inserted into the body in order to view the internal organs. The procedure is often uncomfortable but requires conscious participation from the subject. Benzo-diazepines reduce the anxiety of patients, and, because of the induced amnesia, they have less painful memories to deter them from future examinations.

Transient disorders of organic origin arise from a number of causes, including transient cerebral ischemia, toxins, head injury, ECT, and drugs. All these disorders are characterized by anterograde amnesia, but RA depends on the particular condition. At a general level these disorders have the same characteristics as the amnesic syndrome. TGA and drug-induced amnesia appear to be completely reversible phenomena, whereas PTA may result in some residual impairments. ECT does not appear to damage memory perma-nently, although the possibility that some individuals might be peculiarly susceptible must be considered.

10

Psychogenic Disorders of Memory

Loss of memory in the absence of any detectable brain pathology is known as *psychogenic amnesia*, a name that reflects its psychological, rather than organic, cause. To avoid confusion, I should point out that the term *functional amnesia* is often used as an alternative name for disorders of this type. Psychogenic amnesia almost always follows some unpleasant and emotionally disturbing event, and the degree of impairment can vary. For some, amnesia will be restricted to a specific episode, whereas for others, there will be loss of personal identity and total RA.

Despite their variability, some classification of psychogenic memory disorders can be made. Most common is *hysterical amnesia*, in which a disturbing experience results in an individual being unable to recall events from that period. *Hysteria* can be defined as the expression of unusual behaviour in the absence of any physical cause. Amnesia is one of a number of disorders that can be induced by hysteria; others include writer's cramp, paralysis and simulated blindness. In psychiatric circles, the latter are often referred to as *conversion hysterias*, whereas loss of memory is classed as a form of *dissociation hysteria*. The classic studies of hysterical amnesia were carried out by Janet (1904). One case concerned Irene, a 20-year-old girl who nursed her mother through a slow, painful terminal illness under squalid conditions. After her mother's death, Irene's behaviour changed radically. She accepted that her mother was dead, but could not remember how the death had occurred. Another case was Madame D., victim of a tasteless practical joke. While she was sitting at home one day, a man had appeared and said to her: 'Get a bed ready . . . they are carrying your husband home quite dead.' The message was untrue, but Madame D. became very distressed and developed hysterical symptoms.

After two days the hysteria cleared, and it was apparent that Madame D. could remember nothing about the cruel trick that had been played on her. One unusual feature of her case was that she experienced anterograde amnesia as well as RA. In almost every case, hysterical amnesia involves only retrograde loss.

During hysterical amnesia, lost memories can often be recollected under special conditions. Both Irene and Madame D. were able to recount their traumatic experiences when in a trance-like state which Janet described as 'somnambulism'. Similarly, Freud's Elizabeth von R., through psychoanalysis, came to recall her wish that her sister might die so that she could marry her brother-in-law. However, as Erdelyi and Goldberg (1979) point out, there are difficulties in accepting such recall as the unequivocal return of lost memory. Many cases of hysterical amnesia involve matters of personal embarrassment, so the initial failure to remember might reflect a response bias, in that the individual cannot face telling the examiner certain things that they have always been fully aware of. In addition, much of what is supposedly recalled in such situations may not be true, but unless the examiner has knowledge of what actually happened, this cannot be verified.

Amnesia regarding combat experience provides a more convincing demonstration of memory recovery. The amnesia has a straightforward origin, and the circumstances can often be verified independently. Grinker and Spiegel (1945) studied a large number of men who had developed amnesia following traumatic wartime episodes. They made use of the *sodium pentothal interview*, in which the patient is sedated by slow intravenous injection of the drug. Its first effect is to relieve any anxiety that the patient may have. This is followed by the onset of drowsiness. At this point the injection is halted, and the interview begins. Because the interviewer knows the circumstances he can start to cue the patient about the traumatic incident. As recall becomes more detailed, the subject may become more and more agitated, as this passage shows:

The terror exhibited in moments of extreme danger, such as the imminent explosion of shells, the death of a friend before the patient's eyes ... is electrifying to watch. The body becomes increasingly tense and rigid; the eyes widen and the pupils dilate, while the skin becomes covered in fine perspiration. The hands move about convulsively, seeking a weapon, or a friend to share the danger. The breathing becomes incredibly rapid and shallow. The intensity of the emotion sometimes becomes unbearable; and frequently, at the height of the reaction, there is collapse and the patient falls back in bed and remains quiet . . . usually to resume the story at a more neutral point. (p. 80)

Sodium pentothal is one of a number of barbiturates that have been found to facilitate the recall of emotionally disturbing memories. The most commonly used alternative to pentothal is sodium amytal (amylbarbitone). These drugs are assumed to have their effect by reducing anxiety so that the patient can tolerate the recollection of experiences which are too painful to recall in the normal conscious state.

A more extensive form of hysterical amnesia is encounterd in a condition known as *fugue*. It can be defined as the 'sudden onset of wandering with clouding of consciousness and a more or less complete amnesia for the event' (Berrington et al., 1956). During a fugue, the patient is unaware that anything is wrong and will often adopt a new identity. Fugues are identified only when the patient 'comes to', days, months, or even years after the precipitating event, usually some distance from where he or she was living originally.

Most patients emerging from a fugue regain their normal identity and past history, and the amnesia is only for events of the fugue period itself. Less commonly, patients may become aware that they have lost their identity, but progress no further. In these circumstances, the patient has to adopt a new permanent identity and relearn skills. Akhtar and co-workers (1981) describe the case of a middle-aged American woman found unconscious in a bookshop. On admission to hospital, the only sign of abnormality was a small bump on her head, presumably caused when she passed out. She showed no signs of mental impairment except a total inability to remember who she was and her past history. The investigators went to extreme lengths to discover her identity; the FBI was contacted; her fingerprints were taken; and the police circulated her picture to local hotels. Under hypnosis, the patient never mentioned relatives but frequently gave the names of friends and acquaintances. However, when these were traced, none of them could identify her. After two months she was discharged, at which time she 'guessed that she was 58 . . . unmarried, childless, Christian, and a legal secretary from somewhere in Illinois'. Being a competent secretary, she contacted various employment agencies and, somewhat amusingly, turned up at the hospital where she had been studied to work for the day. As the authors note, 'She still did not know who she was or where she came from, but she was not a bad typist!'

A more typical fugue is illustrated in a recent report by Schacter and associates (1982) involving a 21-year-old man (PN) found wandering in Toronto. When stopped by the police, he had no identification and could provide little useful information about himself. His picture was published in the local newspaper and was identified by his cousin. PN did not recognize his cousin, but she was able to tell the hospital that the patient's grandfather, to whom he had been very close, had died the previous week. When questioned, PN could not remember anything about his grandfather or the recent funeral. The next evening PN was watching a funeral sequence in the serial *Shogun*. This prompted him to remember his grandfather's death and the funeral. Over the next few days his RA cleared, and the only residual deficit was an inability to recall events that occurred during the fugue state itself.

The investigators were able to test various aspects of PN's memory, both during and after the clearance of his fugue. On standard memory and intelligence tests, PN's ability changed little after he emerged from his fugue. However, his response on the autobiographical cueing procedure was markedly different on the two occasions. While amnesic, almost all the memories he recalled referred to events during his four-day fugue state. Of those that referred to earlier experiences, most related to one specific time, suggesting that some 'islands' of past memory survived the fugue. When the fugue cleared, the cueing procedure elicited very few memories from the fugue period, the vast majority relating to the patient's previous life.

Before leaving this topic, we should note that fugue can sometimes have an organic origin. Epileptics who suffer from complex partial seizures can experience long periods of aimless wandering, which is referred to as *poriomania* (Mayeux et al., 1979). When a patient presents a fugue state, the possibility of an epileptic origin should not be overlooked.

EXPLANATIONS OF HYSTERICAL AMNESIA AND FUGUE

Since hysterical amnesia and fugue both involve disruption of episodic memory, there is a temptation to make comparisons with temporary organic amnesias. However, there are important differences, which rule out a common explanation. First, organic disorders almost always produce anterograde amnesia; cases of pure RA of organic origin are remarkably uncommon. Psychogenic disorders, by contrast, show the reverse situation, being almost exclusively retrograde in nature. Second, loss of personal identity, the defining feature of fugue, rarely occurs in even the most severe organic disorders. Finally, the observation that psychogenic amnesia can often be alleviated by procedures such as the pentothal interview has no parallel in organic disorders.

Janet (1904) was probably the first to offer a comprehensive account of hysterical amnesia and fugue. Under normal conditions, psychological functions, including memory, were assumed to be integrated within a unified personality. However, under adverse conditions, such as an emotionally disturbing experience, it was thought that memories became detached from personal identity, thereby rendering recall impossible. Janet believed that the appearance of hysterical amnesia was determined genetically, that each individual possessed a certain amount of energy which bound together different elements of the personality. Psychogenic amnesia was most likely to occur, therefore, in individuals with low levels of energy.

Janet's theory was physiological, in that the prime determinant of hysterical amnesia was the individual's innate level of 'mental energy'. Modern accounts of hysterical disorders are more Freudian in outlook, attributing them to the operation of repression. According to this idea, memory is a dynamic system, in which memories containing information injurious to the ego can be repressed. In this way the memory system can produce a 'defence reaction' that represses unpleasant experiences. In Freud's system, the appearance of hysterical memory disorders is thus determined by the individual's psychological history, rather than his or her physical constitution. The idea that memory has a self-defence capability provides a useful framework for understanding psychogenic memory disorders. It explains why hysterical disorders occur only following adverse events, and, moreover, it is consistent with the high incidence of depression and other psychiatric disorders in patients who subsequently develop psychogenic memory disorders. This correlation has led some people to suppose that psychogenic disorders may be a means of avoiding depression or suicide, a fact expressed in the term 'fugue' which derives from the latin *fugere*, meaning to run away or flee.

Even if we accept the 'defence reaction' interpretation of fugue, it is still necessary to explain how memory can be organized to produce sudden and selective forgetting of past events and, in more extreme cases, loss of personal identity. In chapter 2 we saw that a crucial property of episodic memories was their self-referential quality – that they have meaning only because they relate to the individual. Similarly, the fact that an individual can reflect on a set of personal experiences provides an essential component of identity. In an argument that has some similarities to the argument that Janet proposed 80 years earlier, Schacter and colleagues (1982) suggested that personal identity serves as a 'control element' under which episodic memories are organized. The process of repression might exert its effect by forcing a dissociation between episodic memory and personal identity. Where this dissociation is partial, a limited hysterical amnesia will arise, but, when it is total, a fugue develops, in which episodic memories can no longer be utilized because their frame of reference is unavailable; personal identity is then lost, because it cannot be anchored to any set of personal memories. This is a plausible theory, but we have yet to explain how memory is organized so as to allow these degrees of dissociation.

PSEUDODEMENTIA

In *pseudodementia* the patient presents symptoms similar to those of dementia, but shows no evidence of brain dysfunction. This condition is encountered most frequently in distressed elderly patients, in whom its appearance can lead to the false diagnosis of Alzheimer's Disease. Pseudodementia can also be observed in patients who have suffered a minor organic brain injury, which, on recovery, appears to have produced a degree of impairment far in excess of what one would expect. Pratt (1977) provides an illustrative case. A young soldier was involved in a car accident shortly before he was due to take up a dangerous post abroad. He was unconscious for only two minutes and showed no signs of neurological abnormality; however, he appeared to have lost his personal identity and had a dense RA. He even seemed unable to perform simple motor skills and recognize objects. Over the next six months he relearned his former skills and information about his past life. The patient's brief period of unconsciousness ruled out PTA, and suggested instead that his deranged symptoms were of psychogenic origin. To confirm this, he was interviewed under amylbarbitone narcosis, which revealed that his psychological functions, including memory for his accident, were normal.

Pseudodementia, like hysterical amnesia and fugue, can be seen as a defence reaction in the individual. In the elderly it is often interpreted as a means of avoiding depression or of gaining more help. When it occurs following a minor brain injury, it can often be linked to an individual's desire to avoid some unpleasant experience. In the example above, the soldier's pseudodementia can be seen as a means of avoiding a dangerous assignment.

A related condition is *accident* or *compensation neurosis* (Guthkelch, 1980). This is most often found in head-injured victims who are awaiting settlement of compensation claims. These 'victims' exaggerate the extent of their memory defect in an attempt to gain higher compensation. However, this form of neurosis may manifest itself in other ways. The British comedian Tony Hancock was involved in a car accident in which he suffered mild concussion. Following the accident, he claimed that his memory was defective and insisted on performing 'The Blood Donor' almost entirely from mug boards. It is unlikely that he performed in a state of PTA; more likely, his brief experience of memory loss caused him a disproportionate loss of confidence.

Identification of malingering can be a difficult business. In 1930 a journal reported 'the first pure case of . . . complete and isolated loss of memory retention'. The patient, known as B, had been found unconscious at work, overcome by carbon monoxide (CO) fumes. He quickly regained consciousness, and on initial assessment did not show evidence of memory impairment. He was discharged from hospital after a week, but reappeared about five weeks later, disoriented and complaining that his memory for recent events was 'nil'. His memory span was so poor that it was necessary to ask questions in very short forms and repeat them many times. He forgot instructions immediately, and seemed totally unable to remember anything new. By contrast, he was capable of remembering most of his life up until the accident, including events on the day itself.

The discovery of such a 'pure' memory deficit attracted considerable attention, but also aroused suspicion. It was noted that B was atypical of other CO-poisoning cases and had no signs of neurological impairment. Furthermore, the fact that compensation had still to be agreed on shed further doubt on the authenticity of his amnesia. Initially B was co-operative with investigators, but after some years, he refused to be examined further. This led two psychiatrists to adopt a rather devious means of observing him. Posing as tourists, they visited B's home town and made contact with him. At first B behaved normally, but when the 'tourists' revealed their true identity he began to exhibit his amnesic symptoms and adopt an evasive manner (Zangwill, 1967).

The procedures used to investigate the true nature of B's amnesia were at times underhand and are vulnerable to ethical criticism. Unfortunately, not much progress has been made in devising ways of detecting malingering, and clinicians still have to rely on common sense and intuition. However, in a later section, will see that work has begun on how to identify simulated amnesia.

MULTIPLE PERSONALITY

No discussion of psychogenic memory disorders is complete without some discussion of multiple personality. This is an extremely rare psychiatric condition in which the individual appears to have two or more distinct personalities. Within a multiple personality, it is often reported that each personality is unable to remember the activities of the others. Because of their dramatic nature, multiple personalities have been the subject of intense media interest, and a number of popular books describing individual cases have appeared – for example, *The Three Faces of Eve* (Thigpen and Cleckley, 1957).

The nature of multiple personality is illustrated by the recent case of the 'Hillside Strangler' in Los Angeles. Kenneth Bianchi was charged with the rape and murder of several women but, despite strong evidence against him, he persistently denied his guilt and claimed that he knew nothing about the crimes. Under hypnosis, however, another personality called 'Steve' emerged. He was very different from Ken, and claimed responsibility for the murders. When removed from the hypnotic trance, Ken could remember nothing of the conversations between Steve and the hypnotist.

If two or more personalities can coexist wihin the same individual, it creates difficult legal problems. In Bianchi's case, prosecution of Ken could be seen as unjust, because it was Steve who had committed the crimes. However, the ruling went against Bianchi, because the court refused to accept that he genuinely possessed two personalities. A number of psychologists pointed out that Bianchi's other personality emerged only in hypnotic sessions in which the examiner had already informed him that he would reveal another part of himself. In the discussion of hypnosis in chapter 3, we saw that a major problem in trying to interpret the effects of hypnosis on memory is the phenomenon of compliance. In Bianchi's case, hypnosis allowed the suggestion that another personality could exist, and Bianchi may have seized the opportunity to confess by complying in this manner. Furthermore, his general knowledge of psychiatric diagnosis and the features of multiple personality may have provided Bianchi with a basis for responding more convincingly.

The general consensus is that multiple personality is a means of compartmentalizing different aspects of memory, the most usual reason being the need to repress unpleasant experience. The use of multiple personality as a defence reaction is demonstrated by the case of 'Lucy' (Coons et al., 1982). Hospitalized on account of a drug overdose, Lucy had been suffering from amnesia and hallucinations for two years as a result of being raped. Psychological examination revealed that she had four 'personalities'. Aside from her normal friendly personality there was 'Linda', an aggressive person who emerged when she recounted the physical and sexual abuse she had endured as a young child; 'Sally', a distrustful, isolated person who gave the accounts of the rape incident; and 'Sam', an imaginary man who rescued her when she was feeling suicidal. EEG readings taken during the expression of each personality were very similar, a finding which Coons and his associates interpreted as consistent with one person adopting different modes of expression, rather than the existence of different personalities.

AMNESIA AND CRIME

Amnesia for crime, especially homicide, has been widely documented. Surveys have shown that between 23 and 65 per cent of murderers have, or claim to have, amnesia for their crime. Other crimes appear to elicit amnesia with far less frequency, but where this occurs, the crimes are usually violent. Taylor and Kopelman (1984) examined 203 men on remand for violent and non-violent offences. Of these, 19 reported amnesia for their crimes, of which 9 were homicides, 6 involved personal violence and arson, and 4 involved criminal damage. Amnesia was not observed in any person charged with a non-violent crime.

In a recent review, Schacter (in press, a) has noted that fugue states are rarely associated with crime. A possible exception is the case of Guenther Padola, who was charged with the murder of a policeman, tried, and subsequently executed. Throughout the proceedings, he consistently claimed loss of personal identity and denied any knowledge of the crime. His defence claimed that he was unfit to plead, but the prosecution was successful in convincing the court that his amnesia was not genuine. Interestingly, one of the arguments was that Padola could not be amnesic because he had retained his general knowledge and skills. Such a view would not have seemed out of place during the fifties when Padola's case was heard. However, if it were heard today, expert knowledge of the known characteristics of amnesia would support the argument that such a dissociation is possible.

Amnesia for a crime could be considered as the repression of an experience likely to cause feelings of guilt and anxiety. In cases where crimes are particularly horrific, suppression of their memory may be the only way an individual can continue living. Recently Ian Brady, one of the Moors Murderers, was contacted by parents of children he is suspected of killing. He refused to reply, noting that 'I have to keep the mental blocks up and keep control'. However, not all amnesia for crime has a psychogenic origin. First, there is a high incidence of schizophrenia and depression among criminals who cannot remember their crimes. In these cases, the amnesia may be intimately bound up with their mental illness. Another line of explanation stems from the fact that many murders are committed during 'alcoholic blackouts'. These blackouts are a common phenomenon among both alcoholics and normal drinkers who over-indulge. During a blackout, the individual is not incapacitated, and he is usually in possession of most mental faculties; the person is thus drunk, but not stuporous or unconscious. Two forms of blackout can be identified. The first is an '*en bloc*' form, in which the blackout has a clear start and a clear finish, with amnesia for the intervening events. Here, the individual knows he has a 'lost period', whereas in the second form the individual is not aware of any amnesia. In this case the individual may have exhibited memory lapses during a drinking bout (e.g. asking the same question repeatedly) but have no recollection of it.

In chapter 3 we considered the phenomenon of state-dependent learning, in which memories formed in one particular state were more easily remembered when subjects were in the same state at the time of testing. Furthermore, a number of studies have shown that alcoholic intoxication is an effective means of inducing these effects. This being so, alcoholic blackouts could be a form of state-dependent forgetting. A number of studies have explored this possibility, including a unique study by Wolf (1980). If amnesia for crime committed during a state of drunkenness is due to state-dependent learning, then it should be possible, under appropriate conditions, to reinstate memory for the events. Wolf studied five Eskimos with a history of alcoholism who had been convicted of murder. All five were known to have been drunk when they committed their crimes, and all claimed amnesia for that period. One subject

drank 22 cans of beer over about 5 hr. He remembered leaving the bar with friends and later being held on the floor and choked.... He remembered nothing more until the next morning. In the first interval he went home, got his gun, came back the half mile to the bar, walked in, and without saying anything, raised his gun and shot the man next to him. He was then thrown to the floor and choked. Subsequently he was arraigned, booked and transported to the nearest jail, but remembered nothing of this.

During the course of Wolf's experiment the convicts were allowed to become highly intoxicated again. As they did, they became increasingly angry, and their conversation was often accompanied by intense emotion, but at no time did any of them recall the circumstances of their crime. When they sobered up, they had varying degrees of amnesia for the events of the experiment.

On the assumption that Wolf's subjects were intoxicated at levels similar to those at which they committed their crimes, the above findings argue against a state-dependent explanation of amnesia for crime. This conclusion agrees with those of other studies (c.g. Goodwin, 1974; Lisman, 1974) which have also failed to confirm a state-dependent explanation of alcoholic blackouts.

These findings leave us with two possible explanations of alcohol-induced amnesia. It could be of psychogenic origin, as some have argued, in that the individual represses knowledge of shameful acts committed during a blackout. There seem to be a number of arguments against this, however. Blackouts do not appear to be related to the nature of the events occurring during the amnesic period. If the amnesia were of psychogenic origin, one would expect blackouts to be more frequent for unpleasant and embarrassing events. The behaviour of individuals observed during blackouts also argues against a psychogenic cause. Ryback (1971) observed a number of alcoholics during blackouts and noted a profound anterograde amnesia. As we saw earlier, psychogenic disorders almost always involve a selective RA (see also Hashtroudi et al., 1984). Finally, if blackouts were psychogenic in origin, it should be possible to reinstate memory for the lost period under conditions that have been effective with other disorders, but this is not the case. The generally accepted explanation is that blackouts arise because the original level of alcohol intoxication was sufficient to disrupt the physiological process involved in memory formation.

This would explain why studies of alcoholic murderers provide no support for a state-dependent learning interpretation of amnesia for crime. However, this conclusion does not lead us to entirely reject state-dependent learning as an explanation of amnesia for crime. In most circumstances, crimes of violence are associated with states of extreme emotion that are unlikely to be experienced at any other time. There is some evidence that emotion itself can cause state-dependent learning. Briefly, it was shown that memories congruent with a subject's mood state were more easily remembered than those associated with a different mood (chapter 3). Given this relationship, is it possible that some instances of amnesia for crime might be explicable in the same way?

At present, there is little evidence to support this possibility. One problem is re-creating the emotional state presumed to have existed at the time a crime was committed, a much more difficult task than achieving a comparable level of intoxication! Recently, Bower (1981) reported observations of Robert Kennedy's assassin, Sirhan Sirhan. Throughout his trial and subsequent imprisonment, Sirhan denied any memory of the assassination. By means of hypnosis, however, a psychiatrist was able to induce in him a highly agitated state in which he began to 'scream out the death curses, "fire" the shots, and then choke as he re-experienced the Secret Service bodyguard nearly throttling him after he was caught'.

Sirhan's behaviour suggests that his amnesia may have been of state-dependent origin: he was unable to remember because, without hypnotic assistance, he could not re-create the highly emotional state associated with his memory for the crime. At this point we might recall combat amnesia, which, as we saw earlier, can be overcome by sodium pentothal narcosis. One interpretation of this phenomenon might be that the narcosis allows the patient to reinstate the extreme emotion experienced at the time, thereby 'unlocking' the forgotten event.

AMNESIA AND THE LEGAL SYSTEM

If a defendant is amnesic for a crime with which he is charged, it can have important implications for his trial. First, it may be argued that the defendant is unfit to plead. The case of Padola cited earlier seems to have served as a precedent in recent times. During the trial there was much discussion about the origin of Padola's fugue state. He had sustained a minor head injury at the time of arrest, but the jury felt that his amnesia was not genuine. On appeal, the original court decision was upheld, with the additional point being made that, even if Padola's amnesia had been genuine, he would still have been fit to plead.

A second issue is that amnesia for a crime can provide the basis for a plea of *automatism*. This term refers to behaviour that is carried out involuntarily and without conscious intent. Two forms of automatism can be identified. The first involves conscious involuntary movements, such as reflex actions carried out under duress. An example of crime resulting from this form of automatism might be a driver attacked by a hornet who, by taking reflexive evasive action, unintentionally steers his car on to the pavement. In this case the charge of reckless driving could be countered by arguing that the driver was out of control through no fault of his own.

The second and less straightforward kind of automatism arises when an individual is unconscious during an act or when his or her actions can be considered 'purely automatic' because they cannot remember what took place. A plea of this form of automatism has been accepted in a variety of circumstances, including crimes committed while sleep-walking or as a result of organic brain dysfunction caused by illnesses such as epilepsy, tumour, and hypoglycaemia. Hill and Sargent (1943) described a well-known case in which a man was on trial for murdering his mother. He offered the defence that he committed the murder while in an epileptic state brought on by consuming four pints of beer on an empty stomach. To test this, the defendant was given the same amount of 'mild ale' under controlled conditions; this produced an abnormal EEG and other symptoms of an epileptic attack. With this evidence in mind, the jury found the man 'guilty but insane'. Crimes committed during an alcoholic blackout do not fall in the category of automatism, the argument being that an individual is aware of the effects of alcohol and should therefore accept responsibility for acts carried out while drunk even though he has no recollection of them.

No case of acquittal due to an organic amnesic state appears to have been recorded in the professional literature. However, a recent British case provides a possible example. On 11 October 1984 a slow-moving goods train was hit from behind by a passenger train. The driver of the passenger train had passed through a number of red signals, each time cancelling the automatic warning signal. When questioned by the police, it became clear that the driver had no memory for events in the two or three minutes preceding the accident. There were no abnormal signs, and the driver had appeared well at the start of the journey. Neurological examination subsequently revealed that the driver suffered migraine-like symptoms, had lost his sense of smell, and had received a blow on the head three months prior to the accident. The investigators concluded that the accident occurred because a sudden attack of TGA led him to forget that he was going through stop signals (HMSO, 1986). The train driver was acquitted because of circumstantial neurological evidence.

More difficult are cases in which the alleged period of automatism has a purely psychological cause. In 1970 the Canadian courts considered the case of K, a 'devoted father and husband' who suffered from a mild neurotic condition. A family friend informed him that his wife was about to leave him. When his wife entered the room, he engaged her in an embrace and begged her not to leave him. After about 15 minutes, K emerged from a blackout to find that his embrace had suffocated his wife. In his defence it was argued that K had suffered 'a tremendous emotional blow, as forceful as any external blow to the head'. The jury accepted that the crime was committed during a period of automatism, and K was acquitted.

Cases such as K's present courts with a particularly difficult kind of decision. Judges and juries have to distinguish between genuine cases of automatism induced by psychological trauma and those in which amnesia does not rule out conscious intent at the time the crime was committed. We have seen earlier that amnesia for crime may be a form of defence reaction which serves to repress the unpleasant memories of the violent act. Thus the amnesia arises *after* the event, and does not imply a lack of conscious involvement during the amnesic period itself. The ways in which judges and juries deliberate on such matters does not appear to follow any clear precedent, a fact which may explain the variable outcome of trials in which amnesia is the only basis for a plea of automatism.

THE PROBLEM OF MALINGERING

Perhaps the biggest problem facing a jury confronted with an apparently amnesic defendant is whether the memory loss is genuine. The characteristics of amnesia are very easy to feign, so detection is bound to be difficult. However, Schacter (in press, a) has summarized a number of factors which might allow a distinction to be made. Amnesia for crimes that have been well planned should be regarded as highly suspect, while an inability to remember an impulsive and emotionally charged crime should be given greater credibility. Also, amnesia in persons with a psychiatric history is more likely to be genuine than that in those with no record of mental illness.

Another approach is to use our general knowledge of amnesia to detect malingerers, the assumption being that a malingerer may not know the exact characteristics of amnesia and may thus produce an atypical simulation. The case of B described above is an example of this. His reduced memory span is completely atypical of organic amnesia, and the presence of severe anterograde amnesia without accompanying RA is also very unusual. Another factor is that studies of hysterical amnesia and fugue show that the onset tends to be gradual rather than sudden. Thus a defendant presenting symptoms of sudden memory loss should be regarded with suspicion. Consistency may also be a useful indicator in that simulators may vary what they remember across time or even contradict themselves. However, our knowledge of consistency in genuine amnesic states, especially psychogenic ones, is minimal, so this kind of evidence must be treated with caution.

An alternative approach is to question the defendant under hypnosis or while attached to a polygraph. We have already considered the controversial issues surrounding hypnosis, and 'lie-detection' appears to be no more reliable (British Psychological Society, 1986). Pentothal and amylbarbitone interviews have also been used on some occasions, on the assumption that they promote confessions. However, there are doubts about this 'truth serum' theory; moreover, these interviews have attendant medical risks and cannot be given without voluntary consent.

A rather different approach has been described by Schacter (in press, b). He has explored the differences between simulated and real amnesia under laboratory conditions. Subjects watched a video film which, along with the main theme, included a number of trivial incidents which would not normally be noticed. One group was then told about one of these incidents, the other was not, the assumption being that the latter group would genuinely have no knowledge of the incident described. Subjects in both groups then had to convince a third party that they knew nothing about the incident. There was little difference between the 'malingerers' and the genuine 'amnesics' except that the former rated themselves as significantly less likely to benefit from hints than the subjects who genuinely did not know.

Although in a laboratory setting, Schacter's study opens up the possibility that malingerers could be detected because their portrayal of amnesia is inaccurate to a trained observer. In a more practical setting, Brandt and co-workers (1985) investigated LG, a man on trial for murdering his wife who claims total amnesia. He was shown a list of 20 words, and then given a forced-choice recognition test in which a list word was paired with a new word and he had to indicate which one he had seen before. On this task, pure guessing would produce a score of 50 per cent, but LG's score was significantly below this, indicating that he really remembered the words and was trying to simulate amnesia. However, being unaware of the level of chance performance, he overdid the amnesia, thereby revealing his malingering.

Returning to Schacter's study, he also showed that people experienced at dealing with the testimony of amnesic defendants were extremely poor at detecting simulators. Again, Schacter suggested that this might reflect false beliefs about the nature of amnesia. The idea that malingering might be detectable by developing a more sophisticated account of the differences between genuine and simulating amnesics is promising, but, as Schacter concedes, greater knowledge in this area would provide more information for the would-be malingerer too, enabling him to make his performance more convincing.

INFANTILE AMNESIA

Few people can remember events in their lives before the age of about three and a half. This phenomenon is known as *infantile amnesia*, and its inclusion in this chapter is a consequence of early attempts to explain it in terms of repression, rather than any general belief that it has a psychogenic origin. According to Freudian theory, certain crucial stages in personality development take place during early childhood, and repression of these early experiences was thought to be part of normal development. In a more modern approach, more recently, people such as Neisser (1967) have suggested that infants construct a record of their experience that is organized differently from the record of later experiences. This discontinuity would mean that adults could no longer access information acquired during early childhood.

More recently it has been suggested that infants lack a particular form of memory. Nadel and Zola-Morgan (1984) characterize this form 'as one that represents environments and their contents, the "time-and-place" of things'. Without this, infants would very rapidly forget what had happened to them. Like a number of previous researchers, Nadel and Zola-Morgan argue that developmental changes in memory are linked with specific maturational changes in the brain; furthermore, they propose that the hippocampus is the key region undergoing change.

It should not have escaped the reader's attention that the form of memory thought to be absent in infants is rather similar to the type of deficit found in the amnesic syndrome; and Schacter and Moscovitch (1984) have suggested that infantile amnesia and the amnesic syndrome show certain similarities. One feature of infant memory is the so-called $A\bar{B}$ error. An object is hidden at location A, and the child is allowed to search for it there a number of times. In full view of the child, the object is then relocated at a different place; yet the child continues to look for the object in the original location. Schacter and Moscovitch have suggested that this phenomenon is due to rapid forgetting, because the number of $A\bar{B}$ errors can be reduced by decreasing the delay between placing the object in its new location and allowing the child to search. The basis of the child's error, therefore, is forgetting that the object has been relocated. The authors further demonstrate that adult amnesics make the same kind of error, suggesting a common deficit in the two groups.

The commonality between infant memory and adult amnesia provides converging evidence for a particular form of memory concerned with recording events. The absence of this memory would explain infantile amnesia, because no record of specific events would have been formed during infancy. One problem, however, is that the ability to remember events begins to emerge

around 10 months (Schacter and Moscovitch, 1984), whereas the
infantile amnesic period covers at least the first three years.

Psychogenic memory disorders constitute a fascinating, but poorly
understood, set of phenomena. There are only a handful of
objective studies, the bulk of the information coming from
anecdotal case histories. Most psychogenic disorders take the form
of defence reactions, in which various devices are employed to
repress part or all of a person's memory. Episodic memory seems to
be most vulnerable, but in the case of pseudodementia, other
aspects of LTS are affected. In hysterical amnesia only one part of
memory becomes inaccessible, but in fugues there is a complete
loss of episodic memory. Multiple personalities serve to divide up
episodic memory by attributing different components of episodic
memory to different personalities. Psychogenic disorders cannot
be explained in the same way as organic disorders. Most disorders
appear to be forms of defence reaction that suppress unpleasant
experiences or allow them to be recalled only under conditions
which do not reflect the individual's normal personality. Amnesia
for crime occurs predominantly following violent crimes, and in
the case of crimes carried out during a period of alcoholic blackout,
is almost certainly caused by physiological disruption of memory
processes during the blackout period. Where it occurs under other
circumstances, memory loss may be related to some psychotic
disorder, be of psychogenic origin, or reflect state-dependent
forgetting. Amnesia presents a challenge to the legal system; in
particular, reliable means for detecting malingering need to be
devised.

11

Remediation

Loss of memory following brain damage is a common occurrence, and its effects on a victim's life can be devastating. Normal employment is usually impossible, because the patient is a hazard both to himself and to others. The home becomes a dangerous environment for amnesic patients, and they need constant supervision to ensure that accidents do not occur. Amnesic patients may easily become bored and frustrated, since reading a book, watching a film, or following a conversation all require an intact memory, and the patient may be reduced to low-level activities to pass the time. Amnesia can also affect a patient's social life, since extreme forgetfulness and the tendency to repeat the same question over and over again can create frustration in even the most sympathetic relative or friend. Problems in remembering new information present the major difficulty, but RA can also have disturbing consequences. Some patients, such as those with Korsakoff's Syndrome, seem to accept their impairment; but for others, loss of memory is a source of distress which can lead to psychiatric illness. A person with impaired memory is therefore likely to be unemployed, at risk, bored, frustrated, and even anxious or depressed.

The debilitating effects of amnesia have been commented on ever since the study of amnesia began, but serious consideration of remediation has occurred only during the last five years or so. Miller (1984) attributes this to the changing role of neuropsychologists, in whom the traditional preoccupation with assessment has been replaced by a belief that psychology can play an important part in rehabilitation of brain-damaged patients. Assessment is still an essential part of the neuropsychologist's function, but, with the development of more sophisticated neuro-imaging techniques, neuropsychologists are becoming increasingly concerned with evaluating a patient's potential for rehabilitation rather than merely locating lesions.

The development of memory therapy may also have been held back by the mistaken belief that nothing can be done about organic memory impairments. We will see later that the achievements of memory therapy are modest, but their importance within the therapeutic setting must not be underestimated. Patients and their relatives can often gain considerable satisfaction from even minor improvements in memory. Moreover, memory therapy can reduce depressive symptoms in memory-disordered patients (e.g. Zarit et al., 1981).

In trying to help someone with memory difficulties, one problem is knowing where to start. In aphasia, there is usually some residual function that can be identified immediately and serve as the foundation for improvement. Amnesics have residual memory functions, of course, such as the ability to acquire new procedural memory. However, only clinicians with a specialized knowledge of amnesia are aware of this. Thus a relative or therapist faced with an amnesic might be surprised to hear that learning to program a computer is a possible therapeutic option for that patient (see below). One of the goals of neuropsychology, therefore, is the dissemination of knowledge about amnesia and potential therapeutic options.

Confronted with an amnesic person, it is useful to have some idea of the various treatment possibilities. Apart from the physical treatments discussed in the final section, the various options, although psychological, do not need to be carried out by a qualified psychologist.

EXTERNAL AIDS

We all use external memory aids to some extent: we use diaries to remember appointments, write lists when we go shopping, and use alarms as reminders. Amnesics must make more extensive use of these aids, because without them, independent existence would be virtually impossible. The range of external aids is vast, but we can start our discussion by dividing them into those that store information and those that act as cueing devices.

Diaries and daily timetables are very useful to amnesic patients, since they can store information about what the patient has to do at certain times. Successful use of a diary or timetable can enable a patient to remember a routine, keep appointments, and thereby reduce day-to-day management problems considerably. Lists and plans can be displayed in prominent places so that the patient can have easy access to general information. In addition, photographs and other memorabilia can be displayed in cases if the patient has retrograde as well as anterograde amnesia.

External stores of information are fine, provided the patient remembers to use them. But having a diary or timetable is no use if you do not remember to consult it regularly. Harris (1984) lists three criteria which external cueing devices must meet to be maximally effective. First, the cue must be given as close as possible to the time at which a desired act is required, since it is no good reminding an amnesic in the morning that he or she must do something at lunchtime. Second, it must be active rather than passive – that is, it must alert the individual to the fact that something needs to be done. Third, it should specify as clearly as possible what needs to be done. Cues such as a knotted handkerchief are inadequate, because they provide no information about what should be done.

With the development of microelectronics, a number of useful cueing devices have come onto the market (for a review of these, see Harris, 1984). Briefly, the ideal mechanism is a timer which can be programmed to display specific messages at set times. Devices of this kind exist, and there is no doubt that modern technology could produce a machine tailored to the specific needs of a particular amnesic patient. However, as is so often the case with specialized aids for the disabled, demand will be low, and production costs correspondingly high. In addition, people with impaired memories may not be able to learn the detailed sequence of operations required to enter new information in the machine.

An alternative approach is to combine a simple timing mechanism with a timetable or diary. The patient has only to learn that the alarm means that he should look at his timetable. Kurlychek (1983) taught a man in the early stages of AD to consult his diary every time his watch alarm sounded. Davies and Binks (1983) used a similar procedure to teach a Korsakoff patient certain commands. Interestingly, they found that he could learn to consult a book when prompted by the cue, but could not associate the cue with different commands that he had committed to memory. The combination of an external memory store with a simple cueing device such as a watch alarm has considerable promise. It is cheap to produce and makes minimal new learning demands on the patient. Future applications of this approach are therefore awaited with interest.

MEMORY AS A MUSCLE?

It is often assumed that an analogy can be drawn between the workings of memory and those of a muscle. The latter, as we all know, will improve in strength with repeated exercise, and a similar view has been taken of memory. Harris and Sunderland (1981) surveyed a number of hospitals offering memory therapy, and found that the 'memory as a muscle' idea was surprisingly common among therapists. This belief may well derive from the fact that repeated practice may reduce the severity of other neuropsychological deficits such as aphasia, leading therapists to generalize that this will be true of memory disorders. The experimental evidence, however, provides little indication that repeated practice leads to any *general* improvement in memory performance.

Godfrey and Knight (1985) gave Korsakoff patients 32 hours of practice on paired-associate learning, but found no improvement in performance. In a more extensive study, Prigatano and colleagues (1984) put a group of head-injured patients through a rehabilitation program which included repeated practice on a number of memory tasks. To evaluate the effectiveness of the program after six months, the patients' performance on three subcomponents of the WMS – logical memory, hard paired associates, and visual reproduction – and other tests was compared with their ability on the same tests before treatment. The program produced modest, but statistically significant, improvements in memory performance, of approximately one item on each component of the WMS. Discussing this study, Schacter and Glisky (in press) note that as some 625 hours of training were involved in the program, the improvement rate was 1/625th of an item per patient per hour – hardly cost-effective!

A number of studies involving normal subjects have shown that repeated practice improves memory performance. Ericsson and Chase (1980) recruited an undergraduate (SF) and asked him to spend one hour a day, three to five days a week, practicing the digit span task. At the outset his digit span was 7, but by the end of the training it had increased to almost 80. Although this involved 230 hours of training, the gains were enormous, but what exactly had been achieved? Digit span is assumed to reflect the operation of STS, so one conclusion might be that training had increased his STS capacity. If this were so, then SF should have shown superior performance on any memory span task; but when digits were replaced by consonants, his performance was only seven items. Analysis of SF's performance indicated that his enhanced memory span for digits stemmed from a complex strategy that he had developed which allowed him to group numbers into 'chunks', making them easier to remember. There was no suggestion that his STS had undergone any general increase in capacity.

A number of computer programs have been developed in an attempt to help amnesic patients. These programs run on micro-processors, and allow the patient to engage repeatedly in a number of memory tasks. A typical program might involve the learning of face-name associations, in which the subject attempts to recall the name and occupation of a fictitious character. If successful, the patient can try a harder task in which more information has to be remembered. This is a potentially attractive form of therapy, since the equipment is relatively inexpensive, it is automated, and the patient may find it more enjoyable than conventional therapy in which memory failures in the presence of others may serve as a source of embarrassment or frustration. However, from the evidence we have reviewed, there is little reason to believe that repeated practice using computer-based procedures will be any more effective than other techniques.

An alternative to repetitive practice is to consider how the 'expanding' retrieval technique of Landauer and Bjork (see chapter 4) might be applied to amnesic patients. Schacter et al. (1985) found that amnesics' retention of fictional information was improved by repeated testing of the same fact at increasing retention intervals. Furthermore, they found some evidence that this technique was applied spontaneously by the patients at a subsequent stage. As we will see later, most memory strategies acquired by amnesics are of limited value because the patients fail to implement them unless told to do so. The preliminary findings using the expanding retrieval technique suggest that this may not always be the case.

MEMORY STRATEGIES

An alternative to practice is to equip the amnesic patient with more efficient memory strategies, the aim being to make any residual memory capacity more effective. In chapter 4 we reviewed a number of mnemonics — artificial strategies for remembering information more efficiently. Therapists have seized on these as a means of improving defective memory. Gardner (1977) taught an amnesic the following song to help him learn his personal details:

> Henry's my name;
> Memory's the game;
> I'm in the VA in Jamaica Plain;
> My bed's on 7D;
> The year is '73;
> Every day I make a little gain.

Rhymes are easier to learn than prose, because they constrain the possible responses that a patient can make. However, the range of situations in which they could be used would seem to be rather restricted.

First-letter mnemonics, especially acronyms, are a more general way of teaching amnesics information they would otherwise find difficult to remember. Thus a shopping list might be remembered by arranging it so that the first letters of each item form a word (e.g. carrots, yoghurt, cucumber, lentils, eggs, spinach). Glasgow and associates (1977) used a first-letter mnemonics to help a head-injured victim remember a strategy for studying prose more effectively. Known as PQRST, it instructed the patient to

> P – Preview (preview material quickly)
> Q – Question (ask key question)
> R – Read (read thoroughly)

S – State (state answers)
T – Test (test yourself on answers)

It was found that the patient remembered selected prose passages much better using PQRST. Furthermore, the patient was able to generalize the method to newspaper articles. Wilson (1982) used PQRST with Mr B, a man rendered amnesic by a stroke. He remembered what each letter meant and was able to retain 80–100 per cent of the information studied using the strategy for half an hour.

Of all the techniques used by memory therapists, those based on mental imagery are the most popular. In our discussion of mental imagery (chapter 4), we noted that imagery is an effective means of promoting paired-associate learning, provided the image is inter-active. Lewinsohn and co-workers (1977) found that similar instructions given to amnesic patients improved their performance (see also Cermak, 1975). Robertson-Tchabo and associates (1976) taught elderly people with memory problems the method of loci. The patients used the mnemonic to learn three different word lists presented on different days, and no evidence of interference between lists was found. However, the authors note that the subjects never employed the technique unless specifically in-structed to do so. Wilson has provided evidence that the method of loci may be an effective memory strategy for head-injured patients, although she notes considerable individual variation. In an early study, Patten (1972) used the peg word system to help memory-disordered patients learn paired associates. The findings are somewhat anecdotal, but they suggest that the method was more effective than other learning strategies. However, the peg word system is rather elaborate, and only Evans (1981) has reported its use in a clinical setting.

There seems little doubt that amnesic patients remember more when instructed to use mental imagery mnemonics, but whether these strategies can be of any value to the patient in everyday life is another matter. The method of loci is often considered to be a good way to remember a shopping list, but wouldn't a written list be easier? However, in one sphere it is possible that imagery mnemonics do have a practical value. Learning new names is something that amnesic patients find particularly difficult, and a written name is not much help if you are trying to recognize a number of different people.

Wilson's (1982) patient Mr B was successfully taught new names using an imagery technique similar to that of Lorayne and Lucas (1975, chapter 4). To remember the name 'Barbara', for example, the patient was told to imagine a barber holding a large letter A and associate this image with her face. Within 12 days the patient could name 12 people with 100 per cent accuracy. The technique was also used to provide him with correct orientation information. At the outset of therapy, he invariably gave 'Harold Wilson' as the name of the Prime Minister, but successful learning of an image depicting a woman thatching the roof of 10 Downing Street resulted in him learning the correct response – Mrs Thatcher. Lewinsohn and associates (1977) also used a variant of the Lorayne and Lucas strategy on their patients, and found significantly better face-name learning than that achieved by other means.

The association of distinctive images with faces in order to learn names seems an effective strategy for some amnesic patients. There are limitations, however. Coming up with a suitable image may sometimes require a considerable degree of ingenuity (proponents of the imagery method have an uncanny knack of picking suitable names to illustrate their method), and this may be beyond the scope of many brain-damaged people. Even when a name suggests a suitable image, there may be difficulties in making it precise enough for the patient to decode it unambiguously.

The above review is not exhaustive, but illustrates the range of mnemonics that can promote learning in brain-damaged patients. Within the therapeutic setting, any success at remembering must be regarded as valuable, but if we are interested in the broader issue of rehabilitation, we must consider whether these strategies have any application to the patient's normal life. We have already noted studies in which amnesics fail to implement strategies they have found successful in the laboratory, and this would generally seem to be the case. Wilson's Mr B, for example, learnt a number of useful strategies in the laboratory, but implemented them only occasionally when he returned home. Parkin and Wilson (in preparation) report a similar case of a man (JB) who made excellent use of mnemonics when instructed to do so, but never used them on his own.

A related problem is that amnesics often feel somewhat 'detached' from knowledge they have acquired. Cermak (1976) reports that the PE amnesic SS learnt a number of useful facts about current affairs, as well as a number of useful instructions. One of these involved the question 'What do you do when you enter your house?', to which SS learnt the response 'Put on my sweater'. But, although able to reproduce this and many other responses three months later, he never made use of them. Cermak describes the manner in which SS recalled these facts and instructions as 'automatized', in that the patient did not realize that they related to him. A further example of this is reported by Parkin and co-workers (in preparation), who describe the case of a severely amnesic woman (Mrs T) who, after many repetitions, was able to name one of her doctors correctly. She retained this information for over eight months, but never volunteered it, claiming that she had never met the doctor before. On one occasion she was tempted to guess the doctor's name and got it correct without any prompting. When asked how she knew, she became agitated, and said: 'I'm sorry, I don't know how or why I know that.'

That patients fail to implement strategies or utilize facts they have learned during rehabilitation programs reflects a failure of *metamemory*, that aspect of memory function that allows us to know that we know something. Thus Mrs T's failure to utilize her knowledge stems from her inability to recognize having seen the doctor before. Without this information, she has no basis for knowing that she knows the doctor's name, because he seems a complete stranger. Thus, even though amnesic patients may learn new facts, they find it difficult to use them because they are unable to recognize the situations in which they are appropriate.

Problems like this could be overcome if there were some means of alerting a patient to the fact that he or she knows something about a given situation. One approach might be the development of self-help techniques (Moffat, 1984). These would resemble 'help' files on a computer, the idea being that the patient could learn some form of mnemonic which he would recall when confronted with a memory problem; this, in turn, would present the patient with a range of different strategies that might be used to overcome the difficulty.

Schacter and Glisky (in press), echoing a point made earlier by

Wilson (1984), has argued that teaching amnesics mnemonic strategies in the hope that this will lead to general improvements in memory is unrealistic. Instead, he argues that therapy should be aimed at teaching *domain-specific knowledge* – that is, information relating to a particular setting in which the amnesic patient currently experiences difficulty. In the next section we will consider an example of this approach, but before doing this, we must return briefly to more theoretical matters.

DIRECT PRIMING AND MEMORY REMEDIATION

Tulving and colleagues (1982) report an experiment in which normal subjects were shown a list of words such as 'yoghurt' and 'pendulum'. Memory was tested twice, after one hour and after seven days. Two forms of retention test were used: a standard yes/no recognition procedure and a 'fragment completion' test. In the latter, an incomplete version of one of the targets was presented (e.g. –o–hur–, –e–d–l–m), and the subject was instructed to complete it. Recognition accuracy declined markedly across the seven-day retention interval, whereas successful fragment completion rate remained unchanged. To estimate the extent to which subjects' general knowledge contributed to performance, the researchers included a condition in which subjects completed fragments based on words they had never seen before. The subjects were not as successful on these as they were on fragments based on words presented in the learning phase. This indicates that performance on the completion task is enhanced by exposure of the target word during the learning phase; but the basis of the effect is unclear. One might think that subjects remember the list, and that this limits the alternatives they consider when trying to complete the fragment. However, the fact that the fragment completion rate is unaffected by the decline in recognition performance suggests that fragment completion has nothing to do with conscious recollection. Instead, it would appear that the phenomenon relies on some form of memory other than episodic memory, and for this reason it has been termed *direct priming*.

A reasonable interpretation of direct priming effects is that they arise from some temporary activation of information in semantic memory. It is generally assumed that we have an individual representation for each word that we know, and that exposure of a word in a learning list leads to that representation becoming more active. As a result, it is more easily retrieved than comparable words that have not been pre-exposed. We should then expect to see evidence of direct priming in amnesic patients, because semantic memory is spared in this condition. In a number of experiments, Warrington and Weiskrantz (e.g. 1970) showed that amnesic patients could identify words when given partial cues such as the first three letters, even though they were totally unable to recall or recognize them. The original interpretation of these findings was that the partial information served to reduce the number of response alternatives, thereby facilitating recall. However, there is no indication that the subjects were in any sense recollecting the words (Parkin, 1982), and a more likely interpretation is that the results reflect direct priming.

Several studies have confirmed the existence of direct priming in amnesic patients. Cermak and associates (1985) showed Korsakoff patients a list of 10 words and then gave them a yes/no recognition test. Their recognition performance was very poor, but a subsequent identification test in which subjects had to name words presented very briefly on a screen showed that the patients responded much faster to words that had been on the study list, even though they had previously failed to recognize them. In a second experiment they explored whether direct priming depended on a pre-existing representation in semantic memory. The procedure was repeated but included non-words (e.g. 'numby') which, by definition, cannot have a representation in semantic memory. The results showed that direct priming was restricted to words, which suggests that the phenomenon occurs only with pre-existing associations.

If direct priming is restricted to pre-existing associations, it will have only limited value in the therapeutic setting, because the main problem is getting the patient to acquire new information. Schacter and Graf (in press) have questioned this conclusion, and have presented data in which amnesics appear to show direct priming based on novel associations. They presented patients with arbitrarily associated word-pairs such as WINDOW–REASON and then gave them a word completion task. Completion of the second word was compared under two conditions: 'same context', in which the fragment was accompanied by the word paired with it originally (e.g. WINDOW–REA), and 'different context', in which it was paired with a different word (e.g. RIPE–REA). Schacter and Graf found that completion was more accurate in the 'same context' situation, thus indicating that the amnesics were able to retain some information about a novel association.

On the assumption that direct priming can be used to establish novel associations, Glisky and co-workers (1986) examined the possibility that amnesics might be able to learn computer terminology. They employed the *method of vanishing cues*, which is a variant of the direct priming procedure. At the start, the patient was presented with a definition – e.g. 'to store a program' – and the name of the command that enables that to happen – 'SAVE'. On the next trial the definition was repeated, but only the first letter of the command was presented. If the patient could not answer, a second letter was presented, and so on until a correct response occurred. On the next trial the definition was presented again, alongside a fragment of the command containing one less letter than that needed for successful recall on the previous trial; thus, if a subject had been successful with SAV– he or she would see SA— on the next trial.

The results were impressive: all the patients were able to learn the appropriate command for 15 different definitions without any cues being available. Encouraged by these findings, Glisky and associates (in press) carried out a further study to determine whether amnesics could learn to use computers. Their results showed that amnesics could be taught a variety of computer skills, including editing, writing, and data storage operations. With this degree of success, one might wonder whether these patients were genuinely amnesic. Glisky and her colleagues have countered this by describing their most severe patient, who, although unable to remember any of fifty or so visits to the rehabilitation unit, was able to succeed on even the most complex of the programming tasks.

Direct priming, as reflected in the method of vanishing cues, is a potentially interesting development. It is simple to administer and could be applied in any situation in which a patient needs to acquire new terminology. Furthermore, if amnesics can learn to operate computers, it may be possible to use them as external memory aids and for amusement. However, judgement must be reserved. Glisky and co-workers report that their patients acquired very specific knowledge; thus they could give the appropriate term when given exactly the same definition as that used in the learning phase, but could not do so if the definition was expressed in a different manner. This inflexibility was not found in normal subjects trained in the same way, which suggests that the amnesics have acquired the knowledge in a specific manner which prevents them from generalizing to similar situations. Another problem is that remediation based on direct priming of new associations may be possible only in less severe cases. In the Schacter and Graf study described earlier, a reanalysis showed that it was only patients with relatively mild amnesia who showed priming of novel associations. The implication, therefore, is that direct priming in remediation might only be effective for milder cases. Despite these problems, direct priming techniques are a useful addition to the therapist's options.

Remediation procedures have been concerned almost exclusively with improving patients' ability on memory tasks such as learning a word list, remembering someone's face, or learning commands, which a normal person would rely partly or wholly on episodic memory. An alternative approach is to consider the remedial potential of the preserved procedural memory of amnesics. Chapter 6 reviewed a number of studies showing that amnesics can acquire motor and perceptual skills very effectively, because these do not require episodic information. Preserved perceptual learning may contribute to the successful learning of Glisky's patients, but, generally speaking, there has been little attempt to exploit amnesics' procedural memory within a therapeutic setting. With a view to occupational therapy, Talland (1965) showed that a Korsakoff amnesic could learn how to use a novel device for picking up beads, but this was not generalized to any practical setting. More recently, Wilson and Moffat (1984a) have shown that a word list in which each item has been associated with a distinctive movement is recalled better than one that has not. This is encouraging, but once again we see that the aim is to ameliorate impaired episodic memory, rather than directly exploit any benefits that preserved motor memory might bring to the patient. In particular, the possibility that even severe amnesics might make use

of computer-based amusements seems to have been largely un-
explored.

PSYCHOLOGICAL APPROACHES TO MEMORY THERAPY
– AN OVERVIEW

In this chapter we have considered a number of different
approaches to memory therapy. External stores and cueing devices
are extremely useful, especially if the two can be combined in a
simple and effective way such as a watch alarm and a diary.
Repeated practice does not seem to have a significant role, although
it may exert some general beneficial effect on recovery. Amnesics
have shown improved memory performance using a wide range of
different strategies, most notably those based on visual imagery.
However, there is no evidence that amnesic patients use these
strategies unless instructed to do so. Because of this, the teaching of
strategies is unlikely to produce any general alleviation of patients'
memory problems. With this difficulty in mind, a more realistic
approach is to concentrate remedial efforts on the acquisition of
information relating to specific situations in which the patient
currently faces difficulty.

PHYSICAL TREATMENTS FOR MEMORY DISORDERS

Memories are assumed to be formed by changes in the pattern of
synaptic connectivity between neurones. The transmission of
neural impulses depends crucially on neurotransmitters, chemicals
which are released from pre-synaptic membranes and diffuse to
post-synaptic membranes, where they stimulate a new impulse.
Modern experimental techniques have shown that various
neuronal pathways exist, each identified by the presence of a
specific neurotransmitter. It is now known that memory deficits are
associated with reduced levels of particular neurotransmitters,
indicating that specific neuronal pathways are implicated in the
process of memory.

It has been estimated that AD affects between 3 and 4 per cent of
the population of the USA over 65. With the continuing expansion

of this age-group, the incidence of AD will soon reach epidemic proportions. Faced with this prospect, there has been an enormous effort to find ways in which the progress of AD within an individual might be arrested or reversed.

About ten years ago, a number of scientists reported that patients with AD had abnormally low levels of the neurotransmitter acetylcholine (ACh). This deficit is known to be caused by the degeneration of *cholinergic* (acetylcholine-containing) neurones, particularly in a region of the basal forebrain known as the *nucleus basalis of Meynert* (NbM). Experiments on normal subjects have shown that blocking the action of ACh causes memory impairments (see chapter 1). Given this, one can suppose that the memory deficit in AD patients is linked directly to their depleted levels of ACh. Support for this theory comes from a study by Johns and co-workers (1985). They examined the cerebro-spinal fluid of 14 AD patients and found a strong correlation between their level of mental impairment, as measured by a memory and information test, and the extent of ACh depletion.

The first attempts at therapy were inspired by work on Parkinson's Disease. This disease is known to be associated with depleted levels of another neurotransmitter, *dopamine*. The symptoms of this disease can be dramatically ameliorated by administering a drug known as *L-dopa*, which acts by stimulating the remaining dopaminergic cells to produce enough additional dopamine to counteract the deficit. It was hoped that a similar strategy might work with cholinergic deficits. One approach has been to give AD patients large amounts of choline, either directly or in the form of lecithin. Choline provides the basis for manufacturing ACh, and it was hoped that administering it in large quantities would increase ACh levels. The outcome of these experiments has been disappointing, with no indication of significant improvements except, perhaps, in younger patients with a short history of the disease.

The failure of choline therapy suggests that cholinergic neurones, unlike their dopaminergic counterparts, cannot increase their level of activity in a compensatory manner. An alternative strategy is to enhance the efficiency of the ACh that the depleted system can still produce. One way to achieve this is to administer drugs which inhibit the action of an enzyme called *acetyl-*

cholinesterase (AChE). This is present at all cholinergic synapses, and its role is to break down ACh once its action at the synapse has finished. Reducing AChE levels should therefore increase the amount of ACh available.

The most widely investigated AChE inhibitor is *physostigmine*, and a number of studies have looked at whether increasing its level can affect AD. A problem with physostigmine is that it has a narrow 'therapeutic window' – that is, the dose range over which it has a beneficial effect is limited. Johns and associates (1985) were able to establish the optimal dose of physostigmine for 20 AD patients and to examine their performance on a famous faces test, on digit span, and on recognition of verbal and pictorial information. Physostigmine enhanced performance on the recognition task, but not on the famous faces or digit span tests. Failure to improve digit span with physostigmine is to be expected, given that ACh inhibitors do not impair digit span in normal subjects, but some improvement on the famous faces task would have been expected.

These findings are in line with a number of others that have shown modest improvements with physostigmine. However, there is evidence that administration of physostigmine might inhibit the release of ACh. All neurones have *receptors* located on their synaptic membranes, and these are the sites at which neuro-transmitters exert their effect. Cholinergic neurones have two types of receptor, known as M1 and M2, and these are thought to be largely unaffected in the early stages of AD. M2 receptors are located on the pre-synaptic membranes, and are thought to regulate the flow of ACh, stimulating more production when ACh levels are low and reducing it when levels are high. ACh has a strong affinity for M2 receptors; thus, what ACh is available will be attracted to them in preference to other sites. As a result, the M2 receptor will sense a higher level of ACh than is really the case, and thus inhibit ACh release (Mash et al., 1985). Administration of physostigmine may therefore be more effective if a drug that reduces the activity of M2 receptors is also given. M1 receptors are found on post-synaptic membranes, and their role is to receive the ACh released from pre-synaptic membranes. M1 receptors are therefore responsible for conveying the impulse within a cholinergic pathway. This opens up a new possibility for therapy, for, if a drug could be found that selectively enhanced the operation of M1 but not M2 receptors,

ACh available in the system could operate more effectively.

A third strategy is to administer *cholinomimetic* agents, which, as the name suggests, are substances which mimic the activity of ACh. One such drug is *arecoline*, which has been found to enhance learning in normal humans and ageing primates (Sitaram et al., 1978; Bartus et al., 1982). Despite these findings, therapy aimed at restoring or simulating cholinergic activity has had only limited success in alleviating the psychological deficits of AD. One problem is that AD is much more than a deficit in cholinergic activity. AD patients also have depleted levels of *catecholamine* neuro-transmitters, including dopamine and *norepinephrine* (the latter is also known as *noradrenalin*, and pathways in which it is involved are termed *noradrenergic*). Arnsten and Goldman-Rakic (1985) have shown that *clonidine*, a substance that promotes the activity of catecholamines, improves the learning capability of ageing monkeys. This drug may therefore be an additional means of relieving the symptoms of AD.

Although the principal focus has been AD, there have also been a number of attempts to alleviate memory problems in the amnesic syndrome. McEntee and Mair (1978) assessed the amount of noradrenergic activity in a group of Korsakoff patients, and found that the degree of memory impairment was directly related to the level of norepinephrine depletion. Following this up, the same authors (McEntee and Mair, 1980) administered a number of drugs assumed to enhance noradrenergic activity to eight Korsakoff patients. Only clonidine was found to enhance memory per-formance, and the benefits were relatively small, being restricted to tasks involving short-term retention of information. There was no benefit at all in tasks such as remembering unfamiliar faces and paired-associate learning, which amnesics perform notoriously badly. More recently, McEntee and colleagues (1984) have argued that norepinephrine depletion is the prime cause of memory impairments in Korsakoff's Syndrome. However, a recent neuro-pathological study by Arendt and his associates (1983) has indicated that Korsakoff's Syndrome can cause neuronal loss in the NbM. As we saw earlier, this is a primary source of cholinergic activity, and allows for the possibility that Korsakoff's Syndrome may have a cholinergic component.

Attempts to alleviate memory disorders by attempting to

compensate specific deficiencies in individual neurotransmitters have achieved only limited success. The reason for this is that it is unlikely that such a complex process as memory relies on only a few of the many neurotransmitters known to exist in the mammalian brain.

BRAIN TRANSPLANTS

One of the greatest problems in overcoming brain damage is the fact that the brain has little regenerative capability. Furthermore, when some region of the brain is damaged, other regions do not seem to be able to take over its function. Recent research has highlighted ways of promoting recovery in the peripheral nervous system, but these techniques, such as reconnecting nerves by microsurgery, cannot as yet be applied to more central components of the nervous system (Freed et al., 1985). An alternative approach involves the use of brain transplants. Dunnett and associates (1982) surgically destroyed connections in the septo-hippocampal region of young rats. The rats had previously learnt several mazes, and the effect of the damage was to reduce their performance. The impaired rats were then given grafts of septo-hippocampal tissue taken from rat fetuses. It was found that the grafts reduced the animals' impairments on the maze-learning tasks, which suggests that the grafts had become effective parts of the animals' memory system. In a subsequent study, Gage and co-workers (1984) showed that suspensions of neural tissue taken from the septo-hippocampal region of rat fetuses can alleviate age-related learning deficits in rats. Transplants present us with an interesting therapeutic option, but the moral and philosophical issues surrounding their use in humans present immense problems. Furthermore, the fact that successful transplants depend on the availability of fetal brain tissue only adds to the ethical dilemma.

Suggestions for
Further Reading

Chapters 1, 2, 3 and 4

There are a large number of textbooks covering normal human memory. Recommended are Klatzky, 1980; Zechmeister and Nyberg, 1981; and Eysenck, 1984. Although quite old, Baddeley, 1976, is still very useful. Richardson, 1980, provides a comprehensive account of imagery, as does Kosslyn, 1983. The history of memory models and their emphasis on spatial metaphors is described in some detail by Roediger, 1980. The effects of emotion on memory have recently been reviewed by Blaney, 1986. Wagstaff, 1981 and 1984, are good sources for work on hypnosis and memory.

Chapter 5

Lezak, 1985, provides a definitive account of neuropsychological testing, and Brooks and Lincoln, 1984, and Mayes, 1986, present evaluations of clinical memory tests. Good general accounts of clinical neuropsychology can be found in Heilman and Valenstein, 1985, and Strub and Black, 1981. Walsh, 1985, gives some detailed case histories involving different degrees of amnesia. Kolb and Whishaw, 1985, is an excellent account of human neuropsychology, and parts I and II are particularly recommended to those unfamiliar with the organization of the nervous system.

Chapters 6 and 7

Whitty and Zangwill, 1977, covers the different aspects of amnesia, and Talland, 1965, is worth browsing through. Butters and Cermak, 1980, provides a detailed overview of more recent experimental work on Korsakoff's Syndrome. A large number of multi-author volumes concerned with amnesia have appeared in the last few years. These include Cermak, 1982; Squire and Butters, 1984; and Weinberger et al., 1985. Squire and Butters, 1985, also covers recent developments in both human and animal research. Recent research on consolidation theory is covered in Weingartner and Parker, 1984. Mayes, forthcoming, provides a more detailed account of the various kinds of organic amnesias.

Chapter 8

Light and Zelinski's review (1983) covers work done in the seventies on ageing, and Rabbitt, 1986, provides an account of more recent developments. Miller, 1977, gives a comprehensive account of dementia, and supplementary reading can be found in volume 42 of the *British Medical Bulletin*, which is devoted exclusively to recent research on AD.

Chapter 9

Markowitsch, 1983, provides a detailed review of transient global amnesia. Russell, 1971, provides a good account of PTA, and Schacter and Crovitz, 1977, gives a clear account of more recent memory research. Brooks (1984) presents a very wide-ranging account of closed-head injury. Weiner, 1984, is an excellent source for most of the recent ECT research, and the commentaries that follow his review enable the reader to grasp the complexity of the debate in this area.

Chapter 10

Rappaport, 1942, is an interesting source regarding older research on hysterical disorders, but for more recent research the volume edited by Kihlstrom and Evans (1979) is probably the best. Schacter (in press, b) is a thorough review of the amnesia and crime literature and Gibbens and Hall Williams (1977) provide an authoritative account of medicolegal issues. A good place to start reading about infantile amnesia is Moscovitch, 1984.

Chapter 11

Wilson and Moffat, 1984, gives a comprehensive account of the difficulties surrounding memory remediation. Miller, 1974, has a good discussion of the factors influencing recovery from brain damage. Richardson et al., in press, gives a balanced view of the value of imagery in memory remediation. Background reading for the physiological aspects of memory therapy can be found in Thompson, 1985, and, at a more detailed level, in Kandel and Schwarz, 1985.

References

Abel, E. L. (1971) Marijuana and memory: Acquisition or retrieval? *Science*, 173, 1038–40.

Abernathy, E. M. (1940) The effect of changed environmental conditions upon the results of college examinations. *Journal of Psychology*, 10, 293–301.

Akhtar, S., Lindsey, B., and Kahn, F. L. (1981) Sudden amnesia for personal identity. *Pennsylvania Medicine*, 84, 46–8.

Albert, M. S., and Moss, M. (1984) The assessment of memory disorders in patients with Alzheimer's Disease. In L. R. Squire and N. Butters (eds), *Neuropsychology of Memory*, 236–46. New York: Guildford.

Albert, M. S., Butters, N., and Levin, J. (1979) Temporal gradients in the retrograde amnesia of patients with alcoholic Korsakoff's disease. *Archives of Neurology*, 36, 211–16.

Alzheimer, A. (1907) Uber eine eigenartige Erkranskung der Hirnrinde. *Allgemeine Zeitschrift für Psychiatrie Psychoisch-Gerichtliche Medicin*, 64, 146–8.

Anderson, J. R. (1985) *Cognitive Psychology and its Implications*, 2nd edn. New York: Freeman.

Anderson, J. R., and Bower, G. H. (1972) *Human Associative Memory*. Washington, DC: Winston.

Andrews, E., Poser, C. M., and Kessler, M. (1982) Retrograde amnesia for forty years. *Cortex*, 18, 441–58.

Arendt, T., Bigl, V., Arendt, A., and Tennstedt, A. (1983) Loss of neurones in the nucleus basalis of Meynert in Alzheimer's Disease, paralysis agitans and Korsakoff's Disease. *Acta Neuropathologica*, 61, 101–8.

Arnsten, A. F. T., and Goldman-Rakic, P. S. (1985) α2-Adrenergic mechanisms in prefrontal cortex associated with cognitive decline in non-human primates. *Science*, 230, 1273–6.

Atkinson, R. C., and Shiffrin, R. M. (1968) Human memory: A proposed system and its control processes. In K. W. Spence and J. T. Spence (eds), *The Psychology of Learning and Motivation*, vol. 2. New York: Academic Press.

Baddeley, A. D. (1966a) Short-term memory for word sequences as a function of acoustic, semantic and formal similarity. *Quarterly Journal of Experimental Psychology*, 18, 362–5.

Baddeley, A. D. (1966b) The influence of acoustic and semantic similarity on long-term memory for word sequences. *Quarterly Journal of Experimental Psychology*, 18, 302–9.

Baddeley, A. D. (1976) *The Psychology of Memory*. New York: Basic Books.

Baddeley, A. D. (1984a) Memory theory and memory therapy. In B. Wilson and N. Moffat (eds), *The Clinical Management of Memory Problems*, 5–27. London: Croom Helm.

Baddeley, A. D. (1984b) Reading and working memory. *Visible Language*, 18, 311–22.

Baddeley, A. D. (1986) *Working memory*. Oxford: Churchill Livingstone.

Baddeley, A. D., and Hitch, G. J. (1974) Working memory. In G. A. Bower (ed.), *The Psychology of Learning and Motivation*, vol. 8, 47–90. New York: Academic Press.

Baddeley, A. D., and Warrington, E. K. (1970) Amnesia and the distinction between long and short-term memory. *Journal of Verbal Learning and Verbal Behavior*, 9, 176–89.

Baddeley, A. D., and Warrington, E. K. (1973) Memory coding and amnesia. *Neuropsychologia*, 11, 159–65.

Bartus, R. T., Dean, R. L., Beer, B., and Lippa, A. S. (1982) The cholinergic hypothesis of geriatric memory dysfunction. *Science*, 217, 408.

Bayles, K. A. (1982) Language function in senile dementia. *Brain and Language*, 16, 265–80.

Beatty, W. W., Salmon, D. P., Bernstein, N., Martone, M., Lyon, L., and Butters, N. (in press) Procedural learning in a patient with amnesia due to hypoxia. *Brain and Cognition*.

Bennett-Levy, J., and Powell, G. E. (1980) The subjective memory questionnaire (SMQ): An investigation into the self-reporting of real-life memory skills. *British Journal of Social and Clinical Psychology*, 19, 177–83.

Benson, D. F., and Geschwind, N. (1967) Shrinking retrograde amnesia. *Journal of Neurology, Neurosurgery and Psychiatry*, 30, 539–44.

Benson, D. F., Marsden, C. D., and Meadows, J. C. (1974) The amnesic syndrome of posterior cerebral artery occlusion. *Acta Neurologica Scandinavica*, 50, 133–45.

Berlyne, N. (1972) Confabulation. *British Journal of Psychiatry*, 120, 31–9.

Berrington, W. P., Liddell, D. W., and Foulds, G. A. (1956) A Re-evaluation of the fugue. *Journal of Mental Science*, 102, 280–6.

Biber, C., Butters, N., Rosen, J., Gerstmann, L., and Mattis, S. (1981) Encoding strategies and recognition of faces by alcoholic Korsakoff and other brain-damaged patients. *Journal of Clinical Neuropsychology*, 3, 315–30.

Blakemore, C. (1977) *Mechanics of the Mind*, Cambridge: Cambridge University Press.

Blaney, P. H. (1986) Affect and memory. *Psychological Bulletin*, 99, 229–46.

Block, R. I., and Wittenborn, J. R. (1985) Marijuana effects on associative processes. *Psychopharmacology*, 85, 426–30.

Boller, F., Mizutani, T., Roessmann, U., and Gambett, P. (1980) Parkinson's Disease, dementia and Alzheimer's Disease: Clinicopathological correlations. *Annals of Neurology*, 7, 329–35.

Bolles, R. C. (1975) *Learning Theory*. New York: Holt, Rinehart and Winston.

Botwinick, J. (1978) *Aging and Behavior*, 2nd edn. New York: Springer.

Bower, G. H. (1970) Imagery as a relational organizer in associative learning. *Journal of Verbal Learning and Verbal Behavior*, 9, 529–33.

Bower, G. H. (1981) Mood and memory. *American Psychologist*, 36, 129–48.

Bower, G. H., Gilligan, S. G., and Monteiro, K. P. (1981) Selectivity of learning caused by affective states. *Journal of Experimental Psychology: General*, 110, 451–73.

Bradshaw, J. L., and Nettleton, N. C. (1983) *Human Cerebral Asymmetry*. Englewood Cliffs, NJ: Prentice-Hall.

Brandt, J., and Butters, N. (1986) The neuropsychology of Huntingdon's disease. *Trends in Neurosciences*, 9, 118–20.

Brandt, J., Rubinsky, E., and Lassen, G. (1985) Uncovering malingered amnesia. *Annals of the New York Academy of Sciences*, 444, 502–3.

British Psychological Society (1986) Report of the working group on the use of the polygraph in criminal investigation and personnel screening. *Bulletin of the British Psychological Society*, 39, 81–94.

Brooks, D. N. (1974) Recognition memory and head injury. *Journal of Neurology, Neurosurgery and Psychiatry*, 37, 794–801.

Brooks, D. N. (1975) Long and short term memory in head injured patients. *Cortex*, 11, 329–40.

Brooks, D. N. (1984) *Closed-Head Injury*. Oxford: Oxford University Press.

Brooks, D. N., and Lincoln, N. B. (1984) Assessment for rehabilitation. In B. Wilson and N. Moffat (eds), *The Clinical Management of Memory Problems*, 28–45. London: Croom Helm.

Brown, J., Brown, M. W., and Bowes, J. B. (1983) Effects of lorazepam on rate of forgetting, on retrieval from semantic memory and on manual dexterity. *Neuropsychologia*, 21, 501–12.

Brown, R., and McNeill, D. (1966) The 'tip-of-the-tongue' phenomenon. *Journal of Verbal Learning and Verbal Behavior*, 5, 325–37.

Burke, D. M., and Light, L. L. (1981) Memory and aging: The role of retrieval processes. *Psychological Bulletin*, 90, 513–46.

Butters, N. (1984) Alcoholic Korsakoff's Syndrome: An update. *Seminars in Neurology*, 4, 226–44.

Butters, N. (1985) Alcoholic Korsakoff's Syndrome: Some unresolved issues concerning aetiology, neuropathology, and cognitive deficits. *Journal of Experimental and Clinical Neuropsychology*, 7, 181–210.

Butters, N., and Cermak, L. S. (1980) *Alcoholic Korsakoff's Syndrome. An Information Processing Approach to Amnesia*. New York: Academic Press.

Butters, N., and Miliotis, P. (1985) Amnesic disorders. In K. M. Heilman and E. Valenstein (eds), *Clinical Neuropsychology*, 2nd edn, 403–52. Oxford: Oxford University Press.

Butters, N., Miliotis, P., Albert, M. S., and Sax, D. S. (1983) Memory assessment: Evidence of the heterogeneity of amnesic symptoms. In G. Goldstein (ed.), *Advances in Clinical Neuropsychology*, vol. 1, 127–59. New York: Plenum Press.

Butters, N., Wolfe, J., Martone, M., Granholm, E., and Cermak, L.S. (1985) Memory disorders associated with Huntingdon's Disease: Verbal recall, verbal recognition and procedural memory. *Neuropsychologia*, 23, 729–43.

Butters, N., Martone, M., White, B., Granholm, E., Wolfe, J. (in press) *Clinical Validators: Comparisons of Demented and Amnesic Patients*.

Buzan, T. (1972) *Use Your Head*. London: BBC Publications.

Calloway, S. P., Dolan, R. R. J., Jacoby, R. J., and Levy, R. (1981) ECT and cerebral atrophy. A computer tomographic study. *Acta Psychiatrica Scandinavica*, 64, 442–5.

Cermak, L. S. (1975) Imagery as an aid to retrieval in Korsakoff patients. *Cortex*, 11, 163–9.

Cermak, L. S. (1976) The encoding capacity of a patient with amnesia due to encephalitis. *Neuropsychologia*, 14, 311–26.

Cermak, L. S. (ed.) (1982) *Human Memory and Amnesia*. Hillsdale, NJ: Erlbaum.

Cermak, L. S., and O'Connor, U. (1983) The anterograde and retrograde retrieval ability of a patient with encephalitis. *Neuropsychologia*, 21, 213–34.

Cermak, L. S., Talbot, N., Chandler, K., and Woolbarst, L. R. (1985) The perceptual priming phenomenon in amnesia. *Neuropsychologia*, 23, 615–22.

Claparède, E. (1911) Recognition et moiité. *Archives de Psychologie Genève*, 11, 79–90.

Clark, D. M., and Teasdale, J. D. (1981) Diurnal variation in clinical depression and accessibility of positive and negative experiences. *Journal of Abnormal Psychology*, 91, 87–95.

Cohen, N. J. (1984) Preserved learning capacity in amnesia: Evidence for multiple memory systems. In L. R. Squire and N. Butters (eds), *Neuropsychology of Memory*, 83–103. New York: Guildford.

Cohen, N. J., and Squire, L. R. (1980) Preserved learning and retention of pattern-analyzing skills in amnesia: Dissociation of knowing how from knowing that. *Science*, 210, 207–10.

Conrad, R. (1964) Acoustic confusions in immediate memory. *British Journal of Psychology*, 55, 75–84.

Coons, P. M., Milstein, V., and Marley, C. (1982) EEG studies of two multiple personalities. *Archives of General Psychiatry*, 39, 823–5.

Cooper, S. J. (1984) Drug treatments, neurochemical change and human memory impairment. In B. Wilson and N. Moffat (eds), *The Clinical Management of Memory Problems*, 132–47. London: Croom Helm.

Corkin, S. (1965) Tactually guided maze-learning in man: Effects of unilateral cortical excisions and bilateral hippocampal lesions. *Neuropsychologia*, 3, 339–51.

Corkin, S. (1982) Some relationships between global amnesias and the memory impairments in Alzheimer's Disease. In S. Corkin et al. (eds), *Alzheimer's Disease: A Report of Progress*, 149–64. New York: Raven Press.

Corkin, S., Sullivan, E., Twitchell, T., and Grove, E. (1981) The amnesic patient HM: Clinical observations and test performance 28 years after operation. *Abstracts of the Society for Neuroscience*, 80(1), 235.

Craik, F. I. M. (1968) Short-term memory and the aging process. In G. Talland (ed.), *Human Aging and Behavior*, 131–68. New York: Academic Press.

Craik, F. I. M. (1977a) Depth of processing in recall and recognition. In S. Dornic (ed.), *Attention and Performance*, vol. 6, 679–98. London: Wiley.

Craik, F. I. M. (1977b) Age differences in human memory. In J. E. Birren and K. W. Schaie (eds), *Handbook of the Psychology of Aging*. New York: Van Nostrand Reinhold.

Craik, F. I. M., and Lockhart, R. S. (1972) Levels of processing: A framework for memory research. *Journal of Verbal Learning and Verbal Behavior*, 11, 671–84.

Craik, F. I. M., and Simon, E. (1980) Age differences in memory: The roles of attention and depth of processing. In L. W. Poon et al. (eds), *New Directions in Memory and Aging*. Hillsdale, NJ: Erlbaum.

Craik, F. I. M., and Tulving, E. (1975) Depth of processing and retention of words in episodic memory. *Journal of Experimental Psychology: General*, 104, 268–94.

Crovitz, H. F., Harvey, M. T., and McClanahan, S. (1981) Hidden memory: A rapid method for the study of amnesia using perceptual learning. *Cortex*, 17, 273–8.

Crowder, R. G. (1982) General forgetting theory and the locus of amnesia. In L. Cermak (ed.), *Human Memory and Amnesia*, pp. 33–42. New York: Erlbaum.

Dakof, G. A., and Mendelsohn, G. A. (1986) Parkinson's disease: The psychological aspects of a chronic illness. *Psychological Bulletin*, 99, 375–88.

Damasio, A. R., Damasio, H., and Tranel, D. (1986) Prosopagnosia. In H. D. Ellis et al. (eds), *Aspects of Face Processing*. Dordrecht: Martinus Nijhoff.

Daniel, W. F., and Crovitz, H. F. (1983a) Acute memory impairment following electroconvulsive therapy: A review of the literature. 1. The effects of electrical stimulus waveform and number of treatments. *Acta Psychiatrica Scandinavica*, 67, 1–7.

Daniel, W. F., and Crovitz, H. F. (1983b) Acute memory impairment following electroconvulsive therapy: A review of the literature. 2. The effects of electrode placement. *Acta Psychiatrica Scandinavica*, 67, 57–68.

Darley, C. F., Tinklenberg, J. R., Roth, W. T., Hollister, L. E., and Atkinson, R. C. (1974) Influence of marijuana on storage and retrieval processes in memory. *Memory and Cognition*, 1, 196–200.

Davidoff, D. A., Butters, N., Gerstman, L. J., Zurif, E., Paul, I. H., and Mattis, S. (1984) Affective/motivational factors in the recall of prose passages by alcoholic Korsakoff patients. *Alcohol*, 1, 63–9.

Davies, A. D. M., and Binks, M. G. (1983) Supporting the residual memory of a Korsakoff patient. *Behavioural Psychotherapy*, 11, 62–74.

Denney, N. W. (1974) Clustering in middle and old age. *Developmental Psychology*, 10, 471–5.

De Wardener, H. E., and Lennox, B. (1947) Cerebral beri-beri. *Lancet*, 1, 11.

Digman, J. M. (1959) Growth of a motor skill as a function of distribution of practice. *Journal of Experimental Psychology*, 57, 310–16.

Dillard, A. (1982) *Teaching a Stone to Talk*. London: Picador.

Drachman, D. A., and Leavitt, J. (1972) Memory impairment in the aged: Storage versus retrieval deficit. *Journal of Experimental Psychology*, 93, 302–8.

Drachman, D. A., and Leavitt, J. (1974) Human memory and the cholinergic system. *Archives of Neurology*, 30, 113–21.

Dunnett, S. B., Low, W. C., Iversen, S. D., Stenevi, V., and Bjorkland, A. (1982) Septal transplants restore maze learning in rats with fornix-fimbria lesions. *Brain Research*, 251, 335–48.

Ebbinghaus, H. (1885) *Über das Gedachtnis*. Leipzig: Dunker.

Eich, J. E. (1980) The cue-dependent nature of state-dependent retrieval. *Memory and Cognition*, 8, 157–73.

Eich, J. E. (1984) Memory for unattended events: Remembering with and without awareness. *Memory and Cognition*, 12, 105–11.

Erdeyli, M. H., and Goldberg, B. (1979) Let's not sweep repression under the rug: Toward a cognitive psychology of repression. In J. F. Kilhlstrom and F. J. Evans (eds), *Functional Disorders of Memory*, pp. 355–402. Hillsdale, NJ: Freeman.

Ericsson, K. A., and Chase, W. G. (1980) Acquisition of a memory skill. *Science*, 208, 1181–2.

Erikson, R. C., and Scott, M. I. (1977) Clinical memory testing: A review. *Psychological Bulletin*, 84, 1130–49.

Evans, C. D. (1981) *Rehabilitation of the Head Injured*. London: Churchill Livingstone.

Eysenck, M. W. (1984) *A Handbook of Cognitive Psychology*. London: Erlbaum.

Fedio, P., and Van Buren, J. M. (1974) Memory deficits during electrical stimulation of the speech cortex of conscious man. *Brain and Language*, 1, 29–42.

File, S. E., and Bond, A. J. (1979) Impaired performance and sedation after a single dose of lorazepam. *Psychopharmacology*, 66, 309–13.

Fink, M. (1984) ECT – verdict. Not guilty. *The Behavioral and Brain Sciences*, 7, 26–7.

Frank, G. (1981) *Amnestiche Episoden*. Berlin: Springer.

Freed, W. J., de Medinaceli, L., and Wyatt, R. J. (1985) Promoting functional plasticity in the nervous system. *Science*, 227, 1544–52.

Freeman, C. P. L., Weeks, D., and Kendell, R. E. (1980) ECT: Patients who complain. *British Journal of Psychiatry*, 137, 17–25.

Freud, S. (1914) *Psychopathology of Everyday Life*. In A. A. Brill (ed.), *The Writings of Sigmund Freud*. New York: Modern Library, 1938.

Fukuda, T., and Matsuda, Y. (1969) Comparative characteristics of slow wave EEG, autonomic functioning and clinical picture in typical and atypical schizophrenia during and following ECT. *International Pharmacopsychiatry*, 3, 13–41.

Gabrieli, J. D. E., Cohen, N. J., and Corkin, S. (1983) The acquisition of lexical and semantic knowledge in amnesia. *Society for Neuroscience Abstracts*, 9, 238.

Gage, F. H., Bjorklund, A., Stenevi, U., Dunnet, S., and Kelly, P. A. T. (1984) Intrahippocampal septal grafts ameliorate learning impairments in aged rats. *Science*, 225, 533–6.

Gardner, H. (1977) *The Shattered Mind: The Person after Brain Damage*. London: Routledge and Kegan Paul.

Gibbens, T. C. N., and Hall Williams (1977) Medicolegal aspects of amnesia. In C. W. M. Whitty and O. L. Zangwill (eds), *Amnesia*, pp. 245–64. London: Butterworth.

Gilmore, M. (1970) *A World Away. A Memoir of Mervyn Peake*. London: Victor Gollancz.

Glanzer, M., and Cunitz, A. R. (1966) Two storage mechanisms in free recall. *Journal of Verbal Learning and Verbal Behavior*, 5, 351–60.

Glanzer, M., and Razel, M. (1974) The size of the unit in short-term storage. *Journal of Verbal Learning and Verbal Behavior*, 13, 114–31.

Glasgow, R. E., Zeiss, R. A., Barrera, M., and Lewinsohn, P. M. (1977) Case studies on remediating memory deficits in brain damaged individuals. *Journal of Clinical Psychology*, 33, 1049–54.

Glisky, E. L., Schacter, D. L., and Tulving, E. (1986) Computer learning by memory-impaired patients: Acquisition and retention of complex knowledge. *Neuropsychologia*, 24, 313–28.

Glisky, E. L., Schacter, D. L., and Tulving, E. (in press) Learning and retention of computer-related vocabulary in memory-impaired patients: Method of vanishing cues. *Journal of Experimental and Clinical Neuropsychology*.

Godden, D., and Baddeley, A. D. (1975) Context-dependent memory in two natural environments. *British Journal of Psychology*, 66, 325–31.

Godden, D., and Baddeley, A. D. (1980) When does context influence recognition memory? *British Journal of Psychology*, 71, 99–104.

Godfrey, H. P. D., and Knight, R. G. (1985) Cognitive rehabilitation of memory functioning in amnesic alcoholics. *Journal of Clinical and Consulting Psychology*, 53, 555–7.

Goodwin, D. W. (1974) Alcoholic blackout and state-dependent learning. *Federation Proceedings*, 33, 1833–5.

Graff-Radford, N. R., Eslinger, P. J., Damasio, A. R., and Yamada, T. (1984) Nonhemorrhagic infarction of the thalamus: Behavioral, anatomic, and physiological correlates. *Neurology*, 34, 14–23.

Grinker, R. R., and Spiegel, J. P. (1945) *Men Under Stress*. New York: McGraw-Hill.

Guthkelch, A. N. (1980) Post-traumatic amnesia, post-concussional symptoms and accident neurosis. *European Neurology*, 19, 91–102.

Hamilton, E. (1961) *Plato: The Collected Dialogues*. New York: Bollingen Foundation.

Harris, J. (1984) Methods of improving memory. In B. Wilson and N. Moffat (eds), *The Clinical Management of Memory Problems*, 44–62. London: Croom Helm.

Harris, J. E., and Sunderland, A. (1981) A brief survey of the management of memory disorders in rehabilitation units in Britain. *International Rehabilitation Medicine*, 3, 206–9.

Hasher, L., and Zacks, R. T. (1979) Automatic and effortful processes in memory. *Journal of Experimental Psychology: General*, 108, 356–88.

Hashtroudi, S., Parker, E. S., de Lisi, L. E., Wyatt, R. J., and Mutter, S. A. (1984) Intect retention in acute alcohol amnesia. *Journal of Experimental Psychology: Learning, Memory and Cognition*, 10, 156–63.

Hebb, D. O. (1949) *The Organization of Behavior*. New York: Wiley.

Heilman, K. M., and Sypert, G. W. (1977) Korsakoff's Syndrome resulting from bilateral fornix lesions. *Neurology*, 27, 490–3.

Heilman, K. M., and Valenstein, E. (1985) *Clinical Neuropsychology*, 2nd edn. Oxford: Oxford University Press.

Her Majesty's Stationery Office (HMSO) (1986) *Railway Accident. Report on the Collision that Occurred on 11th October 1984 near Wembley Central Station*.

Hermann, D. J., and Neisser, U. (1978) An inventory of everyday memory experiences. In M. M. Gruneberg et al. (eds), *Practical Aspects of Memory*. New York: Academic Press.

Hess, T. M. (1985) Aging and context influences on recognition memory for typical and atypical script actions. *Developmental Psychology*, 21, 1139–51.

Hewitt, K. (unpublished manuscript) Context effects in memory: A review. Cambridge University Psychological Laboratory.

Higbee, K. (1977) *Your Memory: How it Works and How to Improve it*. Englewood Cliffs, NJ: Prentice-Hall.

Hill, D., and Sargent, W. (1943) A case of matricide. *Lancet*, 1, 526–7.

Hirst, W. (1982) The amnesic syndrome. Descriptions and explanations. *Psychological Bulletin*, 91, 435–60.

Holding, D. H. (1965) *Principles of Training*. Oxford: Pergamon.

Hulicka, I. M., and Grossman, J. L. (1967) Age-group comparisons for the use of mediators in paired-associate learning. *Journal of Gerontology*, 22, 46–51.

Hunter (1977) Imagery, comprehension and mnemonics. *Journal of Mental Imagery*, 1, 65–72.

Huppert, F. A., and Piercy, M. (1976) Recognition memory in amnesic patients: Effect of temporal context and familiarity of material. *Cortex*, 4, 3–20.

Huppert, F. A., and Piercy, M. (1977) Dissociation between learning and remembering in organic amnesia. *Nature*, 275, 317–18.

Huppert, F. A., and Piercy, M. (1978a) The role of trace strength in recency and frequency judgements by amnesic and control subjects. *Quarterly Journal of Experimental Psychology*, 30, 346–54.

Huppert, F. A., and Piercy, M. (1978b) Recognition memory in amnesic patients: A defect of acquisition? *Neuropsychologia*, 15, 643–52.

Huppert, F. A., and Piercy, M. (1979) Normal and abnormal forgetting in organic amnesia: Effect of locus of lesion. *Cortex*, 15, 385–90.

Hunter, I. M. L. (1977) Imagery, comprehension and mnemonics. *Journal of Mental Imagery*, 1, 65–72.

Hyden, H., and Egyhazi, H. (1962) Nuclear RNA changes of nerve cells during a learning experiment in rats. *Proceedings of the National Academy of Sciences*, 48, 1366–75.

James, W. (1890) *Principles of Psychology*, vol. 1. New York: Henry Holt.

James, W. (1899) *Talks to Teachers on Psychology: And to Students on Some of Life's Ideals*. New York: Henry Holt.

Janet, P. (1904) *Neuroses et Idées Fixes*, 2nd edn. Paris: Felix Alcan.

Janis, I. (1950) Psychological effects of electroconvulsive treatments: I. Post-treatment amnesias. *Journal of Nervous and Mental Disease*, 111, 359–82.

Jaynes, J. (1976) *The Origins of Consciousnes in the Breakdown of the Bicameral Mind*. Boston: Houghton Mifflin.

Jenkins, J. J., Mink, W. D., and Russell, W. A. (1952) Associative clustering as a function of verbal association strength. *Psychological Reports*, 4, 127–36.

Johns, C. A., Haroutunian, V., Greenwald, B. S., Mohs, R. C., Davis, B. M., Kanof, P., Horvath, T. B., and Davis, K. L. (1985) Development of cholinergic drugs for the treatment of Alzheimer's Disease. *Drug Development Research*, 5, 77–96.

Jones, M. (1974) Imagery as a mnemonic aid after left temporal lobectomy: Contrast between material specific and generalized memory disorders. *Neuropsychologia*, 12, 21–30.

Kahn, E. A., and Crosby, E. C. (1972) Korsakoff's Syndrome associated with surgical lesions involving the mamillary bodies. *Neurology*, 27, 117–25.

Kandel, E. R., and Schwartz, J. H. (1985) *Principles of Neural Science*. Amsterdam: Elsevier.

Kapur, N., and Coughlan, A. C. (1980) Confabulation and frontal lobe dysfunction. *Journal of Neurology, Neurosurgery and Psychiatry*, 43, 461–2.

Kapur, N., Heath, P., Meudell, P., and Kennedy, P. (1986) Amnesia can facilitate memory performance: Evidence from a patient with dissociated retrograde amnesia. *Neuropsychologia*, 24, 215–22.

Kausler, D. H. (1970) Retention-forgetting as a nomological network for developmental research. In L. R. Goulet and P. B. Baltes (eds), *Life Span Developmental Psychology: Research and Theory*, 306–57. New York: Academic Press.

Kausler, D. H., and Hakami, M. K. (1983) Memory for activities: Adult age differences and intentionality. *Developmental Psychology*, 19, 889–94.

Kihlstrom, J. F. and Evans, F. J. (1979) *Functional Disorders of Memory*. Hillsdale, N. J.: Freeman.

Kinsbourne, M., and Wood, F. (1975) Short-term memory processes in the amnesic syndrome. In J. A. Deutsch (ed.), *Short-Term Memory*, 258–91. New York: Academic Press.

Kintsch, W. (1970) Models for free recall and recognition. In D. A. Norman (ed.), *Models of Human Memory*, 333–74. New York: Academic Press.

Klatzky, R. L. (1980) *Human Memory*, 2nd edn. New York: Freeman.

Kolb, B., and Whishaw, I. Q. (1985) *Fundamentals of Human Neuropsychology*, 2nd edn. New York: Freeman.

Kopelman, M. D. (1985) Rates of forgetting in Alzheimer-type dementias and Korsakoff's Syndrome. *Neuropsychologia*, 23, 623–38.

Kosslyn, S. M. (1983) *Ghosts in the Mind's Machine: Creating and Using Images in the Brain*. New York: Norton.

Kurlychek, R. T. (1983) Use of a digital alarm chronograph as a memory aid in early dementia. *Clinical Gerontologist*, 1, 93–4.

Landauer, T. K., and Bjork, R. A. (1978) Optimum rehearsal patterns and name learning. In M. M. Gruneberg et al. (eds), *Practical Aspects of Memory*, 625–32. New York: Academic Press.

Laurence, J., and Perry, C. (1983) Hypnotically created memory among highly hypnotizable subjects. *Science*, 222, 523–4.

Lehman, E. B., and Mellinger, J. C. (1984) Effects of aging on memory for presentation modality. *Developmental Psychology*, 21, 1210–17.

Leng, N. (in preparation) *Heterogeneity in the Amnesic Syndrome*.

Levin, H. S., High, W. M., Meyers, C. A., von Laufen, A., Hayden, M. E., and Eisenberg, H. (1985) Impairment of remote memory after closed head injury. *Journal of Neurology, Neurosurgery and Psychiatry*, 48, 556–63.

Lewinsohn, P. M., Danaher, B. G., and Kikel, S. (1977) Visual imagery as a mnemonic aid for brain-injured persons. *Journal of Clinical and Consulting Psychology*, 45, 717–23.

Lezak, M. D. (1985) *Neuropsychological Assessment*, 2nd edn. New York: Oxford University Press.

L'Hermitte, F., and Signoret, J. L. (1972) Analyse neuropsychologique et differenciation des syndromes amnesiques. *Revue Neurologique*, 126, 86–94.

Light, L. L., and Carter-Sobell, L. (1970) Effects of changed semantic context on recognition memory. *Journal of Verbal Learning and Verbal Behavior*, 9, 1–11.

Light, L. L., and Zelinski, E. M. (1983) Memory for spatial information in young and old adults. *Developmental Psychology*, 19, 901–6.

Lilly, R., Cummings, J. L., Benson, F., and Frankel, M. (1983) The human Kluver-Bucy Syndrome. *Neurology*, 33, 1141–5.

Lishman, W. A. (1981) Cerebral disorder in alcoholism. *Brain*, 104, 1–20.

Lisman, S. A. (1974) Alcoholic blackout: State-dependent learning? *Archives of General Psychiatry*, 30, 46–53.

Lloyd, G. G., and Lishman, W. A. (1975) Effect of depression on the speed of recall of pleasant and unpleasant experiences. *Psychological Medicine*, 5, 173–80.

Loftus, E. F., and Loftus, G. R. (1980) On the permanence of stored information in the human brain. *American Psychologist*, 35, 409–20.

Lorayne, H., and Lucas, J. (1975) *The Memory Book*. London: W. H. Allen.

Luria, A. R. (1968) *The Mind of a Mnemonist*. London: Penguin.

Madigan, S. A. (1969) Intraserial repetition and coding processes in free recall. *Journal of Verbal Learning and Verbal Behavior*, 8, 828–35.

Mair, W. G. P., Warrington, E. K., and Weiskrantz, L. (1979) Memory disorder in Korsakoff's Psychosis, *Brain*, 102, 749–83.

Mandler, G. (1980) Recognising: The judgement of a previous occurrence. *Psychological Review*, 27, 252–71.

Markowitsch, H. J. (1983) Transient global amnesia. *Neuroscience and Biobehavioral Reviews*, 7, 35–43.

Marslen-Wilson, W. D., and Teuber, H. L. (1975) Memory for remote events in anterograde amnesia. Recognition of public figures from newsphotos. *Neuropsychologia*, 13, 353–64.

Mash, D. C., Flynn, D. D., and Potter, L. T. (1985) Loss of M2 muscarine receptors in the cerebral cortex in Alzheimer's Disease and experimental cholinergic denervation. *Science*, 228, 1115–17.

Mattis, S. E., Kovner, R., and Goldmeyer, E. (1978) Different patterns of mnemonic deficits in two organic amnesic syndromes. *Brain and Language*, 6, 179–91.

Mayes, A. R. (1986) Learning and memory disorders and their assessment. *Neuropsychologia*, 24, 25–40.

Mayes, A. R. (forthcoming) *The Varieties of Human Organic Amnesias*. Cambridge: Cambridge University Press.

Mayes, A. R., and Meudell, P. R. (1983) Amnesia in humans and other animals. In A. Mayes (ed.), *Memory in Animals and Humans*, pp. 203–52. Wokingham: Van Nostrand Reinhold.

Mayes, A. R., Meudell, P. R., and Neary, D. (1980) Do amnesics adopt inefficient encoding strategies with faces and random shapes? *Neuropsychologia*, 18, 527–40.

Mayes, A. R., Meudell, P. R., and Pickering, A. (1985) Is organic amnesia caused by a selective deficit in remembering contextual information? *Cortex*, 21, 167–202.

Mayeux, R., Alexander, M. P., Benson, D. F., and Rosen, J. R. (1979) Poriomana. *Neurology*, 29, 1616–19.

McCarty, D. (1980) Investigation of a visual imagery mnemonic device for acquiring face-name associations. *Journal of Experimental Psychology: Human Learning and Memory*, 6, 145–55.

McEntee, W. J., and Mair, R. G. (1978) Memory impairment in Korsakoff's Psychosis: a correlation with brain noradrenergic activity. *Science*, 202, 905–7.

McEntee, W. J., and Mair, R. G. (1980) Memory enhancement in Korsakoff's Psychosis by clonidine: Further evidence for a noradrenergic deficit. *Annals of Neurology*, 7, 466–70.

McEntee, W. J., Mair, R. G., and Langlais, P. J. (1984) Neurochemical pathology in Korsakoff's Psychosis: Implications for other disorders. *Neurology*, 34, 648–52.

McGeoch, J. A. (1932) Forgetting and the law of disuse. *Psychological Review*, 39, 352–70.

Melton, A. W. (1967) Repetition and retrieval from memory. *Science*, 158, 532.

Metzger, R. L., Boschee, P. F., Haugen, T., and Schnobrich, B. L. (1979) The classroom as a learning context: Changing rooms affects performance. *Journal of Educational Psychology*, 71, 440–2.

Meudell, P. R., and Mayes, A. R. (1981) The Claparède phenomenon: A further example in amnesics, a demonstration of a similar effect in normal people with attenuated memory, and a reinterpretation. *Current Psychological Research*, 1, 75–88.

Meudell, P. R., Northern, B., Snowden, J. S., and Neary, D. (1980) Long-term memory for famous voices in amnesic and normal subjects. *Neuropsychologia*, 19, 133–9.

Meudell, P. R., Mayes, A. R., Ostergaard, A., and Pickering, A. (1985) Recency and frequency judgments in alcoholic amnesias and normal people with poor memory. *Cortex*, 21, 487–511.

Miller, E. (1975) Impaired recall and the memory disturbance in presenile dementia. *British Journal of Social and Clinical Psychology*, 18, 87–94.

Miller, E. (1977) *Abnormal Ageing*. Chichester: Wiley.

Miller, E. (1984) *Recovery and Management of Neuropsychological Impairments*. Chichester: Wiley.

Milner, B. (1966) Amnesia following operation on the temporal lobes. In C. W. M. Whitty and O. L. Zangwill (eds), *Amnesia*. London: Butterworths.

Milner, B. (1971) Interhemispheric differences in the location of psychological processes in man. *British Medical Bulletin*, 27, 272–7.

Mitchell, D. B., and Perlmutter, M. (1986) Semantic activation and episodic memory. *Developmental Psychology*, 22, 86–94.

Mnemonics (1972) London: Eyre Methuen.

Moffat, N. (1984) Strategies of memory therapy. In B. Wilson and N. Moffat (eds), *The Clinical Management of Memory Problems*. London: Croom Helm.

Morris, R. G. (1984) Dementia and the functioning of the articulatory loop system. *Cognitive Neuropsychology*, 1, 143–57.

Morris, R. G. M. (1985) Moving on from modelling amnesia. In N. M. Weinberger, J. L. McGaugh, and G. Lynch (eds), *Memory Systems of the Brain*. New York: Guildford.

Moscovitch, M. (1984) The sufficient conditions for demonstrating preserved memory in amnesia: A task analysis approach. In L. R. Squire and N. Butters (eds), *Neuropsychology of Memory*. New York: Guildford.

Mumenthaler, M., Kaeser, H. E., Meyer, A., and Hess, T. (1979) Transient global amnesia after clioquinol. *Journal of Neurology, Neurosurgery and Psychiatry*, 42, 1084–90.

Nadel, L., and Zola-Morgan, S. (1984) Infantile amnesia: A neurobiological perspective. In D. L. Schacter and M. Moscovitch (eds), *Infant Memory*, 145–72. New York: Plenum.

Nebes, R. D., Martin, D. C., and Horn, L. C. (1984) Sparing of semantic memory in Alzheimer's Disease. *Journal of Abnormal Psychology*, 93, 321–30.

Neisser, U. (1967) *Cognitive Psychology*. Englewood Cliffs, NJ: Prentice-Hall.

Nelson, H. E. (1976) A modified card sorting test sensitive to frontal lobe deficits. *Cortex*, 12, 313–24.

Nelson, H. E., and O'Connor, A. (1978) Dementia: the estimation of premorbid intelligence levels using the New Adult Reading Test. *Cortex*, 14, 234–44.

Nigro, G., and Neisser, U. (1983) Point of view in personal memories. *Cognitive Psychology*, 15, 467–82.

Nyssen, R. (1956) Des capacités de définition et d'evocation des mots dans la psychose de Korsakov alcoholique. *Evolution Psychiatrique*, 1, 303–14.

Ostergaard, A. L. (in preparation) Episodic, semantic and procedural memory in a case of amnesia at an early age.

Paivio, A. (1971) *Imagery and Verbal Processes*. New York: Holt, Rinehart and Winston.

Parkin, A. J. (1979) Specifying levels of processing. *Quarterly Journal of Experimental Psychology*, 31, 175–95.

Parkin, A. J. (1982) Residual learning capability in organic amnesia. *Cortex*, 18, 417–40.

Parkin, A. J. (1984a) Levels of processing, context, and the facilitation of pronunciation. *Acta Psychologica*, 55, 19–29.

Parkin, A. J. (1984b) Amnesic Syndrome: A lesion-specific disorder? *Cortex*, 20, 497–508.

Parkin, A. J., and Goodwin, E. (1983) The influence of different processing strategies on the recognition of transformed and untransformed faces. *Canadian Journal of Psychology*, 37, 272–7.

Parkin, A. J., and Hayward, C. (1983) The influence of trait- and physical-feature-based orienting strategies on aspects of facial memory. *British Journal of Psychology*, 74, 71–82.

Parkin, A. J., and Leng, N. (in press) Comparative studies of human amnesia: Methodological and theoretical issues. In H. J. Markowitsch (ed.), *Information Processing by the Brain*. Toronto: Huber.

Parkin, A. J., and Wilson, B. (in preparation) Amnesia following a ruptured aneurysm of the anterior communicating artery: characteristics, remediation and long-term outcome.

Parkin, A. J., Lewinsohn, J., and Folkard, S. (1982) The influence of emotion on immediate and delayed recall: Levinger and Clark reconsidered. *British Journal of Psychology*, 73, 389–93.

Parkin, A. J., Miller, J. W., and Vincent, R. (in preparation) Quality of survival following severe cerebral anoxia caused by cardiac arrest.

Parsons, O. A., and Prigatano, G. P. (1977) Memory functioning in alcoholics. In I. M. Birnbaum and E. S. Parker (eds), *Alcohol and Human Memory*. Hillsdale, NJ: LEA.

Patten, B. M. (1972) The ancient art of memory. *Archives of Neurology*, 26, 25–31.

Patterson, K. E., and Baddeley, A. D. (1977) When face recognition fails. *Journal of Experimental Psychology: Human Learning and Memory*, 3, 406–17.

Penfield, W. (1958) Some mechanisms of consciousness discovered during electrical stimulation of the brain. *Proceedings of the National Academy of Sciences*, 44, 51–66.

Pezdek, K. (1983) Memory for items and their spatial locations by young and elderly adults. *Developmental Psychology*, 19, 895–900.

Pezdek, K., and Miceli, L. (1982) Life span differences in memory integration as a function of processing time. *Developmental Psychology*, 18, 485–90.

Posner, M. I. (1973) *Cognition: An Introduction*. Glenview, Ill: Scott, Foresman.

Prigatano, G. P., Fordyce, D. J., Zeiner, H. K., Roueche, J. R., Pepping, M., and Wood, B. C. (1984) Neuropsychological rehabilitation after closed head injury in young adults. *Journal of Neurology, Neurosurgery and Psychiatry*, 47, 505–13.

Pratt, R. T. C. (1977) Psychogenic loss of memory. In C. W. M. Whitty and O. L. Zangwill (eds), *Amnesia*, 224–32. London: Butterworths.

Pylyshyn, Z. W. (1979) Imagery theory: Not mysterious – just wrong. *Behavioral and Brain Sciences*, 2, 561–3.

Rabbitt, P. M. A. (1982) Breakdown of control processes in old age. In J. E. Birren and K. W. Schaie (eds), *Handbook of the Psychology of Aging*. New York: Van Nostrand Reinhold.

Rappaport, D. (1942) *Emotions and Memory*. New York: International Universities Press.

Reder, L. M., Anderson, J. R., and Bjork, R. A. (1974) A semantic interpretation of encoding specificity. *Journal of Experimental Psychology*, 102, 648–56.

Regard, M., and Landis, T. (1984) Transient global amnesia: neuropsychological dysfunction during attack and recovery of two 'pure' cases. *Journal of Neurology, Neurosurgery and Psychiatry*, 47, 668–72.

Regenstein, Q. R., Murawski, B. J., and Ingali, R. P. (1975) A case of prolonged reversible dementia associated with abuse of ECT. *Journal of Nervous and Mental Disease*, 161, 200–3.

Ribot, T. (1882) *Diseases of Memory*. New York: Appleton.

Richardson, J. T. E. (1980) *Mental Imagery and Human Memory*. London: Macmillan.

Richardson, J. T. E., and Barry, C. (1985) The effects of minor closed head injury upon human memory: Further evidence on the role of mental imagery. *Cognitive Neuropsychology*, 2, 149–68.

Richardson, J. T. E., and Snape, W. (1984) The effects of closed head injury upon human memory: An experimental analysis. *Cognitive Neuropsychology*, 1, 217–31.

Richardson, J. T. E., Cermak, L. S., Blackford, S. P., and O'Connor, M. (in press) The efficacy of imagery mnemonics following brain damage. In M. McDaniel and M. Pressley (eds), *Imaginal and Mnemonic Processes*. New York: Springer.

Robertson-Tchabo, E. A., Hausman, C. P., and Arenberg, D. (1976) A classical mnemonic for older learners: A trip that works. *Educational Gerontologist*, 1, 215–26.

Robinson, J. A. (1976) Sampling autobiographical memory. *Cognitive Psychology*, 8, 578–95.

Roediger, H. L. (1980) Memory metaphors in cognitive psychology. *Memory and Cognition*, 8, 231–46.

Rose, F. C., and Symonds, C. P. (1960) Persistent memory defects following encephalitis. *Brain*, 83, 195–212.

Rundus, D. (1971) Analysis of rehearsal processes in free recall. *Journal of Experimental Psychology*, 89, 63–77.

Russell, E. W. (1975) A multiple scoring method for the assessment of complex memory functions. *Journal of Consulting and Clinical Psychology*, 43, 800–9.

Russell, W. R. (1971) *The Traumatic Amnesias*. London: Oxford University Press.

Russell, W. R., and Smith, A. (1961) Post-traumatic amnesia in closed head injury. *Archives of Neurology*, 5, 16–29.

Ryback, R. (1971) The continuum and specificity of the effects of alcohol on memory. *Quarterly Journal of Studies in Alcoholism*, 32, 995–1016.

Ryle, G. (1949) *The Concept of Mind*. London: Hutchinson.

Saffran, E. M., and Marin, O. S. M. (1975) Immediate memory for word lists and sentences in a patient with deficient auditory short-term memory. *Brain and Language*, 2, 420–33.

Sanders, H. I., and Warrington, E. K. (1971) Memory for remote events in amnesic patients. *Brain*, 94, 661–8.

Sarter, M., and Markowitsch, H. J. (1985) The amygdala's role in human mnemonic processing. *Cortex*, 21, 7–24.

Schacter, D. L. (1983) Amnesia observed: Remembering and forgetting in a natural environment. *Journal of Abnormal Psychology*, 92, 236–42.

Schacter, D. L. (in press, a) Feeling-of-knowing ratings distinguish between genuine and simulated forgetting. *Journal of Experimental Psychology: Learning, Memory and Cognition.*

Schacter, D. L. (in press, b) Amnesia and crime. *American Psychologist.*

Schacter, D. L., and Crovitz, H. F. (1977) Memory function after closed head injury: A review of the quantitative research. *Cortex*, 13, 150–76.

Schacter, D. L., and Glisky, E. L. (in press) Memory remediation: Restoration, alleviation and the acquisition of domain-specific knowledge. In B. Uzzell and Y. Cross (eds), *Clinical Neuropsychology of Intervention.* Boston: Martinus Nijhoff.

Schacter, D. L., and Graf, P. (in press) Preserved learning in amnesic patients: Perspectives from research on direct priming. *Journal of Experimental and Clinical Neuropsychology.*

Schacter, D. L., and Moscovitch, M. (1984) Infants, amnesics and dissociable memory systems. In D. L. Schacter and M. Moscovitch (eds), *Infant Memory*, 173–216. New York: Plenum.

Schacter, D. L., Harbluk, J. L., and McLachlan, D. R. (1984) Retrieval without recollection: an experimental analysis of source amnesia. *Journal of Verbal Learning and Verbal Behavior*, 23, 593–611.

Schacter, D. L., Rich, S. A., and Stampp, M. S. (1985) Remediation of memory disorders: Experimental evaluation of the spaced-retrieval technique. *Journal of Clinical and Experimental Neuropsychology*, 7, 79–96.

Schacter, D. L., Wang, P. L., Tulving, E., and Freedman, M. (1982) Functional retrograde amnesia: A quantitative case study. *Neuropsychologia*, 20, 523–32.

Schaie, K. W. (1980) Cognitive development in aging. In L. K. Obler and M. L. Albert (eds), *Language and Communication in the Elderly: Clinical, Therapeutic and Experimental Issues*, pp. 7–26. Lexington, MA: Lexington Books.

Schonfield, D., and Robertson, B. A. (1966) Memory storage and aging. *Canadian Journal of Psychology*, 20, 228–36.

Scoville, W. B., and Milner, B. (1957) Loss of recent memory after bilateral hippocampal lesions. *Journal of Neurology, Neurosurgery and Psychiatry*, 20, 11–21.

Shallice, T., and Butterwoth, B. (1977) Short-term memory impairment and spontaneous speech. *Neuropsychologia*, 15, 729–35.

Sheehan, P. W., and Tilder, J. (1983) Effects of suggestibility and hypnosis on accurate and distorted retrieval from memory. *Journal of Experimental Psychology: Learning, Memory and Cognition*, 9, 283–93.

Simon, E. (1979) Depth and elaboration of processing in relation to age.

Journal of Experimental Psychology: Human Learning and Memory, 5, 115–24.

Sitaram, N., Weingartner, H., Caine, E. D., and Gillin, J. C. (1978) Human serial learning: Enhancement with arecholine and choline and impairment with scopalamine. *Science*, 201, 274–6.

Smith, S. M. (1979) Remembering in and out of context. *Journal of Experimental Psychology: Human Learning and Memory*, 5, 460–71.

Spear, N. E., and Miller, R. R. (1981) *Information Processing in Animals: Memory Mechanisms*. Hillsdale, NJ: Erlbaum.

Speedie, L. J., and Heilman, K. M. (1982) Amnestic disturbance following infarction of the left dorsomedial nucleus of the thalamus. *Neuropsychologia*, 20, 597–604.

Sperling, G. (1960) The information available in brief visual displays. *Psychological Monographs*, Whole No. 498.

Squire, L. R. (1981) Two forms of human amnesia: An analysis of forgetting. *Journal of Neuroscience*, 1, 635–40.

Squire, L. R. (1982a) The neuropsychology of human memory. *Annual Review of Neuroscience*, 5, 241–73.

Squire, L. R. (1982b) Comparisons between forms of amnesia: Some deficits are unique to Korsakoff's Syndrome. *Journal of Experimental Psychology: Learning, Memory and Cognition*, 8, 560–71.

Squire, L. R., and Butters, N. (1984) *Neuropsychology of Memory*. New York: Guildford.

Squire, L. R., and Chace, P. M. (1975) Forgetting in very long-term memory as assessed by an improved questionnaire technique. *Journal of Experimental Psychology: Human Learning and Memory*, 104, 50–4.

Squire, L. R., and Cohen, N. (1982) Remote memory, retrograde amnesia, and the neuropsychology of memory. In L. S. Cermak (ed.), *Human Memory and Amnesia*, 275–305. Hillsdale, NJ: Erlbaum.

Squire, L. R., and Moore, R. Y. (1979) Dorsal thalamic lesion in a noted case of human memory dysfunction. *Annals of Neurology*, 6, 503–6.

Squire, L. R., and Slater, P. C. (1975) Forgetting in very long-term memory as assessed by an improved questionnaire taxonomy. *Journal of Experimental Psychology: Human Learning and Memory*, 104, 50–4.

Squire, L. R., and Slater, P. C. (1983) Electroconvulsive therapy and complaints of memory dysfunction: A prospective three-year follow-up study. *British Journal of Psychiatry*, 142, 1–8.

Squire, L. R., and Zola-Morgan, S. (1983) The neurology of memory: The case for correspondence between the findings for human and nonhuman primates. In J. A. Deutsch (ed.), *The Physiological Basis of Memory*, 2nd edn. New York: Academic Press.

Squire, L. R., and Zola-Morgan, S. (1985) Neuropsychology of memory: New links between humans and experimental animals. In D. Olton et al. (eds), *Conference on Memory Dysfunctions*, 137–49. New York: New York Academy of Sciences.

Squire, L. R., Cohen, N. J., and Nadel, L. (1984) The medial temporal region and memory consolidation: A new hypothesis. In H. Weingartner and E. Parker (eds), *Memory Consolidation*, pp. 635–40. Hillsdale, NJ: Erlbaum.

Squire, L. R., Slater, P. C., and Chace, P. M. (1975) Retrograde amnesia: Temporal gradient in very-long-term memory following electroconvulsive therapy. *Science*, 187, 77–9.

Starr, A., and Phillips, L. (1970) Verbal and motor memory in the amnesic syndrome. *Neuropsychologia*, 8, 75–88.

Staton, R. D., Brumback, R. A., and Wilson, H. (1982) Reduplicative paramnesia: A disconnection syndrome of memory. *Cortex*, 18, 22–36.

Stenback, A., and Viitamaki, R. O. (1957) Psychological studies on a patient who received 441 electroconvulsive treatments. *Acta Psychiatrica et Neurologica Scandinavica*, 32, 473–8.

Stern, L. D. (1981) A review of theories of amnesia. *Memory and Cognition*, 9, 247–62.

Stevens, M. (1979) Famous personalities test: A test for measuring remote memory. *Bulletin of the British Psychological Society*, 32, 211.

Strub, R. L., and Black, F. W. (1981) *Organic Brain Syndromes*. Philadelphia: Davis.

Stuss, D. T., and Benson, D. F. (1984) Neuropsychological studies of the frontal lobes. *Psychological Bulletin*, 95, 3–28.

Stuss, D. T., Alexander, M. P., Lieberman, A., and Levine, H. (1978) An extraordinary form of confabulation. *Neurology*, 28, 1166–72.

Sunderland, A., Harris, J., and Baddeley, A. D. (1983) Do laboratory tests predict everyday memory? *Journal of Verbal Learning and Verbal Behavior*, 122, 341–57.

Talland, G. A. (1965) *Deranged Memory*. New York: Academic Press.

Talland, G. A. (1968) *Disorders of Memory and Learning*. London: Penguin.

Tart, C. T. (1972) *Altered States of Consciousness*. New York: Doubleday.

Taylor, P. J., and Kopelman, M. D. (1984) Amnesia for criminal offences. *Psychological Medicine*, 14, 581–8.

Teasdale, J. D. (1983) Affect and accessibility. *Philosophical Trans-*

References

actions of the Royal Society, London, B 302, 403–12.

Teuber, H.-L., Milner, B., and Vaughan, H. G. (1968) Persistent anterograde amnesia after stab wound of the basal brain. *Neuropsychologia*, 6, 267–82.

Thigpen, C. H., and Cleckley, H. M. (1957) *The Three Faces of Eve*. New York: McGraw-Hill.

Thomas, J. C., Fozard, J. L., and Waugh, N. C. (1977) Age-related differences in naming latency. *American Journal of Psychology*, 90, 499–509.

Thompson, R. F. (1985) *The Brain: An Introduction to Neuroscience*. New York: Freeman.

Thomson, D. M., Robertson, S. L., and Vogt, R. (1982) Person recognition: The effect of context. *Human Learning*, 1, 137–54.

Thorndike, E. L. (1913) *Educational Psychology*. New York: Teachers College Press.

Tulving, E. (1962) Subjective organization in free recall of 'unrelated' words. *Psychological Review*, 69, 344–54.

Tulving, E. (1972) Episodic and semantic memory. In E. Tulving and W. Donaldson (eds), *The Organization of Memory*. New York: Academic Press.

Tulving, E. (1983) *Elements of Episodic Memory*. Oxford: Oxford University Press.

Tulving, E. (1985) How many memory systems are there? *American Psychologist*, 40, 385–98.

Tulving, E., and Thomson, D. M. (1973) Encoding specificity and retrieval processes in episodic memory. *Psychological Review*, 80, 352–73.

Tulving, E., Schacter, D. L., and Stark, H. (1982) Priming effects in word-fragment completion are independent of recognition memory. *Journal of Experimental Psychology: Human Learning and Memory*, 8, 336–42.

Vallar, G., and Baddeley, A. D. (1984a) Phonological short-term store, phonological processing and sentence comprehension: A neuropsychological case study. *Cognitive Neuropsychology*, 1, 121–41.

Vallar, G., and Baddeley, A. D. (1984b) Fractionation of working memory: Neuropsychological evidence for a phonological short-term store. *Journal of Verbal Learning and Verbal Behavior*, 23, 151–61.

van der Horst, L. (1932) Über die Psychologie des Korsakowsyndroms. *Monatsschrift für Psychiatrie und Neurologie*, 83, 65–84.

Van Zomeran, A. H., and Van den Berg, W. (1985) Residual complaints of patients two years after severe head injury. *Journal of Neurology, Neurosurgery and Psychiatry*, 48, 21–8.

Victor, M., Adams, R. D., and Collins, G. H. (1971) *The Wernicke-*

Korsakoff Syndrome. Philadelphia: Davis.

Wagstaff, G. F. (1981) *Hypnosis: Compliance and Belief*. Brighton: Harvester Press.

Wagstaff, G. F. (1984) The enhancement of witness memory by hypnosis: A review and methodological critique of the experimental literature. *British Journal of Experimental and Clinical Hypnosis*, 2, 3–12.

Walsh, K. W. (1985) *Understanding Brain Damage*. Edinburgh: Churchill Livingstone.

Warrington, E. K. (1985) *Recognition Memory Test*. Windsor: NFER-Nelson.

Warrington, E. K., and Sanders, H. I. (1971) The fate of old memories. *Quarterly Journal of Experimental Psychology*, 23, 432–43.

Warrington, E. K., and Shallice, T. (1969) The selective impairment of auditory verbal short-term memory. *Brain*, 92, 885–96.

Warrington, E. K., and Weiskrantz, L. (1970) Amnesic syndrome: Consolidation or retrieval? *Nature*, 228, 628–30.

Warrington, E. K., and Weiskrantz, L. (1979) Conditioning in amnesic patients. *Neuropsychologia*, 17, 187–94.

Warrington, E. K., and Weiskrantz, L. (1982) Amnesia: A disconnection syndrome? *Neuropsychologia*, 20, 233–48.

Watson, J. B. (1914) *Behavior: An Introduction to Comparative Psychology*. New York: Holt.

Wechsler, D. (1945) A standardised memory scale for clinical use. *Journal of Psychology*, 19, 87–95.

Weeks, D., Freeman, C. P. L., and Kendell, R. E. (1980) ECT: II. Enduring cognitive deficits? *British Journal of Psychiatry*, 137, 26–37.

Weinberger, N. M., McGaugh, J. L., and Lynch, G. (1985) *Memory Systems of the Brain*. New York: Guildford.

Weiner, R. D. (1984) Does electroconvulsive therapy cause brain damage? *The Behavioral and Brain Sciences*, 7, 1–53.

Weingartner, H., and Parker, E. S. (eds) (1984) *Memory Consolidation: Psychobiology of Cognition*. New York: LEA.

Weiskrantz, L. (1982) Comparative aspects of studies of amnesia. *Philosophical Transactions of the Royal Society, London, B*, 298, 97–109.

Weiskrantz, L. (1985) Issues and theories in the study of the amnesic syndrome. In N. M. Weinberger et al. (eds), *Memory Systems of the Brain*. New York: Guildford.

Wetzel, C. D., and Squire, L. R. (1980) Encoding in anterograde amnesia. *Neuropsychologia*, 18, 177–84.

Wetzel, C. D., Janowsky, D. S., and Clopton, P. L. (1982) Remote memory during marijuana intoxication. *Psychopharmacology*, 76, 278–81.

Whitty, C. W. M., and Zangwill, O. L. (eds) (1977) *Amnesia*. London: Butterworths.

Wilkinson, D. A., and Carlen, P. L. (1982) Chronic organic brain syndromes associated with alcoholism: Neuropsychological and other aspects. In Y. Israel et al. (eds), *Research Advances in Alcohol and Drug Problems*, vol. 6, 107–45. New York: Plenum.

Williams, J. M. G., and Broadbent, K. (1986) Autobiographical memory in suicide attempters. *Journal of Abnormal Psychology*, 95, 145–9.

Williams, M. (1968) The measurement of memory in clinical practice. *British Journal of Social and Clinical Psychology*, 7, 19–34.

Williams, M., and Pennybacker, J. (1954) Memory disturbances in third ventricle tumours. *Journal of Neurology, Neurosurgery and Psychiatry*, 17, 115–23.

Wilson, B. (1982) Success and failure in memory training following a cerebral vascular accident. *Cortex*, 18, 581–94.

Wilson, B., and Moffat, N. (1984a) Rehabilitation of memory for everyday life. In J. E. Harris and P. E. Morris (eds), *Everyday Memory, Actions and Absent-Mindedness*. London: Academic Press.

Wilson, B., and Moffat, N. (1984b) *The Clinical Management of Memory Problems*. London: Croom Helm.

Wilson, B., and Baddeley, A. D. (in press) Identification and remediation of everyday problems in memory impaired adults. To appear in P. Nathan et al. (eds), *Neuropsychology of Alcoholism: Implications for Diagnosis and Treatment*. New York: Guildford Press.

Wilson, R. S., Kaszniak, A. W., and Fox, J. H. (1981) Remote memory in senile dementia. *Cortex*, 17, 41–8.

Winocur, G. (1982) The amnesic syndrome: A deficit in cue utilization. In L. S. Cermak (ed.), *Human Memory and Amnesia*, 139–94. Hillsdale, NJ: Erlbaum.

Winocur, G., and Kinsbourne, M. (1978) Contextual cueing as an aid to Korsakoff amnesics. *Neuropsychologia*, 16, 671–82.

Winocur, G., Kinsbourne, M., and Moscovitch, M. (1981) The effect of cueing on release from proactive interference in Korsakoff amnesic patients. *Journal of Experimental Psychology: Human Learning and Memory*, 7, 56–65.

Winocur, G., Oxbury, S., Roberts, R., Agnetti, V., and Davis, C. (1984) Amnesia in a patient with bilateral lesions to the thalamus. *Neuropsychologia*, 22, 123–43.

Winograd, E. (1976) Recognition memory for faces following nine different judgments. *Bulletin of the Psychonomic Society*, 8, 419–21.

Winograd, E. (1981) Elaboration and distinctiveness in memory for faces.

Journal of Experimental Psychology: Human Learning and Memory, 7, 181–90.

Wolf, A. S. (1980) Homicide and blackout in Alaskan natives. *Journal of Studies on Alcohol*, 41, 456–62.

Wollen, K. A., Weber, A., and Lowry, D. H. (1972) Bizarreness versus interaction of mental images as determinants of learning. *Cognitive Psychology*, 3, 518–23.

Wood, F., Ebert, V., and Kinsbourne, M. (1982) The episodic-semantic memory distinction in memory and amnesia: Clinical and experimental observations. In L. Cermak (ed.), *Human Memory and Amnesia*, 167–94. Hillsdale, NJ: Erlbaum.

Yarnell, P. R., and Lynch, S. (1973) The ding: Amnestic states in football trauma. *Neurology*, 23, 196–7.

Yates, F. A. (1966) *The Art of Memory*. London: Routledge and Kegan Paul.

Zangwill, O. L. (1967) The Grunthal-Storring case of the amnesic syndrome. *British Journal of Psychiatry*, 113, 113–28.

Zarit, S. H., Gallagher, D., and Kramer, N. (1981) Memory training in the community aged: Effects on depression, memory complaint and memory performance. *Educational Gerontology*, 6, 11–27.

Zechmeister, E. B., and Nyberg, S. E. (1981) *Human Memory*. Monterey, CA: Brooks/Cole.

Zelig, M., and Beidelman, W. B. (1981) The investigative use of hypnosis: A word of caution. *International Journal of Clinical and Experimental Hypnosis*, 29, 401–12.

Zelinski, E. M., Light, L. L., and Gilewski, M. J. (1984) Adult age differences in memory for prose. The question of sensitivity to passage structure. *Developmental Psychology*, 20, 1181–92.

Zivian, M. T., and Darjes, R. W. (1983) Free recall by in-school and out-of-school adults: Performance and metamemory. *Developmental Psychology*, 19, 513–20.

Zola-Morgan, S., and Squire, L. R. (1985) Complementary approaches to the study of memory: Human amnesia and animal models. In N. M. Weinberger, J. L. McGaugh, and G. Lynch, *Memory Systems of the Brain*, 463–78. New York: Guildford.

Name Index

Subject Index